THE CHANGING CAREER
OF THE CORRECTIONAL OFFICER

Criminal Justice Titles Available from Butterworth-Heinemann

The Changing Career
of the Correctional Officer

Policy Implications for the 21st Century

DON A. JOSI

Armstrong Atlantic State University
Savannah, Georgia

DALE K. SECHREST

California State University
San Bernardino, California

Butterworth-Heinemann

Boston   Oxford   Johannesburg   Melbourne   New Delhi   Singapore

Butterworth–Heinemann supports the efforts of American Forests
and the Global ReLeaf program in its campaign for the betterment
of trees, forests, and our environment.

Library of Congress Cataloging-in-Publication Data
Josi, Don A., 1946–
    The changing carreer of the correctional officer : policy implications for the
21st century / Don A. Josi, Dale K. Sechrest.
        p.   cm.
    Includes bibiliographical references and index.
    ISBN 0-7506-9962-0 (pbk. : alk. paper)
    1. Correctional personnel—United States. 2. Correctional personnel—Training
of—United States. 3. Prison administration—United States. I. Sechrest Dale K.
II. Title.
HV9740.J67   1998
365'.023'73—dc21   97-49259
                                                         CIP

British Library Cataloguing-in-Publication Data
A catalogue record for this book is available from the British Library.

The publisher offers special discounts on bulk orders of this book.
For information, please contact:

Manager of Special Sales
Butterworth–Heinemann
225 Wildwood Avenue
Woburn, MA 01801-2041
Tel: 781-904-2500
Fax: 781-904-2620

For information on all Butterworth–Heinemann books available, contact our
World Wide Web home page at: http://www.bh.com

10 9 8 7 6 5 4 3 2 1

To render a people obedient and keep them so, savage laws inefficiently enforced are less effective than mild laws enforced by an efficient administration regularly, automatically, as it were, every day and on all alike.

— Alexis deTocqueville

Contents

Foreword

When the French philosopher, Jean Baptiste Alphonse Karr, observed many years ago that "the more things change, the more they are the same," it is doubtful he was speaking prophetically of the changing workplace, roles and policies pertaining to twentieth century correctional officers in America. However, the phrase applies with uncanny accuracy.

Change has become the order of the day for the correctional officer. The correctional workplace has added computers, video cameras, metal detectors, drug detection devices, cellular telephones, and an array of "state of the art" technological devices which were only the talk of "futureologists" just a few short years ago. The role of the "guard" who opens and closes doors and watches the prisoners has evolved into the "correctional officer." Potentially the principal agent of change in the entire institutional system, the officer is asked to deal with a younger, more complex, and often more violence-prone population. The legal rights and responsibilities of staff and inmates are continually reviewed and revised, interpreted and expanded.

At the same time, many important areas with fertile soil for change remain stagnant. While the new correctional officer must drastically adapt from "the old ways" and learn to be proactive in addressing the new complexity of the workplace, inmate population and legal structures, the standards for recruitment and compensation have remained discouragingly static. Although more training for correctional officers is available in most settings, and higher education is encouraged and sometimes subsidized, there is a deadening sameness in the lack of educational requirements, and lack of status and recognition for recruits. In many places, staff is recruited from the bottom of the talent pool.

The dedicated, efficient, intelligent correctional officer who provides an enormous contribution to his chosen profession and to the clientele which he serves remains the exception rather than the rule. This is truly tragic. For three decades, I have been teaching that the position of correctional officer requires the highest degree of professionality. The preparation for this role and the economic rewards to be earned by its successful fulfillment must occupy places of high priority in correctional planning and administration. Unfortunately, as the status and financial rewards of other professions such as medicine and law continue to rise in our class-conscious society, corrections is seen by many as simply "a job" and requires no great preparation and yields little economic reward.

In various public opinion polls, less than 15 percent of the population polled state that they would recommend careers in corrections to their children, and perhaps as little as 1 percent of teenagers expressed interest in a career in corrections. Many correctional officers casually accept the dominance of other "higher professions," and describe themselves as "only correctional officers." The need to enhance the professional status of these essential workers is imperative.

There is strong precedent for the linkage of professionalism and higher education in the field of law enforcement. The American police community, in their intense efforts to receive professional recognition, have long considered a four-year college degree as essential. Thirty years ago, one "blue ribbon" national commission recommended that every police agency should require at least four years of higher education at an accredited college or university as a condition of initial employment. Since that time, educational requirements have not lessened for professional police officers. Although some policy makers and researchers have challenged the overall benefits of higher education in policing, the fact remains that millions of federal, state and local dollars have been spent to provide college education for police officers, and the recognition of police professionalism has increased dramatically since the 1960s.

There has been pessimism concerning the value of education for correctional officers as early as the 1940s. However, since about 1964, some positive research findings emerged which are related to the lessening of occupational stress, and correctional officer impact on the effectiveness of intervention programs in the correctional setting. A large volume of professional observations show that employees who receive their technical training and then are exposed to some form of college-level study tend to make a greater commitment to their work, and also develop greater personal esteem, skill and effectiveness.

The demands of multiculturalism require new skills and attitudinal adjustments. The ability to understand cultural differences, to avoid stereotypes, and to communicate effectively is required to get today's job done properly and to suffer less stress in doing so. Higher education is probably the best way to adequately prepare correctional personnel for these complex tasks.

College and universities are recognized as the "gatekeepers" who determine who is to be considered professional in our society. For example, if I were to perform brain surgery on a colleague, I might be sued and indicted. However, if I had the professional credentials of "brain surgeon," after completing the required curriculum at a recognized university, I would be permitted the discretion to decide when to cut into someone's skull. While correctional officers may not have to make such a drastic life and death decision frequently, they must constantly exercise discretion in dealing with rules enforcement, reporting of infractions, degree of force to be legitimately used, and many other important areas of constitutional concern. In order to do this effectively, correctional officers must be recognized as professional, and up to the present time that recognition has been denied to them.

Professors Josi and Sechrest have looked very carefully at the changing role of the correctional officer; the personnel, management and organizational issues impacting on correctional officer career path development; and the need for professionalization. No issue of major concern is left untouched by their observations. They clearly report the current state of affairs, in which 35 states require only a GED or less education to become a correctional officer, and that 13 states are willing to settle for less than a GED. While many of us have been aware of this tragic condition for years, it needs to be constantly repeated and backed with hard data until it is recognized as a major source of the lack of professionalism and reduced effectiveness among the most important segment of correctional personnel in this country.

The authors conclude that "the importance of education both for the individual and organization cannot be overstated. Knowledgeable, highly skilled, motivated and professional correctional personnel are essential to fulfill the purpose of corrections effectively." Their survey of the existing literature on the subject of the value of higher education for correctional officers (with some mixed findings and a great deal of methodological criticism), combined with their in-depth reporting of the research and current practices in the police community, along with the endorsements of four national "blue ribbon" committees dating back to 1967, all give a high degree of support and validation to their conclusion regarding the efficacy of higher education for correctional officers.

I was pleased to see the following statement in print which I first wrote for the use of the International Association of Correctional Officers several years ago: "Education is a necessary component of and principal cause for universal recognition of any profession." This statement succinctly postulates the basic truth of the need for higher education if the correction officer's profession is to be professionalized. There is general agreement that any profession possesses a systematic body of knowledge that is acquired through academic study and that is generally possessed only by the members of that profession. If we want correctional officers to be professional, we must provide higher education for them.

Both training and higher education are necessary for the complete correctional officer. The body of knowledge and skills related to job performance ("prescriptive" materials) is the proper subject matter of training exclusively. The gray area of "descriptive" material (the "what," "how many," etc.) can be found in both training and in some levels of higher education. There is the conceptual, theoretical, and intellectual subject matter which is exclusively in the domain of higher education, which addresses the questions of "why?" and "should we?" The broader ethical and universal dimensions which provide the necessary background for complex decision-making in a culturally diverse society are offered through higher education.

These important distinctions are clearly incorporated into the two models for career development which are presented in this text. The first model—the "Correctional Peace Officer Certification Program" (C.P.O.S.T.)—is a generic certification project similar in content to the highly successful law enforcement educational certification program. It has many desirable features, including the establishment of minimum selection and training standards, certification of training courses, and the provision of management assistance and research services. It can provide for annual salary increments based upon an employee's achievements, job performance, education progress, and increased value to the organization. It has been extremely successful in police agencies.

The second model—"The Educational Assistance Program"—is based on the belief that professionalism requires a commitment to life-long learning and insists that the modern correctional agency should have a reimbursement program for higher education for those employees who wish to pursue educational goals concurrent with their career goals. In the model's statement of purpose, the authors present seven ambitious, yet realistic goals. Their relationship to professionalizing the correctional officer can be seen in the first statement, "to establish a process for the on-going identification of the necessary knowledge, skills and abilities needed for today's modern correctional professional."

Education is both the sign and the cause of professionality. As the sign, education will gain recognition and status for the correctional officer; as the cause, it will enable him to make a professional contribution to the field and to avoid stagnation and burnout. As a result, the economic rewards can be elevated in direct proportion to professionality.

As the number of truly professional correctional officers who perform well and are recognized for doing so increases through the opportunity for higher education, it will be necessary to create a horizontal promotion structure. In the basically paramilitary structure of the prison, the opportunities to "go up the ladder" are relatively limited. Economic and social rewards must be made available on a horizontal plane so that one can become promoted in salary and status as one does a better job at "being professional." Just as physicians gain income and status by becoming better at what they do without having to become a chief of staff in a hospital, so should correctional officers be able to obtain higher goals and rewards professionally as their career develops, without needing to become lieutenants or captains.

Whether the "horizontal promotion" idea is accepted and implemented is independent of the worth of the authors' recommendations for a career development model based on educational assistance for correctional officers. The time is right for this model to have been submitted to the correctional community. A major breakthrough in the long movement toward professionalizing the correctional officer through higher education took place in 1993, when the International Association of Correctional Officers established a Commission on Correctional Curriculum in Higher Education, which is discussed in the text. This effort is the culmination of the movement, which worked on an informal basis with little public notice and no official sanctioning body since 1970.

More formal steps were taken in 1988, when the International Association of Correctional Officers received a grant from the National Institute of Corrections and formed the Council on Curriculum Development in Corrections. This council included state correctional commissioners, academicians, correctional union representatives and staff of correctional institutions. To provide a broad base of professional and academic input into its deliberations, this council conducted surveys of all fifty states' department of corrections, several large metropolitan areas, and hundreds of higher education institutions offering courses in corrections. The work of the council was concluded in 1990 with the development of a standardized curriculum consisting of eighteen semester-hours of basic corrections course work.

In 1991, with a grant from the U.S. Department of Health and Human Services, a task force composed of representatives of the American Correctional Association, the American Jail Association, academics and corrections administrators from several states, reviewed and endorsed the curriculum. In 1992, the Corrections Employee Committee of the American Correctional Association gave its endorsement. In 1993, the Board of Directors of the International Association of Correctional Officers formally established a Commission on Correctional Curriculum in Higher Education to promote the adoption of the standardized curriculum in all college and universities teaching courses in corrections. As a result of this commission and its certification program, it is hoped that the transferability of credentials will be available to correctional officers who complete the standardized curriculum.

This should only be the beginning. The American police community, in their intense efforts to receive professional recognition, have long considered a four-year college degree as essential. Millions of federal, state and local dollars have been spent to provide college education for police officers, and as a result, the recognition of police professionalism has increased dramatically since the 1960s. Hopefully, the same scenario can be painted for the correctional profession as we move into the next century. The work of the International Association of Correctional Officers is a giant step forward. This work of professors Don Josi and Dale Sechrest strongly supports that effort by painting a clear picture of where we are and by presenting its recommendation for an "educational program model for correctional officer career development."

If we finally come to realize the necessity of effective career development, including the importance of higher education, realistic economic rewards and professional recognition for correctional officers, perhaps we will be able to look back in a few years and say that "the more things have changed, the more they really have changed," much to the benefit of the profession, the confined population served, and for all of us in society.

Paul H. Hahn, Chair (Retired)
Department of Criminal Justice
Xavier University
Cincinnati, Ohio

Preface

Outside of line and staff supervisors, relatively little research has been conducted concerning American correctional officers. Much remains to be learned about why some people are attracted to institutional custody work, how and why they remain employed, and why they choose to leave. Those questions are important because correctional officers, who spend more time with inmates than anyone, form the backbone of institutional efforts to secure, control, and rehabilitate offenders in local, state, and federal correctional institutions.

The principles on which correctional practice rests have evolved with time; some are heavily based in tradition, and most are not articulated in any integrated way in a single source in the literature. Our purpose in the development and presentation of this book is to present a comprehensive, timely, issue-oriented perspective on the changing career field of the correctional officer. This text is adaptable as a primary or secondary source or reference book for corrections-related undergraduate classes or as a supplemental reader for graduate seminars. Moreover, students enrolled in practicum or internship courses will find this book of value in gaining a better understanding of the correctional career field.

Within the corrections profession, administrators, management personnel, and line and staff supervisors seeking information to facilitate informed choices about career development options will find the book useful in focusing and placing their careers in perspective and in providing guidance for professional development. Additionally, the nature and scope of this text should provide valuable source material for officials and policy implementors at various levels of public service.

We thank our respective families for the support and encouragement involved in putting together this book. The staff of Butterworth Heinemann, particularly Laurel DeWolf and Stephanie Gelman, were especially helpful in seeing the manuscript through to completion.

Part I

Introduction

1

The Changing Role of the Correctional Officer

Historically, corrections has been viewed as an occupational field, not a profession. The correctional institution was referred to as a *penitentiary*, a facility designed to punish; correctional officers were called *guards*, their duty was strictly custodial, their role was principally that of "turnkey." Without demand for additional skills, little attention was paid to upgrading the position.

Typically, employment as a penitentiary guard attracted white men from rural areas or small towns, many with a limited education and a history of unemployment (Irwin 1980). These "guards" frequently began their careers in their mid- to late twenties, after having tried a variety of other occupations. Many were retired enlisted military personnel who frequently reported an interest in police work and chose corrections because it appeared somewhat related (Philliber 1987). A primary employment motivation factor was job security. The prison system provided the promise of steady work, with little fear of layoff. These individuals frequently did not identify this occupation as a profession; the common tendency was to view the work as "just another job" (Lombardo 1980).

The past 35 to 40 years of research and correctional activity has created an increasingly complex and somewhat contradictory body of knowledge regarding the changing role of the correctional officer. In a 1947 article on the selection process of prison personnel, Lundberg stated, the "methods of selection of the prison guard are generally loose and have little empirical validity" (p. 38). As recently as 1981, Toch wrote, "the correctional officer is a residue of the dark ages. He requires 20/20 vision, the IQ of an imbecile, a high threshold for boredom and a basement position in Maslow's hierarchy" (p. 20). On the other hand, another view has it that the correctional officer can be the single most important person in terms of influencing the inmate and having the potential for enhancing or minimizing, through his or her actions, the effectiveness of the various treatment programs (Glaser 1969; Teske and Williamson 1979; Wicks 1980).

To fully appreciate the unique and conflicting role of the correctional officer in the American workforce, it first is important to understand the dramatic changes that have occurred in penal philosophy during the growth of this nation. The history of society's response to criminal behavior reveals a wide range of reactions that have been employed at one time or another.

3

Large-scale societal devices and procedures for dealing with criminals are of recent origin. Punitive responses to offenders grew in advance of tightly reasoned philosophies of punishment. Offenders have been subjected to death or torture, social humiliation, banishment, imprisonment, and financial penalties. In general, response toward lawbreakers originally was retributive, compelling the criminal to make amends in some way. Later, restraint and punishment became the principal form of reaction to deviants, an approach still dominant in Western societies (Morris 1974).

The forerunner to the modern correctional institution, the penitentiary, is an American invention that arose in the early years of American history. The Walnut Street Jail, a precursor to the modern correctional institution, opened in Philadelphia in 1776. This and the subsequent Pennsylvania Prison at Cherry Hill (1829) operated on the "solitary system," characterized by a distinct architecture intended to isolate prisoners from one another. Auburn Prison (1819), followed a few years later by Sing Sing Prison, both in New York state, provided the architectural model for nearly all penitentiaries constructed in the United States until the last few decades. Referred to as the *silent system*, these prisons were walled institutions in which inmates were incarcerated in cells in multitiered cell blocks with a common work and dining area. However, nearly total silence among convicts was maintained within a repressive regime featuring striped uniforms, lockstep marching, and severe punishment for violation of rules.

Prison reformers of the late 19th century sought to improve conditions within the penitentiary system. Proper supervision of inmates was one area of concern. Many of the early writings on corrections by sociologists were critical of the nature of the relationships between inmates and their keepers. This was often evidenced by the working references to prison guards as "hacks" and "screws" (Sykes 1958). Although few official records were kept, historical accounts of the guards' role portrays them as "cold," "sadistic," and "punitive."

Visitors who toured the early American penitentiaries also were unimpressed with the quality of supervision. According to O'Hare:

> Prison jobs have become the dumping-ground for the inefficient and the unfit relatives and political hangers-on of the professional politicians. These human misfits and failures are thrust into prison jobs because as a rule, they are too worthless for other employment . . . industrially unfit and generally illiterate, human scrubs, mentally defective, morally perverted and very often of much lower type than the prisoners whom they handle. (1923, p. 161)

Little changed from the earliest institutions through the middle of the 20th century. During the Depression of the 1930s, the prison administrators' mandate was to balance their budgets and turn back excess funds to the government. During this period, the prison population was large. Most inmates were placed in minimum or medium security facilities or in prison camps.

During the 1940s prison populations decreased while prison budgets increased—prison administrators often could exceed their budgets and obtain supplemental funding. One result of the increase in available funds was the introduction of the interdisciplinary approach to corrections. Now prison guards were responsible solely for security and custodial duties, and psychologists and psychiatrists handled any counseling or treatment that might be offered to inmates.

With the involvement of social workers, psychologists, and psychiatrists came marked civil service classification and pay scale preference. Prison guards were not classified as "professionals." Higher education was not required and the caste system was strengthened. In-service training programs for guards were rare and had no a "professional" aura. Clemmer, writing in the 1940s, observed that guards had a "retaliatory spirit" toward their charges. This theme was supported some 12 years later by Barnes and Teeters (1952), who referred to guards developing "lock psychosis," the result of continual "numbering, counting, checking, and locking."

In recent decades, the penal environment changed dramatically. Penitentiaries gradually became less severe and more humane "correctional institutions." Since the 1950s, humanitarian reforms designed to lessen the pain of imprisonment and provide constructive inmate "programs" replaced the more repressive penitentiary setting. A rehabilitative philosophy dominated corrections through the mid-1970s. It offered a humanistic approach and corrective action to lead offenders to a law-abiding lifestyle. This was the era of the "rehabilitative ideal" (Morris 1974; Sechrest and Reimer 1982).

Throughout these periods of change, the role of the correctional officer evolved. The rapid growth of "prison systems" into departments of corrections and "prison guards" into correctional officers heightened interest in the role of the correctional officer as a more stable, career-oriented professional. Although recent legislation in several states has emphasized punishment as the primary role of incarceration, the negative and stereotypical connotations associated with corrections employment have been offset by substantial pay increases and a professionalized work environment. Increased training and organization within the field has brought status and readily marketable skills to the workforce.

The 1990s mark a new turning point for correctional systems in the United States. For some time, there has been an intensive effort by the field of corrections to gain the confidence of the public. With increased urbanization, more timely electronic news media reports, and renewed emphasis on human rights, corrections more and more has become the target of a wide variety of attacks. These have included questions on departmental and officer effectiveness of treatment efforts, cost effectiveness of operations, bureaucratic ineptitude, violations of civil rights of offenders, and overcrowding of institutions, among others. To combat this backlash, correctional agencies have devised a plan that has worked very well for law enforcement, a plan best summed up by a single word—professionalization. This movement has been led by an articulate and tactful group of correctional officials, who have stressed a new ideology of the correctional officer occupation.

Historically, policy makers and managers in the criminal justice system have viewed "professionalization" as a favored solution to escalating organizational problems, a panacea used to silence occasional opposition. Public officials generally assume that a "professional staff" will do what is necessary to ameliorate a crisis and better serve the community. While mandating the professionalization of front-line officers, top correctional officials often ignore deeper organizational problems and fail to consider the compatibility of personnel development with the organizational realities of work in contemporary correctional institutions.

Professional development for the correctional officer should be characterized by a concern for departmental performance through higher standards. Moreover, improvement in a number of personnel-related areas need to be addressed. Newer technologies, more sophisticated reporting procedures, and increased legal demands have made it necessary to reconsider the role of the correctional officer. In addition to maintaining the safety and security of the institution, the modern correctional officer must be able to communicate with inmates, supervisors, and the administration to avoid minor issues from escalating into major disturbances or riots. Moreover, the officers must be able to interact with a host of ancillary professionals employed by the institution, including psychologists, counselors, educators, and social workers.

For pedagogical simplicity, we have divided these issues into two main categorical areas: personnel and management/organizational issues. Collectively, these issues are critical to resolving many of the problems encountered by today's correctional officers in performing their duties.

PERSONNEL ISSUES

The correctional officer, like other correctional workers, must often function with conflicting goals. The primary responsibility of the correctional officer is to maintain order and security and to prevent escapes. However, the officer has numerous secondary goals, ranging from assisting troubled inmates to dealing with the general public. Today's modern officer must handle a complex variety of additional tasks and deal with a more sophisticated clientele. The need for additional training and education is a necessary requisite that should be a departmental mandate of every correctional organization.

Institutional changes and improvements have created a new opportunity and job definition for the modern correctional officer. The very dynamics created by wide variations in the operation of today's correctional institutions require an overall improvement in officer performance together with a rudimentary understanding of the behavioral sciences. It has been stated that today's correctional officer is the primary agent for promoting health, welfare, security, and safety within correctional institutions (Rogers 1991). Through direct interaction with accused and adjudicated offenders, the professional correctional officer has the potential to change the correctional process, for good or ill.

The continued development of the profession depends on a sound system of selection, training, and continued education. It is apparent that more than preservice and on-the-job training is required to meet the demands of this increasingly complex job. Correctional systems vary in the quality of their recruitment and selection practices as well as the length and content requirements of their pre- and in-service training mandates. In addition, the successful retention of skilled officers will be contingent on the development and implementation of a career certification program.

Recruitment and Selection

The recruitment and selection process generally is acknowledged as a key event in the operational effectiveness of a state or local correctional agency. All jurisdictions necessarily differ in a variety of unique and important ways regarding personnel selection. Nevertheless, basic principles exist for the development of an efficient, effective, and fair selection process that results in the appointment of those individuals who best possess the skills, knowledge, and abilities necessary for an effective respected correctional agency.

Knowledgeable, highly skilled, motivated, and professional correctional personnel are essential to fulfill the purpose of corrections effectively. Improved recruitment and selection standards of entry level correctional officers can make a positive contribution to the overall performance and operation of the organization. Carlos Sanchez, chief of selection and training for the California Department of Corrections, has questioned the current minimum standards for entry level officers. According to Sanchez, "we should raise our expectations and require a higher competency level for employment. . . . the writing ability of a large segment of our applicant group is deplorable. . . . we should increase our focus on attracting college-trained applicants" (Sanchez 1989, p. 166). Chief Sanchez is not alone in his assessment. In a 1992 nationwide survey of state personnel officers completed by the Robert Presley Institute of Corrections Research and Training, a majority of the respondents favored "some college up to a minimum associate of arts degree" as a prerequisite for entry level correctional officers (Sechrest and Josi 1992). However, respondents on the same study indicated that the minimal educational standard for employment as a correctional officer "was less than a high school diploma for 13 states (25.5%), a GED or high school diploma in 22 states (43.1%), and a high school diploma or more for 16 states (31.4%) [thus] . . . in two-thirds of the states (35 or 68.6%), a GED or less would be sufficient education to become a correctional officer" (p. 8).

Because it is in the "people business," corrections is a very labor-intensive enterprise. But as the numbers of correctional personnel expand to keep pace with growing inmate populations, it also sometimes is difficult to keep in mind that every number on every agency's table of organization represents an individual employee, a person with strengths and weaknesses, capabilities and limitations, satisfactions and frustrations. The field of corrections spends a tremendous amount of money on recruitment and selection of its corrections staff. According to the American Correctional Association, approximately three-fourths of the average operating budget is devoted to personnel. It seems prudent, therefore, to be concerned about the quality of this expensive investment.

Training

Pre- and in-service training often has been cited as one of the most important responsibilities in any correctional agency (Grabow, Sevy, and Houston 1983; McKenna and Pottle 1985; Wahler and Gendreau 1985; Craig 1987; Humphery 1990; Johnson 1990; Morton 1991; Carter 1991). Training serves three broad purposes.

First, well-trained officers generally are better prepared to act decisively and correctly in a broad spectrum of situations. Second, training results in greater productivity and effectiveness. Third, it fosters cooperation and unity of purpose. Furthermore, agencies are consistently being held legally accountable for the actions of their personnel and for failing to provide initial or remedial training (*ACA Training Standards*: American Correctional Association 1990, 1992).

In many respects, corrections has been slow to recognize the value of training and the impact it can have on the total organization (Carter 1991). Poorly trained officers with no prior experience can be a threat to themselves and other staff members. New officers with no prior training have no idea of the proper role or job responsibilities of correctional officers. And yet most new correctional officers have no prior experience in working with inmates, and almost none have any experience that applies to the prison setting (American Correctional Association 1997).

To carry out their security and supervision responsibilities, correctional officers need to understand their agency's correctional philosophy and their institution's regulations and procedures. All officers must be security technicians, with expertise in search, supervision, and inmate management. They must know the limits of their responsibility and authority, as well as how to work as team members with others. Finally, they must understand the judicial and legislative decisions that affect most of their activities. To be knowledgeable in all these important areas, well-developed training programs are necessary.

These concerns are the reasons why training is so critical. In fact, in the 1970s, the American Correctional Association (ACA) Commission on Accreditation for Corrections specified the first national training standards. The ACA not only identified specific standards for new officers but established requirements identifying essential training topics and the number of hours for preservice orientation, academy, and in-service training. Other organizations such as the National Sheriff's Association (NSA), the American Jail Association (AJA), and the International Association of Correctional Officers (IACO) have contributed to the training standards for correctional officers. These standards have contributed to the development of individual officer certification criteria for these organizations.

Training also received an additional boost in the late 1970s when federal judges began ordering correctional agencies to implement or improve existing training programs. By the middle to late 1980s, less emphasis was placed on merely requiring training programs and more on the effectiveness of the training provided (Johnson 1990).

Post-Secondary Education

Does today's correctional officer need a college education? A primary role of education is to instill in individuals the desire, capability, and ability to continue learning throughout life. The world in which the corrections professional operates is continually changing. New discoveries are made, new laws passed, new judicial rulings issued, and new technology is developed on a continuous basis. Adequate development of all skills—technical, human, and conceptual—requires increased amounts of education as society changes and the complexity of the profession and its knowledge base increases. Because higher order skills require more education than lower order skills, those who wish to compete adequately and rise to higher level positions must continue to pursue continuing education opportunities conscientiously.

Despite the increased importance of the correctional officer, little attention has been directed to the fundamental issue of education. Current research studies on the relationship between continued education and correctional officer career development and professionalism are methodologically deficient. This may be because the job of correctional officer over the years has not been seen as requiring education at even the high school level, much less beyond.

Sample data that strive to predict a relationship between higher education and job satisfaction, turnover, attitudinal variables, and substance abuse are relatively small in number and often do not include a significant subset of the target population. For these reasons, any examination of correctional officer education begins with two assumptions. First, there is a need for increasing the educational levels of correctional officers; and second, increased levels of officer education will improve overall correctional operations, including planning, management, and supervisory duties and services.

Career Path Development

This country's burgeoning offender population draws attention to the need for more corrections facilities, programs, and personnel. The current demand for well-trained employees is unprecedented in correctional experience. Simultaneously, the competition for resources to address facility and operational needs is unsurpassed. However, when correctional managers are forced to choose between providing funds for security and custody staff or for training the decision frequently is made in favor of custody requirements. Unfortunately, such circumstances and the lack of training that results can leave members of the corrections community handicapped in their ability to address their performance in efficient, effective, and lawful ways.

It is essential that correctional officers receive adequate preparation for their jobs. This preparation should include appropriate training and orientation to job assignments, and ongoing in-service training to enable them to assume increasing responsibilities. Moreover, training should go beyond preservice orientation and provide an opportunity for the organization to impart its mission, values, vision, and culture. Too often in corrections, only worker skills are targeted for training, and the organization misses a significant opportunity to communicate its vision and mission.

Correctional agencies cannot expect to have a top-notch workforce without having made an investment in career development education and training programs. Organizations clearly communicate how they value training, education, and job development by the resources directed toward staff preparation, both at the preservice and in-service levels and by upper level management's involvement in the entire process.

Career planning is critical to the success of correctional management. Effective career planning is essential to hiring and retaining the most talented employees available and is useful in helping employees avoid career plateaus and obsolescence. From the individual's perspective, career planning is essential if employees are to maintain some self-determination with regard to their own careers. Career planning helps employees make better decisions about their careers, when to seek job mobility and more challenging job assignments and when to stay put. Most important, career planning assists employees in adjusting to the changing personal needs and job demands they face as they pass from one career stage to another.

MANAGEMENT/ORGANIZATIONAL ISSUES

The professional correctional officer will be concerned with a number of management and organizational issues fundamental to the successful operation of the correctional facility. In addition to personnel issues, the correctional officer must learn how to adjust to the day-to-day problems of the job. All officers, for example, should be aware of the problems raised by inmate lawsuits, gang activity, and crowding in their institutions. These are exacerbated by the need to learn how to deal with an increasingly diverse group of coworkers and inmates. The conflict between role ambiguity and the shift toward unionization can be important factors. Learning new technologies can be frustrating as well as rewarding. Finally, the pressure of possible privatization of some operations and well as the entire facility is a constant concern.

Civil Liability

Perhaps the most consequential change in the corrections environment has been a marked increase in court intervention to guarantee the civil rights of inmates. Prior to the early 1960s only a few hundred inmate suits were filed every year in federal courts—judges adhered to a "hands off" policy, accepting the notion that convicted felons lost their rights (Haas and Alpert 1995). By the middle 1960s changes in legal philosophy and case law led to a much greater willingness by judges to hear prisoner petitions. As judicial activism increased, prisoners for the first time gained a source of judicial relief (see Haas 1977, 1981). By 1993, more than 33,000 lawsuits were filed by disgruntled inmates against correctional personnel (Dunn 1994). Needless to say, court decrees to reform unconstitutional practices and conditions have substantially altered standards of prisoner care and custody.

Desiring to acquire compensatory damages and broad equitable relief, inmates increasing have used the litigation process and filed lawsuits for a variety of reasons. Quite often, legal actions arise from inmate allegations against correctional officers for failing to perform their legally assigned duties, performing the duty in a negligent manner, abusing their authority, and accusations of brutality and poor decision making (Ross 1995).

A major challenge for institutional administrators and correctional officers is compliance with court orders. They must ensure that issues that have been resolved in previous court cases do not reappear to set the stage for additional litigation that is extremely costly and time consuming. Critical in defending or reducing the number of inmate lawsuits is that correctional officers exhibit a fundamental working knowledge of the job in accordance with the law and agency policy. The correctional officer must also be conscientious in not violating inmate rights and in remaining within legal guidelines in all interactions with inmates.

The Changing Profile of Inmate Populations

The challenge of operating safe, secure, and orderly correctional institutions has never been greater than in the 1990s. Issues such as inmates with infectious diseases, the increasing frequency of problems with mental or physical disabilities, and other special offender populations make maintenance of institution discipline a difficult task.

Changing laws have mandated concern for disabled and infirm inmates. Perhaps the most significant event in the area of inmates with disabilities was the passage of the Americans with Disabilities Act (ADA) in 1990. Even without an increase in total numbers, the very presence of the ADA ensures that the physically and mentally challenged inmates will become more aware of their rights to equal opportunities for participation in prison life.

The available research indicates that at the present time correctional facilities provide few mechanisms for screening, flagging, and treating disabled inmates. Although a variety of evaluation services and programs are available to at least some inmates in the majority of states, it appears that services specifically addressing the problems faced by disabled inmates are found in only a small number of state institutions. In a few jurisdictions, some program services are not provided to any inmates.

The challenge for correctional personnel will lie in the ability to pool their knowledge and experience to adjust both institutional programs and attitudes of personnel toward these individuals. Failure to comply with the provisions of the ADA may provide inmates with disabilities another source of lawsuits against prison systems.

Task Related Role Conflict

Front-line correctional officers are the backbone of the entire correctional system (Glaser 1969; Corrothers 1992). They perform work that is both complex and demanding, involving considerable physical and psychological resources as well as a diverse array of skills. Despite the crucial role of these individuals, there is a scarcity of information about the variables that affect their occupational functioning (Reid 1982; Patterson 1992).

Correctional officers today must find a balance between the security role and their responsibility to use relationships with inmates to change their behavior constructively. They routinely assume numerous essential yet sometimes contradictory roles (e.g., counselor, diplomat, caretaker, disciplinarian, supervisor, crisis manager), often under stressful and dangerous conditions. The divergent and often incompatible goals can prove problematic; role conflict, role diffusion, and role ambiguity may be difficult if not impossible to avoid. Difficulties in adjusting to the multiple roles and demands that are placed on correction officers can seriously impair occupational responsibility.

Crowding

Prison populations surged during the late 1980s and continue to rise at an alarming rate through the middle 1990s. During this same period of time the chance of going to prison for drug offenses increased fivefold; for weapons offenses, it increased fourfold; and for sex offenses (not rape), larceny/theft, and motor vehicle theft, it doubled. By yearend 1996, there were over 1.2 million state and federal inmates in the United States; on average, state prison systems were operating at 114.7% of their rated capacity; and, the federal prison system was 25% over the rated capacity (Camp and Camp 1997). On January 1, 1997, 8 states reported operating below capacity (less than 95%), 15 at capacity (between 95% and 105%), and 26, the District of Columbia, and the federal prison system reported operating above capacity (greater than 105%) (Camp and Camp 1997).

The population increase that many prison systems experienced during the past few years generally was the result of tougher crime legislation. New guidelines have extended the length of time served in many states. Aggressive legislation that includes "two- and three-strikes" laws and the abolition of parole have had an impact on other states (Shichor and Sechrest 1996). A major cause of the increased population in federal prisons has been stricter drug sentencing laws. In 1994, 61% of all offenders in federal prisons were convicted of drug crimes, compared with 25% in 1980.

Population growth strains correctional personnel as well as housing and support services. Consequently, officers must supervise and control many more inmates on a very tight daily schedule. As the inmate populations exceeds the hiring of new officers, existing staff may find itself spread too thin. At the same time, changes in the composition of prison populations exacerbate the imbalance—between 1980 and 1993, violent criminals accounted for 40% of the growth in state prison populations. As corrections officials divert less serious offenders to community corrections programs, those who actually do time are more apt to be violent as well as young and from a minority group (Toch 1977). Such population shifts add tensions to corrections work.

Cultural Diversity

Although it has been a long-term problem in the correctional arena, cultural diversity has become one of the newest concerns. With the growth of the correctional workforce in recent years, a number of changes in the characteristics of these employees have occurred. According to the American Correctional Association (1997), correctional officers are entering the occupation at a younger age, with higher levels of education, with increasing numbers of women and those in minority groups. The expanding employment of women and members of minority groups in corrections is beginning to produce a workforce more reflective of the people and communities being served. Along with the benefits of a more varied workforce, correctional officers are now faced with the challenge of adapting to the differences they represent. Additionally, this new "generation" of correctional officers are less apt to tolerate the old authoritarian style of command.

Another component of the diverse workforce is the increased number of workers with disabilities. Title II of the Americans with Disabilities Act (ADA), which took effect in January 1992, prohibits discrimination by public entities in the delivery of programs, activities, and services to qualified individuals with disabilities. All state and local governments, including those that do not receive federal assistance, must comply with ADA and section 504 of the Rehabilitation Act of 1973 (as amended). The law applies to state prisons, county jails, and local police lockups, which are considered "public entities" subject to Title II. Many of the provisions of these laws also apply to the employment of correctional officers with disabilities. Although the mandates for serving these special populations are clear, many correctional agencies have failed to provide appropriate opportunities for them.

New Technologies

Advancing technology, more sophisticated reporting procedures, and improved management information systems have made new demands and placed additional burdens on correctional personnel. Critical in the operation of today's correctional institution is the interaction of technology and correctional officers. Technological innovation has spawned a proliferation of new devices. According to Latessa (1996), these devices generally can be categorized into seven areas: perimeter security, locking systems, internal/external surveillance, internal security, fire safety, communications, and management information systems. Correctional officers must work with vendors and suppliers to learn how to use new and often sophisticated mechanical security and video equipment. Training and education must focus on topics such as information needs, data entry, reporting formats, and interpretation of data provided in reports.

Privatization

The increased involvement of the private sector in corrections has presented a variety of challenges to the field (Shichor 1995). Private companies claim they can deliver the same services to corrections as the government. Privatization clearly threatens the civil service concept of job security. Through increased flexibility in hiring and firing of employees, paying lower salaries, providing fewer fringe benefits, limiting promotions, reducing staff, and providing less training, private firms can maximize their profit margins. Moreover, new challenges are presented when correctional officers must work with private vendors in specific areas of the institution, such as food service, medical care, and inmate programs.

Union Ascension

The ascent of unions in corrections is a fairly recent phenomenon that emerged out of the general unionization of civil service employees. Today, almost all states have a correctional officers' union or association, as do many counties. As they have become increasingly a part of corrections, correctional officers' unions have produced mixed results.

Like other labor organizations, unions and associations representing correctional officers seek to improve wages and working conditions and workers compensation for their members. On the downside, they present problems for administrators and supervisors, who must respond to union demands. With the rise of correctional officer unions and associations, the relationships between officers and administrators now are more formalized. When the rights and obligations of each side are stipulated by a labor contract, an old-style warden no longer can dictate working conditions.

Because the members are public employees, most are prohibited by law from engaging in strikes, but during the past 20 years a number of work stoppages and "sick-outs" have occurred. The fact that custody and program staff may be in separate unions has resulted in intraorganizational conflict in some states; in others, the different perspectives on correctional goals cause conflict between union groups, as each seeks to advance the interests of it members.

Recently, the role of the unions in corrections has been stretched beyond simple participation in administrative decision making. Many increasingly have been involved in the political decision process through heavy lobbying and financial support for political candidates. This has not been lost on correctional administrators, for they often can gain the assistance of organized labor at budget time. Unionization has brought correctional officers not only better pay and job security but also greater control over their work. Nonetheless, many people fear that unions and pro-inmate groups may become allies on certain issues against the administration.

SUMMARY

Many correctional systems are trying to meet this broad range of needs in the continuing effort to upgrade the performance of their correctional officers. Scarce resources in the face of increased inmate populations often work to defeat these goals. Nonetheless, the profession has a voice through its International Association of Correctional Officers (IACO), the American Correctional Association, the American Jail Association, and the National Sheriffs' Association. National standards of performance have been developed for institutions and certification programs for individual officers now are being used widely. More training is available through associations and private organizations, most of which can be made part of formal departmental certification programs. Clearly, the "guard" has been replaced by the correctional officer. This officer has learned how to motivate inmates to improve and how to be proactive in addressing the daily problems of institutional operations.

REFERENCES

American Correctional Association. *Standards for Adult Correctional Institutions,* 3d ed. Laurel, MD: ACA in cooperation with the Commission on Accreditation for Corrections, 1990.

American Correctional Association. *Standards for Adult Correctional Institutions,* 4th ed. Laurel, MD: American Correctional Association, 1992.

American Correctional Association. *ACA Correctional Officers Resource Guide* (rev. ed.). Laurel, MD: American Correctional Association, 1997.

Barnes, H.E., and N.K. Teeters. *New Horizons in Criminology.* New York: Prentice-Hall, 1952.

Bureau of Justice Statistics. *Prison and Jail Inmates, 1995.* Washington, DC: U.S. Department of Justice, 1996.

Bureau of Justice Statistics. *Prison and Jail Inmates, 1996.* Washington, DC: U.S. Department of Justice, 1997.

Camp C.G., and G. M. Camp. *The Corrections Yearbook 1997.* Criminal Justice Institute, Inc. New York, 1997.

Carter, D. "The Status of Education and Training in Correction." *Federal Probation* 55 (1991): 17–23.

Clemmer, D. *The Prison Community,* rev. ed. New York: Rinehart and Company, 1958 [1940].

Corrothers, H.G. "Career vs. Job: Why Become a Correctional Officer?" *The Effective Correctional Officer* (1992): 1–10.

Craig R.L. (ed.). *Training and Development Handbook,* 3d ed. New York: McGraw-Hill, 1987.

Dunn, A. "Flood of Prisoner Rights Suits Brings Effort to Limit Filings." *New York Times* (March 21, 1994), pp. A-1 and B-12.

Furniss, J.R. "The Population Boom." *Corrections Today* (1996): 38–43.

Glaser, D. *The Effectiveness of a Prison and Parole System.* Indianapolis: Bobbs-Merrill, 1969.

Grabow, K.M., B.A. Sevy, and J.S. Houston. *Statewide Job Analysis of Three Entry-Level Corrections Positions for the California Board of Corrections Standards and Training for Corrections Program.* Minneapolis: Personnel Decisions, 1983.

Haas, K.C. "Judicial Politics and Correctional Reform: An Analysis of the Decline of the 'Hands-off' Doctrine." *Detroit College of Law Review* 4 (1977): 796–831.

Haas, K.C. "The 'New Federalism' and Prisoners' Rights: State Supreme Courts in Comparative Perspective." *Western Political Quarterly* 34 (1981): 552–571.

Haas, K.C., and G.P. Alpert. "American Prisoners and the Right of Access to the Courts." In K.C. Haas and G.P. Alpert (eds.), *The Dilemmas of Corrections,* 3d ed., pp. 223–246. Prospect Heights, IL: Waveland, 1995.

Humphrey, V. "Training the Total Organization." *Training and Development Journal* (1990): 57–64.

Irwin, J. *Prisons in Turmoil.* Boston: Little, Brown, 1980.

Johnson, E. H. "Preliminary Survey of Personnel Training in American State Prison Systems." Southern Illinois University (mimeographed), 1990.

Latessa, E.J. "Correctional Technology." In M. McShane and F. P. Williams III (eds.), *Encyclopedia of American Prisons,* pp. 457–460. New York: Garland Publishing, 1996.

Lombardo, L.X. *Guards Imprisoned: Correctional Officers at Work.* New York: Elsevier, 1980.

Lundberg, D.E. "Methods of Selecting Prison Personnel." *Journal of Criminal Law and Criminology* 38 (1947): 14–39.

McKenna, D.D., and C. Pottle. *Development of Training Standards, Standards Project: Training Phase Technical Report.* Minneapolis: Personnel Decisions Research Institute, 1985.

Morris, N. *The Future of Imprisonment*. Chicago: University of Chicago Press, 1974.

Morton, J.B. (ed). *Public Policy for Corrections,* 2d ed. Laurel, MD: American Correctional Association, 1991.

O'Hare, K.R. *Remarks on Prisons and Prison Discipline in the United States*. Montclair, NJ: Patterson Smith, 1923, reprinted 1967.

Patterson, B.L. "Job Experience and Perceived Stress Among Police, Correctional, and Probation/Parole Officers." *Criminal Justice and Behavior* 19 (1992): 260–285.

Philliber, S. "Thy Brother's Keeper: A Review of the Literature on Correctional Officers." *Justice Quarterly* 4, no. 1 (1987): 9–37.

Reid, S.T. *Crime and Criminology*. New York: CBS College Publishing, 1982.

Rogers, R. "The Effects of Educational Level on Correctional Officer Job Satisfaction." *Journal of Criminal Justice* 19 (1991): 123–137.

Ross, D.L. "A 20-Year Analysis of Section 1983 Litigation in Corrections." *American Jails* 9 (1995): 10–16.

Sanchez, C.M. "Attracting and Selecting a Top-Notch Staff, The California Experience." *Corrections Today* 58 (1989): 166.

Sechrest, D.K., and D.A. Josi. *National Correctional Officers Education Survey*. Riverside, CA: Robert Presley Institute of Corrections Research and Training, 1992.

Sechrest, D.K., and E.G. Reimer. "Adopting National Standards for Correctional Reform." *Federal Probation* 46, no. 6 (1982): 18–25.

Shichor, D. *Punishment for Profit: Private Prisons/Public Concerns*. Newbury, CA: Sage Publications, 1995.

Shichor, D., and D.K. Sechrest. *Three Strikes and You're Out: Vengeance as Public Policy*. Newbury, CA: Sage Publications, 1996.

Sykes, G. "The Society of Captives." [Princeton University] *Justice Quarterly* 4 (1958): 9–37.

Teske, R., and H. Williamson. "Correctional Officers' Attitudes Toward Selected Treatment Programs." *Criminal Justice and Behavior* 6, no. 1 (1979): 59–66.

Toch, H. *Living in Prison: The Ecology of Survival*. New York: The Free Press, 1977.

Toch, H. "Is a 'Correctional Officer' By Any Other Name a 'Screw'?" *Criminal Justice Review* 3, no. 2 (1981): 19–35.

Wahler, C., and P. Gendreau. "Assessing Correctional Officers." *Federal Probation* 49 (1985): 70–74.

Wicks, R.J. *Guard! Society's Professional Prisoner*. Houston: Gulf Publications, 1980.

Part II

Personnel Issues

2

Recruitment and Selection

While the evolution of the corrections officer has progressed with the evolving criminal justice system, this profession continues to be plagued by the stereotypical portrayal of past decades. The depiction of correctional officers as mindless brutes capable of only taking orders still is ingrained in the minds of a large segment of society whose experiences do not include exposure to this unique field. In fact, according to one author, the correctional institution is somewhat like rape or incest; you know it exists but prefer not to think about it, hoping it will go away (Blydenburgh 1993). Through direct interaction with adjudicated offenders, the modern correctional officer is the essential catalyst of change within the correctional process —knowledgeable, highly skilled, motivated, and professional correctional personnel are essential to fulfill the purpose of corrections effectively. Professionalism is achieved through structured programs of recruitment and the subsequent enhancement of the officer's skills, knowledge, insight, and understanding of the corrections process.

To be sure, corrections has suffered from being the stepchild of the criminal justice system in the United States, from public attitudes of rejection to lack of political support. As we approach a new millennium, correctional officers increasingly will be accountable and therefore will need certain basic credentials and values. Administrators will be required to pay closer attention to character, knowledge base, experience and skill level when hiring future correctional officers. This kind of screening will lead to improvements in hiring and increased professionalism.

The notion of employment as a correctional officer moving from a public service occupation toward the professional end of the occupation-profession continuum has been well established through structured programs of recruitment and enhancement of officers' skills, knowledge, insight, and understanding of the corrections process. Successful careers in corrections clearly require greater commitment to professionalism than was necessary as recently as 15 years ago. Never has there been such a demand for a professionally competent and motivated staff. Although entry level requirements still are comparatively low in some places, advancement often requires higher education, commitment to professional values, and exemplary performance. According to the American Correctional Association (1991), "effective employment practices are based on professional recruiting procedures" (p. 76).

RECRUITMENT

The recruitment of correctional officers refers to the acquisition of applications from persons who want to be on the staff as sworn personnel of the prison or correctional institution. Many of these applications are prompted by notification and advertisements by civil service commissions that an examination will be held for an entry level position. In many other cases, interested persons may initiate the contact by voluntarily approaching the personnel officer or other person at the institution.

Recruitment Standards

A task as important as the recruitment of correctional personnel should be approached from a positive viewpoint. Given the low visibility of corrections as an occupational field and the need to attract staff from a wide cross section of demographic groups, it is essential that agencies undertake aggressive recruitment efforts, both within and beyond their jurisdictional boundaries.

Correctional agencies, through the authority of their respective governments and administrations, need to identify and employ the best candidates available and not merely eliminate the least qualified. All qualified applicants should be considered, without regard to race, sex, age, religion, physical restrictions, political affiliation, or ethnic background. In addition, corrections should serve as a model for other agencies, both public and private, in extending to ex-offenders the opportunity to seek and receive equal consideration for positions for which they are qualified. The benefits of positive recruitment (and selection) policies will result in a lower rate of personnel turnover, fewer disciplinary problems, higher morale, better community relations, and more efficient and effective services.

Basic standards of recruitment provide a framework for both the technical and philosophical details of an efficient and effective correctional recruitment function. It is possible to describe the basic thrust of these standards in summary form.

A written directive should initiate the formal recruitment process. Administrative control for the process should be vested in one identifiable position. All agency personnel, especially women and members of minority groups, should be involved in a recruitment process, based on a written recruitment plan with specific goals and measurable objectives that are evaluated and reevaluated annually. A comprehensive plan will enable the department to conduct an organized and effective search for well-qualified applicants by relating job requirements to recruiting methods. The recruitment directive should set forth measurable recruitment objectives, including actual and forecast vacancies, as well as the strategies and procedures designed to accomplish those objectives. A timetable of key recruitment activities, an itemized recruitment budget, and procedures for obtaining the assistance of community organizations and leaders also should be included.

Recruitment activities may be enhanced by cooperative arrangements with a personnel agency and written recruitment agreements with correctional agencies, community organizations, and key (stakeholders) leaders. Recruiters, armed with literature depicting the cultural diversity of the agency, should be sent on-site to educational institutions, community service organizations, and organizations that represent the minority community.

Any effective and fair recruitment process depends on many technical application requirements, including vacancy announcements that are accurate and based on complete job analyses and the availability of decentralized locations for the application and testing process. An official filing deadline should be established and vacancies advertised through the mass media well in advance of the established deadline. Some form of contact should be maintained with applicants throughout the recruitment, application, and employment process.

Several important assumptions and caveats underlie these recruitment standards. First, the standards generally are applicable only to those agencies with ongoing or active recruitment efforts. In other words, recruitment programs normally take place when actual vacancies exist or when potential vacancies are forecast. However, four basic standards are imperative for all agencies regardless of the job vacancy situation: (1) an Equal Employment Opportunity Plan, (2) cooperative personnel recruitment agreements among correctional agencies, (3) an affirmative action plan, and (4) an Americans with Disabilities (ADA) plan.

A second assumption of the basic standards is that, unless stated otherwise, they apply only to sworn personnel. Similarly, unless specifically stated to the contrary, all standards are applicable to the recruitment of entry-level personnel only.

Third, it is understood that, in certain cases, an agency is required to handle its personnel through a state or local civil service merit system and, therefore, is linked to that system in the recruitment of its correctional personnel.

Agency Administrative Practices

The recruitment process is governed by the economics of the state, county, or municipality responsible for the incarceration of its offenders. Generally, when there are actual or forecast vacancies, the correctional agency initiates an active recruitment campaign for qualified applicants.

To attract the best qualified applicants, a correctional department's recruitment personnel must posses knowledge and skills in the following areas:

1. The agency's recruitment needs and commitments;
2. The agency's career opportunities, salaries, benefits, and training;
3. Federal and state compliance guidelines;
4. The community and its needs (including demographic data, community organizations, educational institutions, etc.);
5. Multicultural awareness or an understanding of different ethnic groups and subcultures;
6. Techniques of informal record keeping systems for candidate tracking;
7. The selection process utilized by the central personnel operation or agency (including procedures involved in background investigations and written, oral, or physical agility examinations);
8. Recruitment programs of other jurisdictions;

9. Characteristics that disqualify candidates;
10. Medical requirements.

An effective agency technique in today's highly competitive job market is to involve all department personnel in the recruitment process and provide incentives for their participation. The benefits of such a program are twofold. First, more personnel become involved in the recruiting than could be assigned specifically to such duties by the agency. Moreover, because of their professional interest, officers generally recruit qualified candidates.

In addition, the placing of women and minority group officers, especially those of supervisory ranks, in recruitment roles achieves several goals. Their involvement can demonstrate the department's commitment to cultural diversity standards, demonstrate promotability by virtue of their rank, enhance the receptivity and support of the community, and increase the potential for recruiting from a diverse cross section of personnel.

State, county, or municipal personnel (human resource) departments often are helpful in the recruitment of qualified applicants. Such agencies, through the years, develop a high degree of expertise in attracting personnel for other government agencies and units. The advantage of utilizing a personnel department's expertise in the recruitment process is twofold. First, the participating agency's likelihood of success actually is multiplied by the number of agencies involved in the agreement. Moreover, an applicant's likelihood of exposure and success, by virtue of applying to any one of the participating agencies, also is multiplied by the number of agencies involved. Cooperative personnel systems facilitate the general exchange of experienced personnel between or among agencies.

Community Outreach

Cooperative assistance from community organizations and key community stakeholders will increase and broaden the agency's exposure within the service community. The cooperation of the community is essential to the recruitment process and will help the department achieve broader dissemination and greater exposure of recruitment information.

Recruiting among the youth is extremely important. So often, youth fail to get the necessary exposure and reinforcement that lead individuals into certain career paths, simply because they are unaware of the opportunities available to them. Career Day on high school, college, and university campuses offers excellent opportunities for setting up displays, passing out recruitment material, and speaking to interested students. Agency recruiters should acquaint college and university career counselors with the benefits and challenges of a correctional officer career. Agencies should nurture student interest in the correctional field by providing them with firsthand experience in corrections, to the degree that their safety and institutional security are ensured. Cooperative student placements through local college and university criminal justice internship programs serve the dual purpose of maintaining the student's interest in corrections while attending college and providing an excellent potential recruitment pool.

Affirmative Action and Equal Employment Opportunity

Affirmative action requires aggressive recruitment of minority group members that are significantly underrepresented in the agency. Preferential recruitment then should be directed toward approximating (within the sworn ranks) the minority composition of the community. If the available minority group workforce is less than the makeup of the minority group service community, the agency should seek the authority to recruit outside its service area to attract a minority group workforce equal to the makeup of that community.

The affirmative action plan should be written in a direct manner so that it easily can be understood and followed. The foundation of a successful recruitment drive should include strong management commitments, an analysis of demographic and geographic features of the agency's service area, and specific knowledge of past efforts to attract minority group members by similar agencies.

The Equal Employment Opportunity Plan should assure equal opportunities for employment and employment conditions for members of minority groups and women. The Equal Employment Opportunity Plan should be based on an annual analysis of the agency's present employment policies, practices, and procedures relevant to their effective impact on the employment and utilization of minority group members and women.

The Americans with Disabilities Act mandates that the disabled have an opportunity to lead productive lives in mainstream society. The agency's employment practices should assure equal opportunities for mentally and physically challenged applicants who fall within the basic standards for employment as a correctional officer.

Job Announcements and Publicity

Detailed job announcements provide a description of the duties, responsibilities, requisite skills, educational level, and physical requirements for the position of correctional officer. The department should provide the most accurate and precise job description possible to avoid undue delay and wasted time on the part of both the agency and the applicant. When the most important performance dimensions are known, the potential applicants are in a better position to relate their particular knowledge, understanding, and skills to those required by the job to be filled. The agency saves the time and expense of making determinations that the applicants could have made, had they been fully apprised.

THE SELECTION PROCESS

Correctional officer selection is the screening of applicants to determine who the prison or correctional institution wants to hire. An appropriate screening process evaluates an applicant in a way that predicts that individual's ability to meet the demands of the job. Employment requirements should be valid, reliable, fair, job related, and nondiscriminatory. Valid tests that measure actual job requirements are the foundation for an objective screening process. In addition, applicants should be thoroughly screened for their ability to relate to others—both staff and offenders—and for their ability to meet any valid physical requirements of the correctional officer position.

Although procedures differ greatly from agency to agency, several procedures are common to most selection processes. Generally, the first step is the administration of a comprehensive written exam. If written tests are used, they must meet the professional and legal requirements of validity (job-relatedness), utility (usefulness), and minimum adverse impact (fairness). Following the successful completion of the written exam, oral interviews of eligible candidates are conducted using uniform questions, evaluation criteria, and rating procedures.

A written background investigation of successful candidates, conducted by trained personnel, generally is recognized as one of the most useful and relevant components of the selection process. Correctional careers require that individuals be of good moral character and not have been convicted of any felony or misdemeanor offenses that involve "moral turpitude." An offense involving moral turpitude usually is interpreted to mean misdemeanor theft or similar, less serious crimes that may suggest an untrustworthy character.

In addition to a criminal record check, the background investigation should include the verification of a candidate's qualifying credentials and the verification of at least three personal references. Some agencies require psychological examinations and polygraph or voice stress examinations as an additional investigative aid. Although the use of psychological testing is questioned by some (see Wahler and Gendreau 1985), Benton (1988) found that 24% of the states use psychological tests to screen entry level candidates.

Prior to the final offer of employment, occupational qualifications such as general health, physical fitness, and agility, emotional stability, and psychological fitness are measured and interpreted by trained personnel, using valid, useful, and nondiscriminatory procedures. A determinant probationary period (ranging from 6 to 24 months) and completion of entry level training are required of all entry level correctional officers.

Jurisdictions necessarily differ in a variety of unique and important ways regarding the selection process of corrections personnel. Nevertheless, basic principles exist for the development of an efficient, effective, and fair selection process that results in the appointment of those individuals who best possess the skills, knowledge, and abilities necessary for an effective, respected correctional agency. A number of basic standards provide a framework for both the technical and philosophical details of an efficient, effective, and fair correctional selection function.

Professional and Legal Requirements

The use of any selection procedure, test, or requirement is subject to statistical analysis and documentation and must satisfy professional and legal requirements for validity, utility, and minimum adverse impact. The linked concepts of the validity (job-relatedness), utility (usefulness), and minimum adverse impact (fairness) of the total selection process and its individual components not only are fundamental management principles of an effective and efficient personnel selection system but also have been incorporated into law through the courts and the regulatory process.

Federal law concerning validity requires proof that a given element of the selection process either will predict job performance or detect important aspects of candidates' work behavior related to the position for which they are applying. If a particular procedure, test, or requirement is not significantly related to an important part of the job, then it is not valid and cannot be used in the selection process. The primary question to be answered in validation is the degree to which the agency makes appropriate assumptions about a candidate's job performance by using a particular procedure, test, or requirement in the selection process. Determining validity is a complicated technical process, and validation research should meet both professional and legal requirements.

Utility is an assessment of the practical value of an element of the selection process based on considerations of validity, selection ratio, the number of candidates to be selected, and the nature of the job.

Adverse impact is a substantially different rate of selection (generally less than 80%) that works to the disadvantage of members of a race, sex, or ethnic group. When two or more alternative components of the selection process are available that have equal validity and utility, the department should use that element with the least adverse impact.

Validity

Three concepts or strategies are accepted by professionals and recognized by the courts for measuring the validity (job-relatedness) of the selection process as a whole or its individual components:

- Criterion-related validation,
- Construct validation,
- Content validation.

The preferred approach is predictive or criterion-related validity. Criteria are identified that reflect successful performance of the job, and test scores then are correlated with the performance ratings for the predetermined criteria: a high correlation demonstrates that the test is a useful predictor of the candidate's job performance. Construct validity involves the identification of the characteristics or traits (e.g., honesty) believed to be important to successful job performance. The test should measure the degree to which the candidate possesses the required characteristics. In content validity, a component of the selection process is justified by showing that it measures a significant part of the job (e.g., a typing test for a typist). In the final analysis, the selection process should be strictly accountable to the following checklist: (1) professionally and legally accepted data collection techniques are used to identify job tasks, (2) measurable candidate characteristics related to predicting job performance are identified, (3) selection components whose measures are job related have been used, and (4) conclusions and inferences about candidates are logical and persuasive. One or more of the validation strategies should be used, as appropriate, to support individual components of the selection process or the selection process as a whole.

Adverse Impact

Adverse impact should be determined by a four-step process. First, calculate the selection rate of each group by dividing the number of persons selected from the group by the number of applicants from that group. An applicant is any person who has indicated an interest in being considered for employment by completing an initial application form. A person who voluntarily withdraws either formally or informally at any stage of the selection process no longer is an applicant for purposes of computing adverse impact. Second, observe which group has the highest selection rate. Third, divide the selection rate for each group by the rate for the highest group. Finally, observe whether the selection rate for any group is less than 80% of the selection rate for the highest group. If so, adverse impact is indicated in most cases, unless a test of statistical significance indicates otherwise. The calculation should be based on a significantly large number of cases to be statistically significant.

A selection rate for any race, sex, or ethnic group that is less than 80%of the group with the highest selection rate generally is regarded as evidence of adverse impact and considered to be discriminatory. Smaller differences in the selection rate may, nevertheless, constitute adverse impact. This occurs when such differences, though small, are significant in both statistical and practical terms or when candidates have been discouraged disproportionately on grounds of race, sex, or ethnic group. On the other hand, greater differences in the selection rate may not necessarily constitute adverse impact. This is the case when such differences are based on small numbers not statistically significant or when special recruiting has caused the pool of minority group or female candidates to be atypical of what normally is expected from such groups.

Written Directives

A comprehensive manual is essential for the proper administration, use, and defensibility of the selection process. In addition, it describes the order of events in the selection process. The manual should include, at the least, information about the purpose, development, validity, utility, fairness, adverse impact, administration, scoring, and interpretation of all elements used in the selection process. The correctional agency may rely on a state or local civil service commission, employment agency, or other public or private external organization to administer or provide one or more elements of the selection process. If so, a copy of all relevant manuals should be maintained on file by the correctional agency.

A Final Word

The entire selection process should be evaluated in terms of its effectiveness in selecting the best qualified candidates in a fair and equitable manner. Elements of the selection process may become obsolete or have new effects over time due to changes in the applicant pool, reclassification of positions, new technology used on the job, and other developments after the selection process has been implemented. All circumstances concerning the evaluation of validity, utility, and adverse impact should be considered in determining when one or more components of the selection process is outdated. This would include a review of the most recent literature and case law on selection, equal employment opportunity, and related selection issues.

Administrative Practices and Procedures

A job-related, useful, and nondiscriminatory selection process depends on a number of professionally and legally accepted administrative practices and procedures, which include informing candidates of all parts of the selection process at the time of formal application; written procedures governing the reapplication, retesting, and reevaluation of unsuccessful candidates; and timely notification of candidates at all critical points in the process.

Written Notification

At the time of their formal application, candidates should be informed, in writing, of all applicable elements and the expected duration of the selection process. A listing of selection guidelines should include all written physical and psychological examinations, polygraph examinations, oral interviews, and background investigations. From the outset, candidates should be made aware that sensitive or confidential aspects of their personal life may be explored. Written notification of the expected duration of the selection process not only is a courtesy but also helps the agency better plan and coordinate its selection process. Candidates should be reasonably informed, in advance, of when and where testing is to take place, in the event they fail to complete the selection process. Moreover, candidates not eligible for appointment to probationary status should be informed, in writing, within 30 calendar days of such a decision. Prompt notification in writing not only is an essential element of an efficient administrative organization but fundamental to a fair and effective selection process.

Reapplication, Retesting, and Reevaluation

A correctional officer candidate who fails the selection process should not necessarily be excluded from further consideration, because (1) no selection component is perfectly reliable; (2) the candidate may acquire new knowledge, skills, and abilities; (3) adverse impact can be reduced through retesting; and (4) the threat of lawsuits or appeals can be minimized through retesting. Nevertheless, alternative forms and reasonable time intervals should be used to prevent overexposure to the selection process. Obviously, a vacancy would have to be available for which a candidate could reapply, and the positions for which vacancies exist would vary over time. Moreover, all candidates not appointed to probationary status should be given a reasonable period of time from the receipt of written notification to present additional information or data concerning the selection decision.

Written Exam

One of the most common screening instruments is a written civil service exam, which, according to the American Correctional Association, is used by almost 80%

of state agencies in the selection of correctional officers. Such tests have the advantage of being easy to administer, relatively inexpensive, and simple to score. Written tests are useful for determining a candidate's general level of knowledge and written communication skills. Good writing capabilities undoubtedly are important in correctional work, where preparing memos, reports, and other forms of written communication are a daily feature of the job.

Additionally, the written exam portion of the selection process should measure an applicant's aptitude for corrections work. That is, the successful accomplishment of corrections work requires that each officer possess certain knowledge, skills, and abilities necessary to perform the job. Ideally, this is accomplished through a job-task analysis, which

- Identifies the tasks being conducted by those already holding the job;
- Determines the knowledge, skills, and abilities necessary to effectively perform job tasks (particularly those that occur frequently or are significant to successful performance).

The relationship between job-task analysis and selection screening is based on a simple concept; that is, if you do not know what you are looking for, how will you know when you find it? The analysis of job tasks therefore is designed to identify what specific types of knowledge and skills are needed to perform the job properly. Then, it is possible to construct written test items that reflect more accurately what a candidate needs to know. The major disadvantage of even the most carefully constructed, job-related written test is that it is limited to measuring knowledge. Written tests can determine what applicants know intellectually but may or may not reflect what they actually are able to do.

In addition, criminal justice agencies that use written exams as part of the employment screening process have faced numerous Title VII (Civil Rights Act of 1964) lawsuits. Written tests generally have been used to reduce the applicant pool to a manageable number of candidates, and as a result of this process, members of minority groups have been eliminated at a higher rate than white candidates. In the past, many agencies avoided Title VII problems with written tests by adjusting scores or using separate white and minority group lists. However, the Civil Rights Act of 1991 specifically prohibits such adjustments. Therefore, correctional agencies are faced with a dilemma. Applicants rejected on the basis of an irrelevant or biased test may have grounds for legal action against the department. For this reason, some agencies have abandoned the written test for other procedures to avoid potential problems.

Oral Interviews

A correctional department's staff is its most important resource. Selecting officers who possess attitudes and personalities consistent with established agency goals sometimes is brushed aside in the haste to complete the interviewing process. The additional time spent selecting the appropriate staff member can save time and money. Even though the goal of interview process is to reduce the numbers (those considered undesirable), it is important not to treat this step lightly. It should be the foundation for making the final selection. A consistent set of guidelines should help determine those applicants best suited for employment as a correctional officer in terms of attitudes and personality.

All elements of the oral interview process should be standardized to be effective and impartial. Uniform questions, a defined set of personal attributes, and a uniform rating scale should be used. Clarification of answers, if needed, may be sought by the interviewer. Rating scales or procedures should be standardized to permit valid and useful distinctions among candidates and their expected job performance. The effectiveness of any process for hiring appropriate employees depends on the degree of care taken in constructing and applying that process.

The oral interview (or personal qualifications appraisal) may be conducted by a board or panel, representative of correctional practitioners, selection professionals, or community representatives. The interview team should have a shared under-standing of the qualities desired in the agency's "ideal" candidate. Such qualities include experience, education, appearance, personality, motivation, creativity, and or-ganization skills. The interview team should identify and rate the qualities in impor-tance, assigning a numerical score to each attribute. The selection or disqualification of an individual on the basis of intangible evidence should be discouraged.

Background Investigations

The background investigation, although costly and time consuming, is considered by many correctional practitioners to be the most useful and relevant component of the selection process. The background investigation serves two purposes: (1) it examines the past work and educational record of the candidate, and (2) it determines if anything in the candidate's background might make him or her unsuitable for work as a correctional officer. The extensiveness of the background investigation is limited only by the number of candidates being investigated and the time available. At a minimum, the investigation should include the verification of a candidate's substance abuse history, a criminal record check, and the verification of facts by at least three personal references.

Investigators must use all data available on the candidate, especially the appli-cation form and the medical history report. It is more reliable to conduct the inquiry in person, although telephone and mail inquiries may be appropriate in cases of crimi-nal history and driving records. The investigation routinely should involve a home visit with the candidate and his or her family and interviews with neighbors.

Minimum qualifying credentials should include educational achievement, em-ployment, age, residence, and citizenship. The verification can be made by telephone, correspondence, computer inquiry, or personal interview and should be backed up by written notations. A candidate's criminal history should be obtained from the National Crime Information Center (NCIC), a Federal Bureau of Investigation (FBI) finger-print check, and appropriate state and local criminal history record information re-positories. Personal references should include at least one employer (if the candidate has an employment history) and may include teachers, landlords, neighbors, friends, and coworkers.

Polygraph Examinations

The use of the polygraph examination as a follow-up to the background investigation is increasingly used as a means of verifying the background of a candidate. Although some states have banned its use for preemployment purposes, when used to screen correctional officer candidates it is necessary to determine why it is being given. Often it can be used only to verify other information, such as reported substance abuse, but not as a primary indicator. If polygraph examinations, or other instruments for the detection of deception, are used in the selection process, they should be administered only by a qualified examiner who is not affiliated with the hiring agency. Moreover, a number of basic "rules" should be observed:

1. Applicants need to be provided with a copy of "relevant" questions used in the examination. For candidates to give their informed consent, it is reasonable for them to know the full nature and extent of the inquiry. "Relevant" questions— those having a bearing on the selection decision—should be provided in advance of the test so that candidates can have sufficient time to review and understand what is going to be asked of them.
2. The administration of examinations and the evaluation of the results are conducted by trained personnel not affiliated with the hiring agency. The sensitive nature of these tests makes it necessary to rely on examiners who possess professional training and credentials in the use and interpretation of these investigative tools.
3. A written directive prohibits the use of results of polygraph examinations or other instruments for the detection of deception as the single determinant of employment status. Polygraph examinations and other instruments used for the detection of deception should be considered only an investigative aid. However, admissions made during pretest, test, or posttest interviews, together with other information, may be sufficient to support decisions relevant to employment status.

Physical Qualifications

Physical qualifications include such things as height, weight, visual acuity, hearing, color blindness, physical agility, and physical fitness. A variety of legal challenges have invalidated many of the specific minimum and maximum qualifications in these areas, because they have not been validated as either job related or as bona fide occupational qualifications. All physical and age qualifications for entry level sworn correctional officer positions should meet the requirements of validity, utility, and minimum adverse impact.

Prior to appointment, the department should check the health and physical fitness of all applicants to reveal any medical problems that might inhibit work performance. Physical fitness is a candidate's body conditioning as measured by examination results, value rated according to the person's age, weight, and height. Such an examination may help identify qualified candidates and reduce the probability of work related disabilities. The use of valid, useful, and nondiscriminatory procedures will support the accuracy and defensibility of the testing process. Moreover, a physical agility examination is helpful to determine a candidate's strength, endurance, coordination, and ease of movement. Although the "events" in such tests may vary considerably, they should be representative of the degree of physical agility that correctional officers are expected to maintain throughout their careers.

Psychological Profile

Correctional work is highly stressful and places officers in positions and situations of heavy responsibility. Psychiatric and psychological assessments are needed to screen out candidates who might not be able to carry out their responsibilities or endure the stress of the working conditions. The department should maintain a report of each emotional stability and psychological fitness examination to ensure proper procedures are followed and to provide data for continuing research and legal defense, if needed.

Once candidates have passed all tests in the selection process, they usually enter a probationary period during which they are observed in basic training and while applying this training in the institutional setting. A one-year probationary period is generally accepted among the correctional community (the ACA probationary period standard for correctional officers is "at least six months but no longer than one year"; ACA standard 3-4057). This probationary period allows for evaluation of the selected candidates. To assure that all probationary candidates have competed equally, the agency should measure the extent of adverse impact, if any, produced by the probationary process. This can be achieved by evaluating the entry level appointment rate (i.e., candidates who achieve permanent status) using the uniform four-fifths (80%) adverse impact indicator. If adverse impact is suggested, it may be necessary to re-evaluate the procedures, techniques, or examinations used during the probationary process.

After the probationary period, the officers should continue to receive periodic in-service training to maintain already acquired skills and to achieve proficiency in new ones (see the following chapter, on training).

REFERENCES

American Correctional Association. *Public Policy for Corrections.* Waldorf, MD: St. Mary's, 1991.

Benton, N. "Personal Management: Strategies for Staff Development." *Corrections Today* 50 (1988): 102–108.

Blydenburgh, J.C. "The Ongoing Battle for Parity." *American Jails* (1993): 51–52.

Wahler, C., and P. Gendreau. "Assessing Correctional Officers." *Federal Probation* 49 (1985): 70–74.

3

Pre- and In-Service Training

Regardless of how good the selection process is at bringing the most qualified recruits into the agency, they cannot be expected to know what is required of them on the job without proper training. Training often has been cited as one of the most important responsibilities in any correctional agency. Poorly trained officers with no prior experience are a threat to themselves and others on the staff. New officers without proper training have no idea of the proper role or job responsibilities of correctional officers. And yet most new officers have no prior experience in working with inmates, and almost none have any training that applies to the prison setting. As we move toward the next century, with all the challenges and changes facing corrections, the need to place greater emphasis on career development through training and education will become more important.

The relative importance of specialized training in corrections has followed a long and strenuous path. Recognition that pre- (basic) and in-service training for correctional officers was required in order that corrections be considered a profession dates back to 1870, when these principles were enunciated at the National Prison Congress meeting in Cincinnati (Silverman and Vega 1996). However, it took more than 100 years before any major attempts were made to realize this objective. In the late 1970s, the American Correctional Association Commission on Accreditation for Corrections specified the first training standards for correctional officers and established requirements identifying essential training topics and the number of hours for preservice orientation, academy, and in-service training (ACA training and staff development standards encompass 3-4070 through 4-4091; ACA 1990).

According to the commission's standard 3-4081, recruit officers should receive at least 40 hours of preservice orientation training. At a minimum, this training should be used to "familiarize new staff members with the purpose, goals, policies, and procedures of the institution and parent agency; working conditions and regulations; responsibilities; inmate rights; and an overview of the correctional field" (ACA 1997, p. 9). In addition, the commission recommended 120 hours of paramilitary-style academy training during the first year of employment and 40 hours of annual in-service training for all officers.

The American Correctional Association standards require that trainers receive adequate preparation for their roles. Standard 3-4071 (ACA, 1990) states that, "The qualified individual coordinating the staff development and training program has specialized training for that position. Full-time training personnel have completed at least

40-hour training-for-trainers course." Standards also call for good planning and co-ordination of training (3-4070), an annual assessment of the program (3-4073), adequate library and reference materials to support training (3-4075), and necessary space and equipment (3-4077).

Consistent with the ACA standards, in 1979 the American Association of Correctional Training Personnel (AACTP) undertook an initiative to develop standards that specified the critical skills required for effective classroom performance of trainers. These included standards for classroom presentation skills, instructional performance objectives, and written lesson plans. This initiative was further expanded in a second project in 1985 to develop standards for the structural support of staff training programs by correctional organizations. In 1987, AACTP initiated a third project to redefine training programs and establish a set of comprehensive standards.

Today, academy training is provided to new correctional officers in virtually all correctional settings. The Federal Prison System has training centers in several institutions in various geographic locations around the country. Many states have correctional academies similar to those developed by police departments. In the opinion of informed experts, this ordinarily requires a training course of a minimum 180 hours (ACA 1997). However, a recent national survey indicated a wide variation in the length of preservice training for correctional officers among state jurisdictions. According to *Corrections Compendium* (August 1996), training hours between state correctional agencies ranged from a low of 0 to a high of 411, "though most respondents indicated training hours closer to the average of 221, and the length of training programs ranges from 17 days (Colorado) to 16 weeks (Michigan)" (p. 13).

In addition to the training received by new recruits, most jurisdictions recognize the importance of continued staff development and require continuous in-service training. Annual training requirements generally involve a specific minimum number of hours of lectures, workshops, seminars, and on-the-job programs. By the middle 1990s, 41 states and the federal Bureau of Prisons required some form of annual in-service training. The annual number of in-service training hours ranged from a low of 16 to a high of 160, but more than 75% of the state jurisdictions required 40 or more hours.

Specialized training programs (pre- and in-service) for correctional officers serve three broad purposes. First, well-trained officers generally are better prepared to act decisively and correctly in a broad spectrum of situations. Second, training results in greater productivity and effectiveness. Third, it fosters cooperation and unity of purpose. Moreover, training programs ensure that the needs of the agency are addressed. In particular, training should be consistent with the agency's goals and objectives. Furthermore, agencies now are being held legally accountable for the actions of their officers and for failing to provide initial or remedial training.

ORGANIZATIONAL GUIDELINES

Organization and Administration

Agency training goals need to be clearly identified and updated on a regular basis. These goals provide the basis for developing all training programs, choosing teaching methods, and evaluating student performance. The training goals should be consistent with the correctional responsibilities of the agency. Specific activities of the training component should include the following:

- Planning and development of the organization's training programs;
- Implementation of training programs;
- Training program coordination;
- Administration of the training academy (if the agency has an academy);
- Officer notification of required training;
- Training program availability;
- Training record maintenance;
- Quality control and training follow-up;
- Selection and training of qualified instructors; and
- Training program evaluation.

Specifying the activities helps assure that all training and training-related activities are being addressed and that there is accountability for the efforts. All training component activities should be conducted within the framework of agency goals and in cooperation with all operational units.

Agency training programs should be reviewed annually to assure that they complement officers and operational needs, legal requirements, and agency policies. The evaluation and updating process should include a review of new laws, court decisions, and agency directives; an evaluation of the training programs; the identification of problems associated with physical facilities, materials, or scheduling; consultation with heads of agency components, the academy director, and the agency's chief executive officer; and a review of the number of persons trained and the extent of training provided. Moreover, a comprehensive annual review process will help maintain the integrity of the departmental training program.

University Affiliation

ACA standard 3-4090 encourages employees to continue their education with the assistance of the organization as well as providing support for professional meetings, seminars, and similar work-related activities. Many correctional agencies conduct some or all departmental training in association with a local college or university. This association may include classroom instruction on campus, teaching by the college faculty at the agency's academy or training site, college credit for training, or assistance in curriculum and lesson plan development. Whatever the level of affiliation selected by the agency, the basis for the relationship as well as the rights and responsibilities of each party should be established through an affiliation agreement.

Training Curriculum

The department should be able to demonstrate the job-relatedness of all training programs. Even though specific requirements for hours of instruction may be imposed, such requirements do not relieve the agency of the responsibility for relating required hours and required course work to a job-task analysis. Along with training curricula based on job-task analyses, the agency should develop performance objectives. The performance objectives should (1) focus on the elements of the job task analysis for which formal training is needed, (2) provide clear statements of what is to be learned, (3) provide the basis for evaluating the participants, and (4) provide a basis for evaluating the effectiveness of the training program.

The use of performance objectives acquaints the training participants with the information they are required to know; the skills that must be demonstrated and the circumstances under which the skills will be used. This approach also enables the instructors to relate training directly to the job performance that will be expected by supervisors.

Lesson Plans

The development of lesson plans help ensure that the subject to be covered in training is addressed completely and accurately and is properly sequenced with other training materials. Lesson plans establish the purpose of the instruction, set forth the performance objectives, relate the training to critical job tasks, and identify the matters that will be taught.

The lesson plans also should include references, teaching techniques (lecture, group discussion, panel, seminars, debate), relationships to job tasks, responsibilities of the participants for the material taught, and plans for evaluation of the participants. The following instructional methodologies should be considered: (1) conferences (debate, discussion groups, panels, and seminars), (2) field experiences (field trips, interviews, operational experiences, and operational observations), (3) presentations (lecture, lecture-discussion, lecture-demonstration), (4) problem investigations (committee inquiry), and (5) simulations (case study, game, and role play).

Testing Policy and Procedures

A written directive should establish the basis for testing, the passing and failing scores in training examinations, and guidelines on development and format of testing. In most instances, agencies should use competency-based testing using performance objectives that measure an officer's knowledge of and ability to use job-related skills. Agency procedures and policies governing remedial training also need to be detailed and updated on a regular basis. Provisions for repertory training should include (1) the circumstances and criteria used to determine the need for remedial instruction, (2) the timetables under which remedial training is provided, and (3) the consequences of participation or nonparticipation on the part of the affected officers.

As officers complete training programs, a training record should be maintained that describes the date of the training, the types of training received, any certificates received, attendance, and test scores. Agency records of each training class should include, at a minimum,

- The course content (lesson plans),
- The names of the officers who attended,
- The overall performance (test scores) of individual officers.

Detailed record keeping will ensure that the agency can demonstrate what instruction was provided, who attended the sessions, and the performance of the attendees.

PRESERVICE (RECRUIT) TRAINING

All newly sworn officers should be required to complete the basic academy training program prior to any routine assignment except as part of a formal field training program. The intent of this standard is to prevent institutional assignment without adequate supervision, prior to successfully completing a structured basic training course. This should not preclude the department's use of individuals who have been hired as correctional officers and not yet trained in the academy in positions within the agency, such as communications, records, or other activities, not in direct contact with the inmate population.

An orientation handbook should be developed and given to all new recruit officers at the time academy training begins. In the new environments of both the correctional profession and a correctional training academy, new officers should be provided with information concerning (1) the organization of the academy; (2) the academy's rules and regulations; (3) the academy's rating, testing, and evaluation system; (4) physical fitness and proficiency skill requirements; and (5) daily training schedules. By providing recruit trainees with this information, the interests of both the agency and the recruit trainees are served.

Academy Curriculum

A comprehensive correctional officer training academy program should include a curriculum based on job-task analyses of the most frequent assignments of officers who complete recruit training and the use of evaluation techniques designed to measure competency in the required skills, knowledge, and abilities. The most significant contribution to recruit training in recent years has been the realization that training to fill a set number of hours may not result in better trained officers. The minimum length and intensity of training should be based on a job-task analysis as measured by competency-based testing. In the opinion of informed experts, this ordinarily requires a training course of a minimum 160 hours (ACA 1997).

The basic training academy curriculum for new recruits generally includes, as a minimum, instruction in the law under which they function, rules of the institution, administrative policies and procedures, elementary personality development, methods of counseling, self-defense tactics and use of firearms, report writing, inmate rules and regulations, inmate's rights and responsibilities, race relations, basic first aid and CPR techniques, radio communication, substance abuse awareness, and how to deal with special inmate populations (e.g., the mentally and physically challenged, those with communicable diseases, and religious variations). The academy may provide the training in any sequence that enhances the presentation of the subject matter. The classroom instruction should be accompanied by recruit participation in practical problems outside the academy setting.

New officers also should receive training in the general procedures used in each of the different duty areas within the institution, including the ways inmates can place them in compromising situations in order to violate institutional rules or corrupt the officer. In addition, the agency may find it beneficial to provide access to psychological counseling services for academy trainees. By the time the new recruit begins an academy training program, the agency has a substantial investment in the trainee. With the stress that may be associated with a new profession, changes in lifestyle, and associated family stresses, recruit trainees may need psychological counseling.

After academy training it will be necessary to provide on-the-job training under the supervision of a training officer. The use of an experienced officer trained as a "mentor" (see page 64) may help defeat many of the stresses of the job, and it may mitigate potentially negative anti-academy attitudes that the officer may find in the work environment.

IN-SERVICE TRAINING

It is the responsibility of the agency to ensure that officers are kept up to date with new laws, technological improvements, and revisions in agency policy, procedures, rules, and regulations. To do so, each agency should require all sworn officers to complete a minimum 40 hours of in-service retraining per year. The mandatory retraining also may be designed to provide supervisory, management, or specialized training to participants. Retraining may be used to supplement (1) prepromotional training, (2) training prior to assignment to a specialized component, or (3) executive development training for higher ranking officers.

In-service training programs should be structured to motivate experienced officers and further the professionalization of the agency. Training curriculum should address, but not be limited to, the following topic areas:

- Review of agency policy, procedures, and rules and regulations (with emphasis on changes);
- Review of statutory or case law affecting correctional operations (with emphasis on changes);
- Review of the functions of agencies in the local criminal justice system;
- Exercise of discretion in the decision to invoke the criminal justice process;
- Agency policy on the use of force, including the use of deadly force;
- Weapons, self-defense, and security procedures training;
- Diversity issues, racial and ethnic sensitivity;
- Supervisor-officer relationships;
- Emergency medical services;
- Review of the performance evaluation system;
- Emergency situation suppression techniques;
- Hazardous materials control and incident management;
- New or innovative technological techniques or methods, if any;

- Review of contingency plans, if any, including those relating to special operations and unusual occurrences;
- Report writing and records system procedures and requirements.

Specialized Training

The agency should identify all of the job positions for which both pre- and post-assignment specialized training is required. Specialized training should include, but not be limited to, the following areas:

- Development or enhancement of the skills, knowledge, and abilities particular to the specialization;
- Management, administration, supervision, personnel policies, and support services of the function or component;
- Performance standards of the function or component;
- Agency policies, procedures, rules, and regulations specifically related to the function or component;
- Supervised on-the-job training.

The department should provide more than traditional "on-the-job training" to officers assigned to specialized activities. The training should be based on the results of a job-task analysis of the specialized assignment, and formal training should be coordinated closely with experienced personnel. Many of the practitioners of correctional specialties have identified specific course content and hours that they believe provide officers with necessary skills. In developing specialized training, these resources represent valuable assets that may be considered along with the job-task analysis in designing curriculum and requiring hours of participation.

In addition to the development of specific skills, personnel assigned to specialized activities should be aware of the administrative requirements and relationships of the specialized function or component to other parts of the agency. Each specialty has associated with it certain legal and policy issues that should be included in training.

REFERENCES

American Correctional Association. *Standards for Adult Correctional Institutions,* 3d ed., pp. 63–64. Laurel, MD: ACA in cooperation with the Commission on Accreditation for Corrections, 1990.
American Correctional Association. *Correctional Officer Resource Guide,* rev. ed., pp. 63–72. Laurel, MD: American Correctional Association, 1997.
Silverman, I.J., and M. Vega. *Corrections: A Comprehensive View.* New York: West Publishing, 1996.
Wees, G. "Fewer Correctional Office Positions Created in 1996." *Corrections Compendium* 21(8) (1996): 12–14.

4

Education

So that agencies can deal effectively with corrections problems in an increasingly complex and sophisticated society, there should be parallel increases in the level of education and training required for correctional officers. Higher education, by itself, is not an absolute answer in achieving improvement in corrections agencies. However, officers who have received a broad general education have a better opportunity to gain a more thorough understanding of society, to communicate more effectively with citizens, and to engage in the exploration of new ideas and concepts.

Officers already appointed should be given the opportunity and incentives to pursue college education. To encourage the recruitment of college-educated officers pay incentives should be given to officers who have achieved education prior to initial employment in the agency.

THE COMMON GOAL

The interest in higher education in criminal justice has been stimulated by previous presidential task forces and commission reports identifying four significantly related national problems (President's Commission on Law Enforcement and the Administration of Justice 1967a; Joint Commission on Correctional Manpower and Training 1969; National Advisory Committee on Criminal Justice Standards and Goals 1973). First is the recognition that crime is a major national concern; second is emphasis on criminal justice career preparation in higher education; third is the need to develop a more diverse correctional officer population by bringing more women and members of minority groups into the field; and fourth is a growing movement within the criminal justice personnel toward achieving professional status. This is true primarily for the police and correctional officers, as the court system personnel (prosecutors, defense attorneys, and judges) possess a high level of expertise and education and have achieved professional status.

Educational issues for the corrections profession are not simple nor interdependent but independent issues related by the cause-and-effect terminology of the various practitioners in correctional service. During the recent prison population explosion, correctional programs emphasized accumulation of hardware and technology while ignoring the most valuable resource of any organization—its personnel. The need exists to increase the individual officer's awareness and knowledge of his or her client population and social situations involving varying degrees of conflict. Mere knowledge is not sufficient; the correctional officer must develop the motivation to learn, acquire new knowledge, read, write, and communicate intelligently. It is incumbent on the organization to develop an adequate delivery system to ensure total support for this endeavor.

A college education, like anything else, is not the total answer. But the officer can become more sophisticated and in touch with a variety of important social science issues and concepts in the college arena, if given an opportunity and some tangible support. This, in turn, can aid in his or her desire to work harder toward becoming a unique professional in the correctional field. The vision is there, and the correctional officer often is willing to act on it, but often little incentive is provided and sometimes the process of trying to improve is fraught with difficulties and roadblocks. This is most unfortunate, given the accepted reality that correction officers are in a position to do such good and prevent such harm.

Therefore, any examination of the possible benefits of postsecondary education for correctional officers begins with two assumptions. First, there is a personal gain for the individual; second, increased levels of officer education will improve overall correctional operations, including planning, management, and supervisory functions and programs and services. The main objective of this chapter is to provide a comprehensive evaluation of the overall effects, both positive and negative, of postsecondary education within the "peace officer" classification of "front line" corrections personnel.

POSTSECONDARY EDUCATION

A primary role of education is to instill in individuals the desire, capability, and ability to continue learning throughout life. The world in which the corrections professional functions is changing continually. New discoveries are made, new laws passed, new judicial rulings issued, and new technology is developed on a continuous basis. Adequate development of all skills—technical, human, and conceptual—requires increased amounts of education as society changes and the complexity of the profession and its knowledge base increases. Because higher order skills require more education than lower order skills, those who wish to compete adequately and rise to higher level positions must continue to pursue continuing education opportunities conscientiously.

The importance of education cannot be overstated. Chernis and Kane (1987) refer to several studies (Bartol 1979; Gurin, Veroff, and Feld 1960; Mannheim 1975; Van Fossen 1979) that support the "view that there is more job satisfaction and less job related strain as one climbs up the occupational, educational, and organizational ladders" (Chernis and Kane 1987, p. 126). Other studies have supported the idea that education reduces burnout and stress (Brown 1987; Carrol and White 1982).

Correctional officers who avail themselves of a program of continued education have the unique opportunity to gain a more thorough understanding of society. In doing so, it is hoped that they will learn to communicate more effectively with their clientele, helping to reduce physical incidents and improve understanding and effective correctional management techniques. A reduction in inmate-officer altercations may lead to fewer officer related compensation claims and, indirectly, reduce employee turnover. The benefits of improved training and communication already are being seen in the adoption of direct supervision models of supervision (Zupan 1991). The benefit of additional education will enable the officer to effectively engage in the exploration of new ideas and concepts within the organization. The importance of education is underscored when one considers competition for promotion and other professional and career development.

The field of corrections in cooperation with higher education should contribute to the improvement of the professional practice of corrections. According to the International Association of Correctional Officers (IACO) Commission on Correctional Curriculum in Higher Education, "Education is a necessary component of and principle cause for universal recognition of any profession" (1995, p. 2). The American Bar Association's (ABA) Public Correctional Policy on Higher Education states, "The purposes of higher education include instruction, public service, and research" (American Bar Association Commission on Correctional Facilities and Services, p. 39). Corrections can and does benefit from academic endeavors in each of these areas.

The application of all relevant knowledge requires that individuals seek continuing education and training opportunities in their primary fields and in related areas. Continuing education and training must be multidisciplinary in their approach (Lawrence 1984). Both training and education are critical. Each has a different role, and each should be a continuing process. Education concentrates on the development of theoretical knowledge, which allows one to understand processes and make decisions in ambiguous situations. Training, on the other hand, is designed to impart specific skills that have direct application in more concrete situations. Education is an important prerequisite to career development and progression; training is an essential function required for minimal performance of duty, although it is an important component of career development.

JUSTIFICATION FOR CONTINUED EDUCATION

Colleges and universities have a distinct advantage in teaching generalized concepts, principles, and techniques that are germane to the broad field of criminal justice and their incorporated occupations. The university environment also is an appropriate setting for arousing the individual's interest in job-related issues and for developing the individual's motivation to search for improvements throughout his or her professional career. Unlike correctional agencies, universities can permit novice decision makers the environment and opportunity to consider the broad range of options, evaluation processes, and more important, the encouragement to improve old procedures and develop new approaches. When the focus is on the process of problem solving, rather than on the generation of immediate and often "short-term" solutions, the individual's awareness of potential resources (personnel, time, and money), legal constraints, and social expectations tends to increase.

Colleges and universities have the expertise and objectivity to encourage the correctional officer, as student, to examine critically the organization's relationship to other entities within the criminal justice system and to society. Few correctional agencies have the resources (staff, money) or the initiative needed to provide this perspective.

Criminal justice programs are relatively new fields of study within the academic environment. Even so, they recognize that the liberal arts have a comparative advantage in teaching certain analytic skills, intellectual pursuits, and personal values and orientations that are desired preconditions for the study of the criminal justice system.

A postsecondary liberal arts or criminal justice education is one way correctional officers can become aware of the many deviations of character within human behavior. These insights would enable the correctional officer to be better prepared to evaluate a difficult and sensitive situation and exercise better judgment. As found with law enforcement officers, it should help to alter the student's working personality and attitudes. Some evidence suggests that education changes attitudes and assists the individual to better recognize complexities and tolerate ambiguity. And, according to Champion (1990), "Some evidence suggests that more highly educated correctional officers can cope with stress more effectively than those with less education . . . [h]owever, more educated correctional officers often have higher levels of job dissatisfaction" (pp. 182 and 238). This is probably due to the lack of job challenge (Cullen et al. 1985; Philliber 1987).

As society increases in complexity it is increasingly important for all criminal justice personnel, especially correctional and law enforcement officers, to develop a cross-cultural awareness. It is evident from a cursory review of statistical data on arrests, convictions, and incarceration that the majority of individuals processed through the system are economically disadvantaged and often of minority groups. Research suggests that the most educated are lower in stereotypical beliefs about members of minority groups and less prejudiced than individuals with less education (Broom and Selznick 1968). The difference results partly from introduction to new perspectives through a varied curriculum and contact with faculty members and other students.

In addition, extended education is becoming more important as a selection criteria for promotion and professional advancement. Successful careers in corrections clearly require greater commitment to the educational process than was necessary as recently as 15 years ago. Although entry level requirements still are comparatively low in some places, advancement through promotion and lateral transfer into other occupational categories (i.e., parole and counseling) often requires higher education (see Jurick 1985; Sechrest and Josi 1992).

With few exceptions (cf. IACO's Commission on Correctional Curriculum in Higher Education 1995), most research relating to the issue of professionalization and continued education of career occupations within the "sworn peace officer" designation have been limited to law enforcement officers. A number of reports indicate that higher education among law enforcement officers provides numerous personnel and organizational benefits.

The Law Enforcement Model

Because we are dealing with the "peace officer" designation in this book, a brief history lesson may help clarify the overall effect of continued education within this occupational milieu. One method of examination is a review of the law enforcement experience that began in the late 1960s. During this time, there was a flurry of activity related to higher education and law enforcement, not unlike the present situation in the field of corrections. According to a Police Executive Research Forum publication, *Police Education and Minority Recruitment: The Impact of a College Requirement*, "the impetus for this activity came from many factors: changing social values, civil unrest and the police response, police relationships with minorities, increasing interest in law enforcement research, and changes to the 'reform' management style in policing" (Carter and Sapp 1991, p. 1).

The education of law enforcement officers long has been a major theme of reformers who have sought to professionalize the police (Vollmer 1936; Fogelson 1977). This reform strategy was particularly emphasized by the President's Commission on Law Enforcement and the Administration of Justice (1967a), which suggested that "the ultimate aim of all police departments should be that all personnel with enforcement powers have baccalaureate degrees" (p. 107). The commission went on to suggest in its *Task Force Report: The Police* (1967b) that only through the requirement of a college degree for police could a significant improvement be expected in the quality of service provided by law enforcement agencies.

The rationale for these recommendations was that police officers who were college educated would be more highly motivated and better able to utilize innovative techniques within the paramilitary organizational structure of law enforcement (Bell 1979). In addition, continued education should provide an improvement in overall job performance and a better understanding of human nature and their client base (Jagiello 1971; Bell 1979). Or, as the American Bar Association concluded in 1973:

> The qualities which law enforcement leaders claim to look for in recruits are the very ones which liberal education is believed to nurture: knowledge of changing social, economic and political conditions, understanding human behavior and the ability to communicate, together with the assumption of certain moral values, habits of mind and qualities of self-discipline which are important in sustaining a commitment to public service. (p. 212)

Interest in police education grew, characterized by increased research and growth in organizations related to criminal justice education. Higher education *seemed* to be a good idea for the police; it *appeared* to be a logical evolutionary step for a profession in its adolescence; many people *believed* that the college experience would make officers perform better. The push for college-educated police was not without controversy, however. Cautious observers of the "education movement" expressed concern that curricula and policy were based on emotion and intuition rather than on empirically tested hypotheses and behavioral criteria (Roberg 1978; Schick 1978; Wycoff and Susmilch 1979). In fact, these criticisms largely were true. Arguments presented in support of various commission recommendations generally were rhetorical and intuitive rather than empirical. This observation does not discount the qualitative arguments; rather, it is a recognition that scientific testing of the concepts also was needed.

As a result of these concerns, increased research on educationally related issues in law enforcement emerged. In a review of the existing research, Carter and Sapp (1991) reported, "[t]he research suggested that higher education provided a number of benefits for law enforcement" (p. 2). In sum, their detailed review found that continued education for law enforcement officers achieved the following:

- Developed a broader base of information for decision making;
- Provided additional years and experiences for increasing maturity;
- Inculcated responsibility in the individual through course requirements and achievements;
- Through general education courses and course work in the major, particularly a criminal justice major, permitted the individual to learn more about the history of the country and the democratic process and to appreciate constitutional rights, values, and the democratic form of government;
- Engendered the ability to handle difficult or ambiguous situations with greater creativity or innovation;
- In the case of criminal justice majors, permitted a better view of the "big picture" of the criminal justice system and a fuller understanding and appreciation for the prosecutorial, judicial, and correctional roles;
- Developed a greater empathy for members of minority groups and their discriminatory experiences through course work and interaction in the academic environment;
- Engendered understanding and tolerance for persons with different lifestyles and ideologies, which could translate into more effective communication and community relationships in the practice of policing;
- Made officers appear less rigid in decision making, to tend to make their decisions in the spirit of the democratic process, and to use discretion in dealing with individual cases rather than applying the same rules to all cases;
- Helped officers to communicate in a competent manner, with civility and humanity;
- Equipped officers better to perform tasks and to make continuous policing decisions with little or no supervision;
- Engendered a more "professional" demeanor and performance;
- Enabled officers to cope better with stress and be more likely to seek assistance with personal or stress-related problems and thereby to be more stable and reliable employees;
- Enabled officers to adapt their styles of communication and behavior to a wider range of social conditions and classes;
- Tended to make officers less authoritarian and less cynical with respect to the milieu of policing;
- Enabled officers to accept and adapt to organizational change more readily.

Performance, Attitudes, and Behavior

The research to date on the positive benefits derived by law enforcement through continued education can be roughly categorized as looking at the effects on (1) performance and job satisfaction, (2) attitudinal variables, and (3) specific police officer behaviors, all of which provide positive organizational benefits as well as personal improvement.

Performance and Job Satisfaction

In studies of the effects of higher education on police performance and job satisfaction, a wide variety of measures were utilized as indicators. Strong positive correlation between years of education and the number of arrests made by police were found by Bozza (1973) and Glasgow, Green, and Knowles (1973). Several other studies reported a positive relationship between education, job performance, and job satisfaction (Marsh 1964; Saunders 1970; Spencer and Nichols 1971; Cohen and Chaiken 1972; Sterling 1974; Gottlieb and Baker 1974; Trojanowicz and Nicholson 1976; Cascio and Real 1976; Finnegan 1976; Cascio 1977; Sanderson 1977; Barry 1978; Weirman 1978; Roberg 1978; Fisher 1981; Murell 1982; Hayeslip 1989). All these studies found moderate to positive relationships between levels of education and specific performance measures.

Finnegan (1976) found that college-educated officers consistently received higher performance ratings from supervisors. Sanderson's (1977) research found college education to have a positive effect on academy performance and career advancement. Cohen and Chaiken (1972) and Sanderson (1977) found a positive relationship between educational levels and officer promotions. College-educated officers tend to have better peer relationships than non-college-educated officers (Madell and Washburn 1978; Weirman 1978) and are more likely to take a leadership role in the organization (Cohen and Chaiken 1972; Trojanowicz and Nicholson 1976; Weirman 1978).

Attitudes

Smith, Locke, and Walker (1967) found that police who went to college tended to be less authoritarian than police who did not attend college. Similarly, police officers who finished college tended to be significantly less authoritarian than those police who did not attend college (Smith, Locke, and Fenster 1970). Dalley (1975) suggests that authoritarianism, conservatism, and rigidity were related to postsecondary education. Parker et al. (1976) also found that education had an effect on dogmatism, in that college-educated police were more open-minded than their respective non-college-educated colleagues. Education also appears to be positively correlated to attitudes of professionalism and had mixed effects on work strain in a study by Miller and Fry (1978). Trojanowicz and Nicholson (1976) found that college-educated officers tend to be more flexible. Other studies show that college-educated officers take fewer leave days, receive fewer injuries, have less injury time, have lower rates of absenteeism, use fewer sick days, and are involved in fewer traffic accidents than non-college-educated officers (Trojanowicz and Nicholson 1976) and have less rigid attitudes about policing (Dalley 1975; Roberg 1978).

A 1989 national study of higher education among police officers by Carter, Sapp and Stephens found that 98% of the responding police departments indicated that law enforcement officers with two or more years of college received fewer citizen complaints than their counterparts who had less education. Further, 96% of the police departments indicated that officers with two or more years of college had fewer disciplinary problems.

Specific Behaviors

A number of other studies report on the positive effects of postsecondary education and specific types of behavior traits common among law enforcement officers. Finckenauer (1975) examined whether college-educated police responded differently than non-college-educated police to hypothetical situations. Sherman and Blumberg (1981) examined the potential effects of higher education on police officers who did or did not shoot their weapons. Professional identity was studied by Greene, Bynum, and Webb (1984) and Regoli and Miracle (1980). Lynch (1976) and Silvester (1990) examined the effects of postsecondary education and officer ethics; the issue of minority relations and officer education was studied by Peirson (1978).

LAW ENFORCEMENT VS. CORRECTIONS: A VALID OCCUPATIONAL COMPARISON?

It seems apparent that correctional personnel, specifically correctional officers, also may be susceptible to certain forms of cynicism and authoritarianism just like police, perhaps for many of the same reasons. It would seem that police and correctional officers share a variety of occupational functions that would produce similar attitudinal reactions. First, both are involved in working with the criminal element in society, and as Goffman (1961) points out, this frequently causes more problems for the worker in comparison with those who work with objects. Jacobs and Retsky (1975) make a similar point when comparing the role of people-oriented prison guards with other guards whose function it is to protect objects. They maintain that, "while Secret Service Agents and Brinks guards may achieve esteem from their contact with the objects they are guarding, close contact with convicted felons seem morally profaning for the [prison] guard" (p. 10).

Second, both police and correctional officers are engaged in socially authorized authoritarian roles. They are charged with keeping society secure and safe: the police maintain law and order on the streets; correctional officers maintain law and order within the prisons. This causes additional problems, because both groups are required to establish authoritarian positions over others, enforce rules or laws, and maintain order (McCorkle and Korn 1954; Sykes 1958). Finally, correctional officers and police officers occasionally have the same clientele. Although under different circumstances, police and correctional officers deal with the same client in the criminal justice system—the criminal.

Other factors tie the correctional officer and the police officer together in similar, yet unique, occupational roles. Among these would be the danger, fear, and isolation first identified by Skolnick (1966) that tend to create an officer subculture. Duffee (1974), Jacobs and Retsky (1975), and Sykes (1958) also point out that a correctional officer subculture is created out of the same factors that affect police.

The situations correctional officers have to deal with sometimes are complicated and explosive, and the proper reaction to them requires a thorough understanding of dyadic and group relations of human and personal behavior, an understanding of what makes prisoners act as they do, and an appreciation of the impact that their actions will have on others.

CONTINUED EDUCATION AND THE CORRECTIONAL OFFICER

As demonstrated by the research conducted on law enforcement officers, the consequences of continuing education for these occupational specialties are positive. Education provides growth and development for the officers, keeps them current regarding developments in the field, and stimulates new procedures for goal accomplishment. Poole and Regoli (1980) argue that "the exposure of officers to higher education may cultivate a flexibility of job definitions and goal redefinition's that could serve as a safeguard against ossified and inappropriate work procedures" (p. 220).

A large segment of the nation's young people now go on to college. In terms of an educational norm, the undergraduate degree today is equivalent in prestige to a high school diploma at the turn of the century. Yet most correctional agencies have failed to take notice. For many agencies, the minimum educational level is still the same as it was 40 years ago, a high school education or less. In a 1992 *National Correctional Officers Education Survey* of state correctional department personnel officers, Sechrest and Josi report that the minimum educational standard for employment as a correctional officer was less than a high school diploma for 13 states (25.5%), a GED or high school diploma in 22 states (43.1%), and a high school diploma or more for 16 states (31.4%). Therefore, in two-thirds of the states (35, or 68.6%), a GED or less would be sufficient education to become a correctional officer (p. 8).

One result of this failure to increase entry level standards is the inability of correctional departments to attract and retain officers in today's highly competitive market for qualified employees. College graduates look elsewhere for employment. The job of correctional officer has often come to be regarded by the public as a second-class occupation, open to anyone with no more than a minimum education, average intelligence, and good health.

It is ironic that correctional agencies have failed to upgrade their basic standards for employment in a era when studies support the general value of higher education for police officers, an occupational group closely aligned with correctional officers. As we approach a new century, upgrading the educational level of correctional officers should be one of corrections most important challenges. Few professions today do not require a college degree. In their quest for greater professionalism, correctional administrators need to take note of this deficiency.

What are the benefits of a college education for the correctional officer? Two important characteristics of correctional organizations influence the behavior of correctional officers. First, most agencies are organized along military lines, with a centralized command structure. This organizational structure traditionally utilizes impersonal management techniques where formal authority is emphasized. Communication normally flows downward. Upward and horizontal communication are suppressed and restricted. This "paramilitary model" provides for strict accountability of individual actions and behavior.

The normal tendency of personnel in a decision-making capacity who operate within a paramilitary structure is to view situations from a zero-sum (win-lose) perspective. This zero-sum attitude often distorts the individual's view of reality—objects are black or white, right or wrong, legal or illegal. Such a simplistic outlook supports the legitimacy of their work role and the smooth functioning of the institution. Decisions are easy and uncomplicated. Officers do what they are told; they do not openly question superiors.

A second influence on behavior is the teaching of officers from early in their careers to observe and evaluate the institution environment. They spend much of their time looking for situations and signals that something is out of place. As experience increases, officers learn to act on their suspicions. They become confident in their ability to identify situations that do not fall in the range of normal behavior that functionally agrees with the environment.

By understanding two major influences on correctional officer behavior—the military structure and the training of officers to critically evaluate their environment—we can begin to understand the systemic impact of the college-educated officer within the correctional organization.

Generally, undergraduate college courses expand the knowledge base. They tend to foster basic critical thinking skills. The result is that students begin to realize that the world is more complicated than being merely black or white, right or wrong. Many upper division courses encourage individual thought and analysis. They require students to analyze phenomena from different viewpoints. Students are encouraged to question the assumptions of ideas and theories. They are asked to analyze accepted procedures and policies.

The stimulation provided by a college education should strengthen the individual's ability to empathize with people in a variety of situations. This awareness is best achieved when officers complete an interdisciplinary degree program that exposes them to a variety of approaches. Vocational training concentrating on specific problems, such as the mentally ill, the cultural differences of ethnically diverse groups, or crisis intervention, also are valuable.

Education is one way correctional officers can be made aware of some of the many difficulties involved with behavior patterns different and unique within the criminal mind. Postsecondary education would enable the officers to be better prepared to evaluate a difficult and sensitive situation to arrive at a more sound and balanced judgment. Moreover, continued education can help alter the student's working personality and reduce the level of cynicism and authoritarianism, both of which are common problems among this occupational group. The overwhelming evidence of police-related research would suggest that education changes attitudes and assists the individual to be better able to recognize complexities and tolerate ambiguity.

Opinions relating to the philosophy of higher education for correctional officers ranged from a focus on the negative effects of academic advancement to a view of higher education as essential to the alleviation of some of the problems caused by the increased complexity of work in a correctional facility. Dissenting voices claim that college education for correctional officers is irrelevant, unnecessary, and essentially impossible to achieve (see Sechrest and Josi 1992).

Basically the recognition of the need for college-educated correctional officers is not new. Over the past several decades, a number of distinguished panels and commissions have been created to address the chronic labor supply problems in corrections. Lengthy reports have been issued by the President's Commission on Law Enforcement and Administration of Justice (1967a, 1967c), the Joint Commission on Correctional Manpower and Training (1969), the National Advisory Commission on Criminal Justice Standards and Goals (1973), the American Bar Association Commission on Correctional Facilities and Services (1973), and Project STAR (1976). Each of these bodies has issued a report strongly recommending *higher educational standards for correctional officers*. National recognition for these standards was realized in 1988 when the IACO received federal funding support to develop a standardized corrections-based higher education curriculum.

The supporting rationale for continued education for correctional officers is that, with a collegiate background, officers will be better motivated and more capable of applying innovative techniques and process to the operations of correctional organizations. Generally, it follows that an increased awareness and competency contribute to increasing effectiveness in performing their tasks. The assessment can be made that the corrections function will continue to change and become more complex as society moves into the 21st century.

As previously stated, several studies have reported differences in performance between police officers with and without college backgrounds. The results of these studies support the position that officers with college experience in fact are better performers, as indicated by reduced citizen complaints, lower stress factors, job satisfaction, and a host of other attitudinal and specific behavior patterns. If such positive results have been reported in law enforcement, is it unreasonable to suggest similar results for the correctional officer?

The importance of education both for the individual and the organization cannot be overstated. Knowledgeable, highly skilled, motivated, and professional correctional personnel are essential to fulfill the purpose of corrections effectively. According to Allen and Simonsen (1986), "no issue in corrections is an important as the training educating, and recruiting of qualified staffs for the various systems" (p. 470). The president of the American Correctional Association made the following statement, "In personal growth for job improvement in corrections, the three most important factors are education, education, and education" (Travisono 1987, p. 4).

CASE STUDY: NATIONAL CORRECTIONAL OFFICERS EDUCATION SURVEY

Background

During the summer of 1992, the California State Legislature commissioned the Robert Presley Institute of Corrections Training and Research to develop, implement, and analyze a national correctional officer education survey (see Sechrest and Josi 1992). Legislative support for this issue had two clear objectives. First, correctional officer hiring practices at the state level did not appear to support the need or necessity for greater education, as previously detailed in a national survey (Corrections Compendium 1990). In addition, the current legislative focus was on California, a state where higher salaries for correctional officers would appear to allow higher entry standards and higher educational levels, a highly speculative and no doubt spurious relationship. This case study is an abridged version of final report submitted to the California State Legislature in October 1992. The results are an accumulation of data retrieved from a comprehensive survey of state correctional agency personnel directors and administrators from all 50 states and the District of Columbia, who were queried on a number of issues relevant to continued education and training for correctional officers.

Introduction

What was the current state of correctional officer education, salary, and benefits for a particular state, and how did it compare with the rest of the nation? Are current department directors and upper level management concerned with the potential benefits of increased correctional officer education? Are correctional administrators willing to support increased education and training mandates for their sworn personnel through the use of financial incentives? A study of state correctional officers by a team from the Robert Presley Institute of Corrections Research and Training attempted to find the answers to these and other questions regarding correctional officer education and training throughout the United States.

For the most part, then current correctional officer compensation throughout the nation was lower than entry level salary for law enforcement officers. This discrepancy may be related to higher entry level requirements for law enforcement personnel, requirements that support higher educational standards and comprehensive preservice training academies. For example, the nationally recognized preservice training standards for entry level correctional officers is 160 hours (American Correctional Association 1990, standard 3-4081). On average, the minimum standard training requirements for police officers, during the same time period, was three to four times greater, with an average of 400 hours (Commission for Police Officers Standards and Training 1990, section D-2).

Methodology

To assess current levels of correctional officer education, a three-page survey questionnaire was mailed to the state department of corrections personnel or training director in all 50 states and the District of Columbia; 51 surveys (100%) were completed and returned.

Areas of Inquiry

Should correctional officers be better educated and, if so, for what purpose? According to one previous survey (Corrections Compendium 1990), hiring practices in the various states did not appear to support the need for greater education. The *Corrections Compendium* survey, however, did not adequately identify the reasons correctional officer education was not a high priority for the agency. Therefore, a more detailed survey was developed to address the following areas:

- What is the minimum educational standard for entry level correctional officers?
- Does the administration support a higher standard?
- Is formal academic education for correctional officers beneficial to the agency's overall mission?
- What is the current educational level of correctional officer staff?
- Do agency policies support continued education for correctional officers?
- Are there educational incentives for correctional officers? That is, is continued education linked with pay or promotion?
- Do agencies provide remuneration for classes and, if so, of what type?
- Is pay for college classes linked to the grades achieved (GPA)?
- Is time off granted to attend classes?
- Are work schedules adjusted for classes?
- Are there any other incentives to go to school?
- What about attitudes of supervisors, direct managers, etc. toward continued office education?
- Are courses taught on agency premises (i.e., at local institutions and training camps, etc.) ?

The study did not explore issues such as the influence of the unions and bargaining agents on educational programs, although respondents were encouraged to comment about these issues.

Survey Results

Respondents were grouped by geographical location into four regions:

- Northeast (10)—Connecticut, Maine, Massachusetts, New Hampshire, New Jersey, New York, Rhode Island, Vermont, Pennsylvania, and Delaware.
- Midwest (12)—Michigan, Ohio, Indiana, Illinois, Iowa, Wisconsin, North Dakota, South Dakota, Minnesota, Nebraska, Kansas, and the District of Columbia.
- South (16)—Virginia, West Virginia, North Carolina, South Carolina, Georgia, Florida, Alabama, Mississippi, Louisiana, Arkansas, Tennessee, Kentucky, Texas, Oklahoma, Missouri, and Maryland.
- West (13)—California, Oregon, Washington, Arizona, Nevada, Utah, Idaho, Montana, Wyoming, Colorado, New Mexico, Hawaii, and Alaska.

Entry Level Salaries

Neither correctional officer pay or current entry level requirements suggested that this is a group that would be looked to for inspiration in better planning mandates, management techniques, or program services for the future. For the most part, correctional officer salaries throughout the nation were substantially lower than salaries for law enforcement officers. Entry level salaries reported in this survey range from a low of $13,520 (South Dakota) to a high of $33,996 (Alaska), with only three states exceeding $30,000 per year. According to the Department of Justice, average entry level salaries for 1990 were $16,427 and $28,033, respectively, for correctional officers and law enforcement (Bureau of Justice Statistics 1991). This reported difference of approximately $12,000 may be related to the recent trend in law enforcement toward occupational "professionalization," through increased educational and training requirements.

Minimum Education Requirements

Data analysis on minimum educational requirements for employment as a correctional officer indicate that in 13 states (25.5%) "less than a high school diploma" was adequate and in 22 states (43.1%) "less than a GED or high school diploma" was sufficient education to qualify for employment. Only 16 states (31.4%) required a high school diploma. In two of every three states (68.6%), a GED or less would qualify as sufficient education to become a correctional officer. When asked about current educational levels for "sworn" staff, 38 states (74.5%) indicated that current staff had "less than 30 units of college," which could mean none. Regional percentages on this question (Midwest, 58%; Northeast, 67%; West, 77%; and South, 88%) indicated a higher emphasis on educational support in the Midwest.

Incentives

Very few state correctional departments supported continued education with financial incentives. Only 3 jurisdictions (5.9%) reported salary step pay incentives linked to continued education. Twelve states (23.4%) supported continued education with additional promotional opportunities; 11 (21.6%) with "one-time" compensation packages (pay, compensation time, or a combination of both). Twenty-one states (41.2%) provided financial reimbursement for tuition and books; and 26 (51%) provided necessary time off or flexible scheduling for officers attending school. Twelve states (23.5%) had on-site courses taught at their institutions.

Agency Policy

Other than financial incentives, about half of the state agencies (24 or 47%) indicated they had a written policy that supported continued education issues. However, only one in four (13 or 25.5%) supported an overall increase in the minimum educational standard for entry level officers. Seven states indicated strong support for a minimum standard that would require "some college" and six supported "other" types (nonspecific) increases above the GED level.

Conclusions

Based on information derived from this survey, it is apparent that correctional staff did not feel the need to attend college classes. Can the need for greater educational attainment by correctional officers be established (i.e., what would be the purpose of increased education for correctional officers)? Because this need was not widely recognized across the United States, perhaps a current need did not exist. This, however, brings us to the question of the individual officer. If the officer saw corrections as a transitional job, perhaps leading to a law enforcement position or another position in the agency, then education would be important. If this were the case for many officers and their respective agencies, what arguments could be employed to stimulate correctional officer education? In what ways could increased educational incentives that increase competencies ultimately meet the needs of the individual, the department, and the larger governmental entity (city, county, or state)? If any of these are concerns, then representative agencies should not hesitate to implement an officer educational assistance program.

Recommendations

Perhaps the most important assets within today's correctional department concerns the human resource development of its correctional officers. Well-planned and well-administered training and education programs are necessary to accomplish departmental goals and objectives. Correctional agencies should place a greater emphasis on the development and systematic delivery of an educational support program.

Recruitment of today's corrections professional should incorporate a highly developed written and oral examination process accessible to all qualified individuals, a testing process designed to identify people who would profit from additional education and training. The newly hired correctional professional would participate in a highly structured, educationally oriented standardized training academy with renewed emphasis on treatment-oriented modification techniques as well as the ever-present self-defense and survival mandates. The overall number of training academy hours should be increased to maximize this enhanced training effort. Veteran staff members would have opportunities for professional development through mandated in-service training requirements in addition to advanced educational opportunities without interference from immediate supervisors and institutional management staff. Professionalism requires a commitment to lifelong learning. The overall purpose of a comprehensive training and education policy should be

- To establish a process for the ongoing identification of the necessary knowledge, skills, and abilities for today's correctional professional.
- To systematically assess the departments curriculum development and lesson plans in conjunction with local colleges and universities.
- To develop standards for staff trainers to ensure consistency in the quality of instruction.
- To enhance career development through increased training and education.

- To ensure compliance with standards that may be developed by the department's administrative staff.
- To provide procedural guidelines for a comprehensive tuition reimbursement program.
- To reduce departmental turnover due to motivational stagnation and reduce employee "burn-out."

REFERENCES

Allen, H.E., and E. Simonsen. *Corrections in America: An Introduction*, 4th ed. New York: Macmillian, 1986.

American Bar Association Commission on Correctional Facilities and Services. *A Survey of Legislation, Regulations and Policies Supportive of Correctional Officer Education.* Washington, DC: American Bar Association, 1973.

American Correctional Association. *Standards for Adult Correctional Institutions*, 3d ed. Laurel, MD: American Correctional Association, 1990.

Barry, D. "A Survey of Student and Agency Views on Higher Education in Criminal Justice." *Journal of Police Science and Administration* 6, no. 3 (1978): 345–354.

Bartol, K.M. "Professionalization as a Predictor of Organizational Commitment, Role Stress, and Turnover." *Academy of Management Journal* 22, no. 4 (1979): 815–821.

Bell, D.J. "The Police Role in Higher Education." *Journal of Police Science and Administration* 7 (1979): 467–475.

Bozza, C.M. "Motivations Guiding Policemen in the Arrest Process." *Journal of Police Science and Administration* 1, no. 4 (1973): 467–475.

Broom, L., and P. Selznick. *Sociology.* New York: Harper and Row, 1968.

Brown, P.W. "Probation Officer Burnout: An Organizational Disease/An Organizational Cure, Part II." *Federal Probation* 51 (1987): 17–21.

Bureau of Justice Statistics. *Sourcebook of Criminal Justice Statistics 1991.* Washington, DC: U.S. Government Printing Office, 1991.

Carroll, J.F., and W.L. White. "Theory Building: Integrating Individual and Environmental Factors Within an Ecological Framework." In W. Paine (ed.), *Job Stress and Burnout: Research, Theory and Intervention Perspectives.* Beverly Hills, CA: Sage, 1982.

Carter, D.L., and A.D. Sapp. *Police Education and Minority Recruitment: The Impact of a College Requirement*, pp. 87 and 89–91. Washington, DC: Police Executive Research Forum, 1991.

Carter, D.L., A.D. Sapp, and D. Stephens. *The State of Police Education: Policy Direction for the 21st Century.* Washington. DC: Police Executive Research Forum, 1989.

Cascio, W.F. "Formal Education and Police Officer Performance." *Journal of Police Science and Administration* 5 (1977): 89–96.

Cascio, W.F., and L. Real. "Educational Standards of Police Officer Personnel." *The Police Chief* 43, no. 8 (1976): 89–96.

Champion, D.J. *Corrections in the United States: A Contemporary Perspective.* Englewood Cliffs, NJ: Prentice-Hall, 1990.

Cherniss, C., and J.S. Kane. "Public Sector Professionals: Job Characteristics, Satisfaction, and Aspirations for Intrinsic Fulfillment Through Work." *Human Relations* 40 (1987): 125–136.

Cohen, C., and J. Chaiken. *Police Background Characteristics and Performance.* New York: Rand Institute, 1972.

Commission for Police Officers Standards and Training. *Police Officers Standards and Training Administrative Manual.* Sacramento, CA: Commission for Police Officers Standards and Training, 1990.

Commission on Accreditation for Law Enforcement Agencies. *Standards for Law Enforcement Agencies.* Fairfax, VA: Commission on Accreditation for Law Enforcement Agencies, Inc., 1984.

Corrections Compendium. "Correctional Officers Education Survey." *Corrections Compendium* 15(10) (1990): 10–19.

Cullen, F.T., B.G. Link, N.T. Wolfe, and J. Frank. "The Social Dimension of Correctional Officer Stress." *Justice Quarterly* 2 (1985): 505–533.

Dalley, A.F. "University and Non-University Graduated Policemen: A Study of Police Attitudes." *Journal of Police Science and Administration* 3 (1975): 458–468.

Duffee, D. "The Correctional Officer Subculture and Organizational Change." *Journal of Research in Crime and Delinquency* 11 (1974): 155–172.

Finkenauer, J.O. "Higher Education and Police Discretion." *Journal of Police Science and Administration* 3 (1975): 450–457.

Finnegan, J. "A Study of the Relationship Between College Education and Police Performance in Baltimore, Maryland." *The Police Chief* (1976): 60–62.

Fischer, R. "Is Education Really an Alternative? The End of a Long Controversy." *Journal of Police Science and Administration* 9, no. 3 (1981): 313–316.

Fogelson, R.M. *Big City Police.* Cambridge, MA: Harvard University Press, 1977.

Glasgow, E.H., R.R. Green, and L. Knowles. "Arrest Performance Among Patrolmen in Relation to Job Satisfaction and Personal Variables." *The Police Chief* (1973): 28–34.

Goffman, E. *Asylums.* Garden City, NY: Doubleday, 1961.

Gottlieb, M.C., and C.F. Baker. "Predicting Police Officer Effectiveness." *Journal of Forensic Psychology* (1974): 35–46.

Greene, J., T. Bynum, and V. Webb. "Patterns of Entry, Professional Identity, and Attitudes Toward Crime-Related Education: A Study of Criminal Justice and Criminology Faculty." *Journal of Criminal Justice* 12(1984): 39–60.

Gurin, G.J., S. Veroff, and S. Feld. *Americans View Their Mental Health.* New York: Basic Books, 1960.

Hayeslip, D. "Higher Education and Police Performance Revisited: The Evidence Examined Through Meta-Analysis." *American Journal of Police* 8, no. 2 (1989): 49–62.

International Association of Correctional Officers Commission on Correctional Curriculum in Higher Education. "Policy Statement Brochure, 1995."

Jacobs, J., and H. Retsky. "Prison Guard." *Urban Life* 4 (1975): 5–29.

Jagiello, R.J. "College Education for the Patrolman: Necessity or Irrelevancy." *Journal of Criminal Law, Criminology and Police Science* 92 (1971): 114–121.

Joint Commission on Correctional Manpower and Training. *A Time to Act.* Washington, DC: Joint Commission on Correctional Manpower and Training, 1969.

Jurik, N.C. "Individual and Organizational Determinants of Correctional Officer Attitudes Toward Inmates." *Criminology* 23, no. 3 (1985): 523–539.

Lawrence, R. "Professionals or Judicial Servants? An Examination of the Probation Officer's Role." *Federal Probation* 48 (1984): 14–21.

Lynch, G.W. "The Contributions of Higher Education to Ethical Behavior in Law Enforcement." *Journal of Criminal Justice* 4, no. 4 (1976): 285–290.

Madell, J.D., and P.V. Washburn. "Which College Major Is Best for the Street Cop?" *The Police Chief* 45 (1978): 40–42.

Mannheim, B. "A Comparative Study of Work Centrality, Job Rewards, and Satisfaction." *Sociology of Work and Occupations* 2 (1975): 79–102.

Marsh, S. "Validating the Selection of Deputy Sheriffs." *Public Personnel Review* (1964): 41–44.

McCorkle, L., and R. Korn. "Resocialization Within Walls." *The Annals of the American Academy of Political and Social Science* (1954).

Miller, J., and L.J. Fry. "Some Evidence on the Impact of Higher Education for Law Enforcement Personnel." *The Police Chief* 43 (1978): 30–33.

Murrell, D.B. "The Influence of Education on Police Work Performance." Doctoral dissertation, Florida State University, Tallahassee, 1982.

National Advisory Commission on Criminal Justice Standards and Goals. *Corrections*. Washington, DC: U.S. Government Printing Office, 1973.

Parker, L., D. Donnelly, J. Gerwitz, J. Marcus, and V. Kowalewski. "Higher Education: Its Impact on Police Attitudes." *The Police Chief* 43 (1976): 33–35.

Peirson, G. *Higher Educational Requirements and Minority Recruitment for the Police: Conflicting Goals?* Washington DC: U.S. Government Printing Office, 1978.

Philliber, S. "Thy Brother's Keeper: A Review of the Literature on Correctional Officers," *Justice Quarterly* 4, no. 1 (1987): 9–37.

Poole, E.D., and R.M. Regoli. "Role Stress, Custody Orientation, and Disciplinary Actions." *Criminology* 18 (1980): 215–226.

President's Commission on Law Enforcement and the Administration of Justice. *Challenge of Crime in a Free Society*. Washington, DC: U.S. Government Printing Office, 1967a.

President's Commission on Law Enforcement and the Administration of Justice. *Task Force Report: The Police*. Washington, DC: U.S. Government Printing Office, 1967b.

President's Commission on Law Enforcement and the Administration of Justice. *Task Force Report: Corrections*. Washington, DC: U.S. Government Printing Office, 1967c.

Project STAR National Advisory Council. *Project STAR: The Impact of Social Trends on Crime and Criminal Justice*. Cincinnati, OH, and Santa Cruz, CA: Anderson-Davis, 1976.

Regoli, R.M., and A.W. Miracle. *Professionalism Among Criminal Justice Educators*. Washington DC: Joint Commission on Criminology and Criminal Justice Education and Standards, 1980.

Roberg, R.R. "An Analysis of the Relationships Among Higher Education, Belief Systems, and Job Performance of Patrol Officers." *Journal of Police Science and Administration* 6 (1978): 336–344.

Sanderson, B. "Police Officers: The Relationship of College Education to Job Performance." *The Police Chief* 44 (1977): 32–35.

Saunders, C. *Upgrading the American Police*. Washington, DC: The Brookings Institute, 1970.

Schick, R.P. *Structural and Attitudinal Barriers to Higher Educational Requirements for Police Officers*. Washington, DC: Police Foundation, 1978.

Sechrest, D.K., and D.A. Josi. *National Correctional Officers Education Survey*. Riverside, CA: Robert Presley Institute of Corrections Research and Training, 1992.

Sherman, L.W., and M. Blumberg. "Higher Education and Police Use of Deadly Force." *Journal of Criminal Justice* 9 (1981): 317–331.

Silvester, D.B. "Ethics and Privatization in Criminal Justice: Does Education Have a Role to Play?" *Journal of Criminal Justice* 18 (1990): 65–70.

Skolnick, J. *Justice Without Trial*. New York: Wiley, 1966.

Smith, A.B., B. Locke, and A. Fenster. "Authoritarianism in Policemen Who Are College Graduates and Non-College Police." *Journal of Criminal Law, Criminology, and Police Science* 6 (1970): 313–315.

Smith, A.B., B. Locke, and W.F. Walker. "Authoritarianism in College and Non-College Oriented Police." *Journal of Criminal Law, Criminology and Police Science* 58 (1967): 128–132.

Spencer, G., and R. Nichols. "A Study of Chicago Police Recruits." *The Police Chief* (1971): 56–59.

Sterling, J. "The College Level Entry Requirement." *The Police Chief* 41, no. 8 (1974): 36–40.

Sykes, G. *The Society of Captives.* Princeton, NJ: Princeton University Press, 1958.

Travisono, A. "Corrections' Most Critical Factors: Education, Education, Education." *Corrections Today* 49 (1987): 4.

Trojanowicz, R., and T. Nicholson. "A Comparison of Behavioral Styles of College Graduate Police Officers v. Non-College-Going Police Officers." *The Police Chief* 43, no. 8 (1976): 56–59.

Van Fossen, B.E. *The Structure of Social Inequality.* Boston: Little, Brown, 1979.

Vollmer, A. *The Police and Modern Society.* Berkeley: University of California Press, 1936.

Weirman, C.L. "Variances of Ability Measurement Scores Obtained by College and Non-College Educated Troopers." *The Police Chief* 45, no. 8 (1978): 34–36.

Wycoff, M.A., and C.E. Susmilch. "The Relevance of College Education for Policing: Continuing the Dialogue." In D. M. Peterson (ed.), *Police Work: Strategies and Outcomes in Law Enforcement.* Beverly Hills, CA: Sage, 1979.

Zupan, L. *Jails: Reform and the New Generation Philosophy.* Cincinnati, OH: Anderson, 1991.

5

Career Development

A major assumption of this book is that career development is driven by job specifications that require increased levels of education and training for advancement. If this were not true and advancement could continue based solely on job experience, there would be no reason or need to pursue the goal of recommending increased education and training for today's correctional officer.

Career development is a structured process utilized by an agency to provide opportunities for individual growth and development at all levels. It is designed to promote productive, efficient, and effective job performance and to improve the overall level of individual job satisfaction. More important, through career development activities, the upward mobility of all personnel may be enhanced by specific opportunities for professional growth and improved job performance.

DEFINITIONS

Career Development

The concept of career development differs from a concept of a career path. Career development encompasses efforts by both the individual employee and the organization in the process of developing work values, crystallizing a vocational identity, learning about opportunities, and implementing work options. The essence of the career development perspective is its focus on the interaction of the individual and the organization over time. Career development is the responsibility of the individual; however, the organization has a responsibility to both advise individuals and make available opportunities for their career development.

Career Path

A career path is the sequence and duration of occupations or jobs in the life span of an individual, in which movement may be lateral, vertical, or horizontal. A U.S. General Accounting Office study (1992) refers to an "occupational path" that an individual will follow to reach a management position. Career and life planning involves personal growth and may be repeated many times in the life of the individual. It is a *process* of self-awareness, career awareness, and decision making that directs the individual in planning and guiding immediate actions, integrating personal and environmental goals, and setting future career goals.

Career Counseling

Career counseling involves the interaction of counselor and employee through guidance that may assist an individual in choosing, preparing, entering, or progressing in a job assignment. Career counseling identifies three elements: (1) the skills, knowledge, and abilities of each individual relative to present and future job assignments; (2) in-service training requirements; and (3) the extent to which the training fulfills employee and departmental expectations.

Formal Education

Continued or postsecondary education through a formal learning experience at a college or university helps the individual meet personal goals and produces a knowledge base for future career application. Training, on the other hand, is carried out by agencies and directed more specifically at enhancing the individual's knowledge, skills, and abilities on the job.

THE IMPORTANCE OF CAREER DEVELOPMENT

According to Foxman and Polsky (1990), "The goal of career development states that each individual in a firm ultimately is responsible for his or her professional development, growth and movement within the organization" (p. 22). This requires employees to know all they can about their strengths and weaknesses, needs, desires and achievements. This also requires that the organization provide career path information and feedback on an employee's potential.

The consequences of inattention to career development by either the employee or the organization has been described as "dysfunctional career drift." In this state, "employees drift along with no goals or plans for self-development, while the job and environment may be demanding new talents or approaches. The organization winds up with. . . obsolete employees" (Glueck 1982, p. 361). In this a situation, both the individual and the organization lose.

The need for career development in corrections exists at all levels. The individual is responsible for self-evaluation to determine his or her desires, abilities, and needs. The organization is responsible for determining career options, career paths, and job requirements. Together, the individual and the organization are responsible for establishing a plan to develop career progression. Career planning involves an understanding between the employee and the organization. The employee needs a career direction, the organization must be aware of its staffing requirements and fit the employee into its structure accordingly (Greller and Nee 1989). The organization should identify a development program to prepare its most valued employees for more challenging positions (Greller and Nee 1989). Career development activities should be directed through a formalized plan that enables the organization to provide a system for identifying and fulfilling the needs of the individual and the agency.

With a detailed and clear career path, however stated, employees can target the positions they desire among the options opened to them. A career path provides access to more prestige and responsibility. It ties together related roles and makes movement between them seem possible. The directions in career paths vary as well as the timing for movement and the length of time required at a role before advancement to the next can occur (Wolf 1983).

Establishing career paths within an organization enables an employee to envision a clear path or opportunity and set individual goals accordingly. Individuals who have opportunities and goals tend to feel rewarded by the organizations they are involved with, and they tend to display more motivation and increased performance. Nesbitt (1988) has concluded that personnel retention has long been a problem in corrections and that career development coupled with career ladders contributes to a positive environment in any organization. Nesbitt promotes a policy for career development that emphasizes both vertical and lateral mobility. In the same publication, Grimm (1988) noted the importance of clearly defined and attainable career paths, which are essential to the retention of motivated employees. Their importance is further demonstrated when considering that individuals deem their careers as less important when those careers offer little opportunity for growth (Wolf 1983). A 1970 study by Gould concluded that individuals who had more extensive career planning ended up with the most effective careers (Glueck 1982).

Unfortunately, existing career development programs in correctional organizations provide or suggest training beneficial for few desired positions. These programs exist largely for individuals within the upper level of management. Few programs have been directed to employees at other levels, due either to cost or the lack of lateral and vertical mobility options available to "front-line" officers.

However, according to Moses (1987), a well-developed, organizationally supported, career planning program is especially helpful to those individuals employed by organizations that offer little opportunity for upward advancement. These organizations can help their employees to remain productive and motivated by making them aware of options open to them, such as lateral moves, skill acquisitions, and job enrichment opportunities "Through career planning, employees learn to evaluate both career opportunities and potential restraints realistically" (p. 25). Individuals provided with this information are less likely to feel that they are trapped. They will come to dwell less on their inability to advance and more on their ability to enrich their current level of opportunity.

Implementing a successful career development program need not require a major commitment of time and resources. But it will require careful planning about what kind of program the department wants, why it wants it, and how management will communicate the initiative to employees.

Issues to consider range from highly philosophical to strictly pragmatic. In many cases, there are no across-the-board right or wrong answers—only answers that fit best wit a particular agency's distinctive culture and goals.

BARRIERS TO EFFECTIVE CAREER DEVELOPMENT

Many career development systems are characterized by barriers to mobility and a lack of information regarding career opportunities (Nesbitt 1988). Traditionally, the public sector employment structure has offered more mobility than the private sector. Programs developed within the pubic sector often provide a variety of career ladders. This would enable frequent occupational moves among program related groups (Wolf 1983). However, information about career choices is not always readily available. In addition, organizations hold many misconceptions and unfounded worries regarding employee career planning. These misconceptions act as barriers to providing employees with the necessary career development information (Moses 1987).

Organizations also fear that career planning will lead to a bombardment of questions by employees and expectations that the organization will provide them with a wide range of career opportunities. This will not be the case, provided that the career-planning process demands realistic career goals. Dramatic career changes become exceptions, shifts in career emphasis become the rule. Within reason, however, the correctional organization should provide its officers with information and counseling to manage their career more effectively.

Organizational hesitation also is based on the notion that, before career planning can be implemented, a whole variety of human resource mechanisms must be established. On the contrary, as explained by Moses (1987), "many organizations have implemented highly successful career planning programs with few mechanisms in place" (p. 26). This can be seen in the relationship between supervisors and employees, which can be a valuable career development tool. In a variety of roles, the same supervisor or several different authority figures can act as coaches, sponsors, and mentors for junior employees. As Shore and Bloom (1986) explain, the "coach" encourages the employees on a daily basis, helping them set goals and improve their job performance. Coaches can help employees by aiding them in obtaining invaluable knowledge for more challenging assignments. The "sponsor" uses job contacts and experiences to help foster the younger employee's placement into new openings and new positions. "Mentors" act as counselors and guides when sharing their professional expertise with a protégé. Mentors can help employees by producing flexible, knowledgeable, and skilled subordinates. Through mentoring, an inexperienced employee gains confidence and insight into the job that the mentor knows so well.

PROGRAM STRUCTURE AND DEVELOPMENT STANDARDS

The structure of a correctional agency's career development program originates through the relationship between two primary components: career counseling and in-service training. Career counseling, involving the interaction of counselor and employee, offers guidance that may assist an individual in choosing, preparing, entering, or progressing in a job assignment. Career counseling identifies three elements: (1) the knowledge, skills, and abilities (KSA) of each individual relative to present and future job assignments; (2) in-service training requirements; and (3) the extent to which the training fulfills employee and agency expectations.

Traditionally, in-service training has ensured a minimum level of proficiency in an assigned job, although such training has not been included as part of career development. The concept of in-service training presented within the framework of these standards embraces more than the traditional definition (i.e., providing an advanced level of instruction that enhances an employee's overall potential for upward mobility or job satisfaction). This concept of in-service training is appropriate for inclusion in an accredited career development program. Two aspects of in-service training are articulated in this program design: proficiency and career specialty.

Proficiency in-service training both maintains and enhances the KSA needed to perform the duties and responsibilities of the assigned job. Career specialty in-service training has two purposes: to stimulate personnel to improve the KSA needed to perform job tasks required in specialized areas and to compete for new areas of interest and specialization that may enhance the potential for upward mobility.

Agency Practices and Procedures

The career development program should foster the improvement of personal knowledge, skills, and abilities of all sworn correctional officers to successfully meet agency tasks. The program should be voluntary and ensure all officers equal access to training and development opportunities. The aim of career development is to highlight specific opportunities for individual growth at all levels and to improve overall job satisfaction and performance. The agency may utilize the career development program to further the professional growth and capabilities of the employee's present or future job role within the agency. The principal components of the career development program are career counseling and in-service training.

The career development program plan objectives should be stated in quantitative terms to facilitate program audits and evaluations. Career development program objectives may specify the potential number of personnel to utilize career development services, the number of personnel assigned to career development services, the number of outside resources for career counseling, and the total number of training hours provided, including technical assistance. A written assessment of Equal Employment Opportunity and affirmative action objectives, if any, should be used to determine whether special training and development opportunities for members of minority groups and women are needed. The assessment should reveal present employment practices, policies, and procedures of the agency relevant to their impact on the employment and utilization of minority group members and women. Moreover, the agency should conduct a continuous review of the career development program plan to provide employees and management with up-to-date information regarding organizational requirements for achieving program goals.

Personnel, such as supervisors and counselors, who are assigned to conduct career development activities should undergo a period of orientation that will provide increased knowledge and skills in the following areas:

- General counseling techniques;
- Knowledge, skills, and abilities assessment techniques;
- Salary, benefits, and training opportunities of the agency;
- Educational opportunities and incentive programs;
- Awareness of the cultural background of ethnic groups in the program;
- Record keeping techniques;
- Career development programs of other agencies;
- Availability of outside resources.

Program Records

An updated record of the knowledge, skills, and abilities of each employee is fundamental to career development planning. The inventory may be derived from a questionnaire or personal interview administered to each employee within the department. Based on the information received, an inventory of the KSA of each officer can be prepared. The inventory may contain information in the following areas: educational background, training courses completed, work experience (past and present), special skills, foreign languages, and a recent performance evaluation report. Along with the job analysis data, the inventory may also be used to determine the department's training requirements.

In addition, the department should maintain an inventory of career specialties, if any, which include the knowledge, skills, and abilities needed for each specialty. Career specialties are derived by the agency from the job analysis and job classification information. More specifically, career specialties may be determined by identifying the most important and frequently performed jobs and jobs that require special training and knowledge to perform the specific duties and responsibilities. By using the catalogue provided by the agency, the officer has an opportunity to examine career specialties available within the agency.

Career Counseling and In-Service Training

Several tools, other than the personal interview, may be utilized in career counseling; for example, a recorded history of the knowledge, skills, and abilities of the employee, those required by the agency; and an inventory of outside resources. These counseling tools may be used to determine individual needs in the program and provide direction that will equate those needs to the needs of the agency. To adequately provide counseling services, personnel assigned to the task should be properly trained to perform the following activities: assessment of the KSA of employees, assessment of the KSA required by the agency, preparation of a career planning schedule, utilization of the resource inventory, administration of a performance evaluation, and the provision of feedback and recommendations to the employee.

An evaluation checklist, utilized as a tool of career counseling, may determine whether the employee has reached an effective level of performance in career development. Moreover, the tool may be used to assess the employee's strengths and weaknesses and alert the counselor to particular areas on which the counseling process must focus.

Management Training

According to Hawkins and Moravec (1989), many correctional agency administrators have been hesitant to develop and support career development programs for correctional officers over a concern that these type of programs place unnecessary emphasis on management positions as the only outcome of career progression. However, management and supervisory training should continue to be an important element in any career development program and a major factor in enhancing an employee's overall potential for upward mobility. Supervision and management positions within a correctional institution requires specialized training in a number of areas, including

- The ability to express and communicate organizational goals and objectives;
- Organizational planning;
- The ability to measure results;
- Decision-making skills;
- Problem identification, prevention, and solution;
- Management information systems;
- Fiscal management;
- Organizational behavior and decision making.

As correctional staff members are promoted, the skills necessary to perform at a given level may change to require supervisory, management, and administrative skills and knowledge. The agency should provide training prior to or immediately following promotions. If budgetary problems preclude formal training in these areas, the department should develop an in-house training network or participate in a regional training program.

In addition, the department should maintain a written record of all proficiency and career specialty in-service training for every officer. The data provide the agency with a ready reference of information for such things as special assignments, reassignments, or advancement. The information recorded should include such items as the title of the course, training, instruction, or workshop completed; date of completion; grade point (if any); and achievement of any special skills or honors.

Annual Review

A yearly review of the officer's training records should be conducted by the career counselor to assess the officer's training progress in achieving career objectives and assess whether the proficiency and career specialty training achieved by the officer adequately meet the KSA's required to perform present and future jobs within the agency. To avoid conflicts that may arise from the counselor's duties as the employee's immediate supervisor, the employee's career facilitator should be someone other than his or her immediate supervisor.

Educational Leave

The department should institute a policy that supports an educational leave program. Educational leave is an absence from duty or employment granted to an officer to undertake academic or vocational instruction as a part of in-service training. Educational leave may be authorized for outside workshops, seminars, attendance at state training academies, or formal educational programs (such as a junior college, college, or university). The agency may support the employee who pursues an educational opportunity by providing salary adjustments, flexible work schedules, or financial aid. Several forms of financial assistance may be offered by the agency, such as reimbursement of money spent in pursuit of college level course work and granting leave with or without pay for credit or noncredit course work or training that is job related.

To further promote academic study, a comprehensive educational leave program should include provisions for tuition reimbursement and preferential shift schedules. The reimbursement may be in full or a percentage based on grades. Where exceptions are made to the regular shift change schedule to facilitate academic study, criteria should be established to minimize controversy. These programs frequently are perceived as preferential to certain individuals and should be administered equitably. In addition, criteria for participation in the program may limit the participants to a specific area of study.

An effective career development program will enable the correctional officer to experience a sense of control over his or her career. Contrary to the fears of many supervisors, the agency that assists its employees in career planning is more likely to retain its best people; such planning promotes learning and helps employees to avoid dissatisfaction, burnout, and other negative outcomes.

In addition, the agency must train line and staff supervisors and managers in career counseling and determine which career management programs are the best for the organization. These responsibilities constitute difficult but intriguing challenges for the future.

CASE STUDY: CAREER DEVELOPMENT—A CASE STUDY OF CALIFORNIA CORRECTIONS

Background

In 1986, the California legislature set out in Penal Code, Title 7, Chapter 3.5, Section 5092 a mandate for the Robert Presley Institute of Corrections Training and Research to develop a career path program for the state department of corrections. It read in part,

> the institute shall develop a detailed and specific program for implementation by the Legislature, the Department of Corrections, and the Department of the Youth Authority that establishes a career path, which is integrated with an educational and training regimen for all youth and adult state corrections personnel in California . . . encourage and foster the attainment of post-secondary educational degrees by correctional officers . . . shall include standards for entry, basic, intermediate, advanced, supervisory, management, and specialized corrections personnel.

In the legislation a specific task was given to the institute: develop a detailed program for implementation by the legislature, the Department of Corrections, and Department of Youth Authority. The purpose of the program was to establish a career path to be integrated with the educational process for all youth and adult state corrections personnel in California. The overall goal was to improve the job and career competence of state correctional officers.

In 1993, the authors developed and presented a comprehensive career development document to the executive board of the Robert Presley Institute (see Sechrest and Josi 1993). To satisfy all three agencies (the state legislature and the Departments of Correction and Youth Authority), the final report had two clear objectives. The first was to gain an understanding of what the California Department of Corrections and the Department of Youth Authority presently were doing in regard to career development. The second goal was to develop two generic career path models, either of which could be adapted to fit the needs of the adult and juvenile correctional departments.

Introduction

Traditionally, California's correctional departments offered jobs, not careers. However, during the 1950s and 1960s, the reputation of the two departments as the most progressive and experimental in the country helped them accumulate bright and dedicated staff members who molded careers in corrections.

Over time, the negative and stereotypical connotations of corrections work were offset by substantial pay increases and a professional work environment. Increased training and organization within the field brought a level of status and readily marketable skills to the workforce. However, the onslaught of facility overcrowding, which began in the middle 1980s, soon forced California's correctional employees into a "survival mentality." Programs and policies that made the California system the hallmark of contemporary corrections were abandoned as line and staff officers devoted all of their energy into simply "keeping up with the numbers." Without experience in some of the problems created in overcrowded conditions, correctional administrators made up solutions as they went along. Long-term planning was a forsaken luxury, and crisis intervention became the trademark of corrections management rather than any conscious movement toward a correctional officer career development program.

Moreover, a number of ancillary issues helped exacerbate the changing environment within California's two correctional agencies. The ascension of a correctional officers' union altered the context of employee-management relations, political interests dominated theoretical goals, and the public knew more about the criminal justice system than ever before, so greater accountability was demanded on all issues, large and small. Employees had to work faster and smarter than in the past and be tougher mentally to face the challenges of the field.

Therefore, the state legislature's interest in a corrections career path program was a well-timed issue. The growth of the employee workforce mandated a new management style to replace the formulas designed for a smaller operation. According to Stohr-Gilmore, Self, and Lovrich (1991), "numerous studies have indicated a clear and consistent relationship between turnover and personnel development programs, opportunities for advancement and related organizational attributes."

Today, both the Department of Corrections and the Department of Youth Authority resemble large corporations, and they must operate as such, particularly with respect to personnel issues. However, in the interests of economy and efficiency, this transition to a new management style had to be planned and systematic.

Moreover, existing career development programs within California's Department of Corrections and Youth Authority provided or suggested training beneficial for a few desired positions. With minor exceptions, these programs existed largely for individuals within the upper level of management. Few programs have been directed to employees at other levels, due to either excessive cost or the large number of persons within the respective agencies.

Questions Addressed

The study focused on career development and related career paths for correctional officers within the California Department of Corrections (CDC) and the Department of Youth Authority (CYA). Several questions regarding career development and career paths within the CDC and CYA were addressed, including

- What *educational requirements* and *related time frames*, if any, should be required beyond entry level job classifications for career development and enhanced job performance?
- How should the CDC and the CYA address the issue of *experience as a substitute for education*, and vice versa, in both entry and career development?

- What should be the relationship between *preservice* (academy) training and *in-service* training, respectively, for job development?
- What is the responsibility of individuals for taking advantage of career development opportunities *within* and *outside* of their work environment?
- Having established the career development expectations for individuals working in the system, what are the related expectations for the organizations involved in implementing such a plan? That is, what must occur in the organizational environment to meet the goal(s) of career development or management education?
- Who should be involved in ensuring the continued development of a career planning program?
- How can the task of career development be best pursued in the CDC and the CYA for the *immediate future*?
- What mechanisms should be created to ensure a *long-term* plan of career development for CDC and CYA employees?
- Is *certification* based on education, training, and job experience a valid goal? If so, who should be responsible for such certification, and how should this task be accomplished?

Some questions could not be addressed. For example, to what extent would a comprehensive career development program improve the performance of correctional officers? Should educational incentives be linked to officer promotions? How could educational attainment best be integrated with training program requirements? To what extent would a comprehensive career development program create better managers or ancillary personnel in specific areas? Would a career development program reduce staff turnover? And, what part, if any, would a career development program play in helping reduce stress related disabilities and workers' compensation claims? The assumption was that improved career development would achieve some, if not all, of these goals.

Current Training Mandates

At the time of the study, there was a correctional officer training academy with a six-week, 240-hour program for the California Department of Corrections (CDC) officers and a five-week, 200-hour program for the California Youth Authority (CYA) officers. The academy training programs are part of a 24-month apprenticeship schedule for correctional peace officers entering the CDC and the CYA (State of California 1988). Permanent status is achieved after a probationary period of 9 months for the CDC or 6 to 12 months (depending on classification) for the CYA. An *apprentice* is defined as "a worker who learns a craft or profession through planned, supervised work on the job in conjunction with receiving planned related technical instruction." The goal is "to further the professionalism of correctional peace officers [by] establishing an monitoring the completion of work processes by apprentices, setting standards for formal training, working with colleges and universities to establish education programs, and by proposing and supporting research" (State of California 1988).

Joint Apprenticeship Committee

A Joint Apprenticeship Committee (JAC) oversees the apprenticeship program. This committee, a joint labor and management undertaking, was made up of voting members from the CDC, CYA, and the California Correctional Peace Officers Association (CCPOA). Nonvoting members include representatives from the Department of Industrial Relations, Division of Apprenticeship Standards, the Community Colleges, legal advisor, and staff from the departments' training and selection programs. The apprenticeship committee addresses nine specific employee classifications: correctional officer, correctional counselor, parole agent for the CDC and CYA, medical technical assistant, casework specialist, CYA youth counselor and group supervisor, and institutional fire fighter.

As part of the apprenticeship for correctional counselor, for example, the individual would receive 3,600 actual hours of training, with 2,403 hours of that training designated to specified areas. These areas include inmate classification, report writing, general counseling, general casework, court order service, and additional experience.

Since January 1, 1988, the JAC "has had the additional responsibility to establish training standards for journey-level staff and supervisors" (State of California 1988). The JAC was proceeding with a plan to require completion of five community college courses by apprentices as part of the completion of the 24-month apprenticeship period. The goal was to implement these courses at five community college sites throughout California as soon as the curriculum can be developed and approved. A draft of the proposed five courses was being considered and curriculum development is beginning. Completion of the courses would lead to a certificate, presumably at the "basic" level.

Apprentices would be required to take these courses on their own time and would not be reimbursed in dollars or time for taking these courses. To the contrary, they would pay regular registration fees at the community colleges. The units taken, however, would be applicable to an associate of arts degree as offered at the participating institution. Prospective employees could take these courses prior to academy attendance. Pay differentials and promotions are *not* tied to course completion. Promotion generally is based on job performance and one's ability to "handle situations." Even though it may be desirable to reward educational attainment with pay or promotions, the respective departments recognized that specific links between job performance and an officer's education, training, and experience could not be established at the time.

Model Program and Policy Proposals

Model 1. Correctional Officer Certification

The Correctional Peace Officer Certificate Program was a "generic" model for a correctional officer certification program. The guidelines for this proposal were developed from and were a composite of the California Peace Officers Standards and Training (P.O.S.T.) program in addition to specific recommendations by the

National Institute of Corrections (NIC) in its proposed correctional officer certification curriculum.

Under this proposal, correctional officers would be encouraged to continue educational pursuits throughout their careers using the dual processes of skills development (on-the-job and in-service training) and postsecondary education. Career development would be encouraged with a three-tiered certification program, based on additional combinations of experience, training, and education.

- The *basic certificate* would be issued on completion of the basic training academy and the probationary apprenticeship program.
- The *intermediate certificate* would represent a combination of experience, training, and continued education.
- The *advanced certificate* would represent accumulation of additional experience and education after having completed the requirements for the intermediate certificate.

The certificate program would not mandate the award of a college degree; however, additional education would reduce the number of years of experience necessary to advance to the next level. The certificate program would not automatically tie pay and other benefits to the levels of certification. Such decisions would be left to the department(s) involved.

Model 2. Correctional Officer Educational Assistance

Individuals within the "peace officer" category, as well as other staff members at all levels already appointed to positions in corrections should be given the opportunity to pursue a college education. The second model, A Model Educational Assistance Policy, provided the details of an officer tuition reimbursement program that would enhance and encourage postsecondary education. Under this proposal the agency would develop a set of workable guidelines to establish and maintain a tuition reimbursement program.

Both model programs were recommended as future goals for all correctional departments. Even though they may not be adopted in their entirety, they provide the basis for future exploration or adoption of peace officer certification programs and for related research. They also should contribute to the development of productive career development and career path programs. The complete text of both programs is discussed at length in Chapter 11, "Conclusions and Recommendations," of this text.

Conclusions

To meet the goals for the establishment of a successful career development program, all components of the personnel process must work together. Recruitment and selection, academy training, and postacademy in-service training and education programs must be included. Each of these was addressed here in relation to the goal of improved individual and agency performance.

Recruitment of today's corrections professional should incorporate a well-developed and validated written and oral examination processes accessible to all qualified individuals. This testing process must be unrestricted by cultural, ethnic, or gender partiality. Sanchez (1989) made two important points about recruitment in California: that the standards for recruits should be raised and that applicant backgrounds should be scrutinized more carefully. He does not believe that the department should be teaching basic writing skills; individuals should be encouraged to achieve these skills elsewhere before applying.

The newly hired correctional peace officer should participate in a structured, standardized academy training program that emphasizes the use of behavior modification techniques and communication skills along with traditional self-defense and survival techniques. The total number of training academy hours should be increased to maximize this enhanced training effort.

Subsequent to academy training and the completion of an apprenticeship (or probationary) period, every correctional officer designate should have clearly defined opportunities for career advancement. These opportunities can and should be structured by the respective departments. Veteran staff members in all classifications should have opportunities for professional development through mandated in-service training requirements in addition to advanced educational opportunities made available with assistance from immediate supervisors and institutional management staff.

Correctional supervisors and "front line" managers are the primary contacts for individuals who wish to learn about and pursue career goals; these individuals should continue to receive training in staff motivation and career development techniques.

Particular emphasis should be placed on motivating women and members of minority groups. As noted by Bush (1977) "Minority administrators recognize that . . . racism continues to operate persistently in America and that their ethnicity alone will account for numerous barriers to their effective and efficient functioning . . . [t]hey will undoubtedly have to 'go it alone' and experience some pain that is not of their own creation" (pp. 21–22). Nesbitt (1988) discusses this issue in the context of women and other members of minority groups, emphasizing that "people who lack opportunity for advancement tend to disengage from the corporation, as manifested in depressed aspirations, lowered commitment to the organization, or a withdrawal from responsibility in the organization" (p. 157).

REFERENCES

Bush, J.A. "The Minority Administrator: Implications for Social Education." *Journal of Education for Social Work* 13, no. 1 (1977): 15–22.

Commission on Peace Officers Standards and Training. *Post Administrative Manual, Commission Procedure D-1, Basic Training*. Sacramento, CA: Department of Justice, 1990.

Foxman, L., Polsky W. "Career Counselor: Aid in Employee Career Development." *Personnel Journal* 69, no. 1 (1990): 22 and 24.

Glueck, W.F. *Personnel: A Diagnostic Approach*. Plano, TX: Business Publications, 1982.

Greller, M., and D. Nee. *From Baby Boom to Baby Bust: How Business Can Meet the Demographic Challenge.* Reading, MA: Addison-Wesley, 1989.

Grimm, C.M. "Compensation." In F.W. Benton and C.A. Nesbitt (eds.), *Prison Personnel Management and Staff Development.* College Park, MD: American Correctional Association and the National Center for Public Productivity, 1988.

Hawkins, M., and M. Moravec. "Career Paths Discourage Innovation and Deflate Motivation." *Personnel Administrator* 34, no. 10 (1989): 111–112.

Moses, B. "Giving Employees a Future." *Training and Development Journal* 41, no. 12 (1987): 25–28.

Nesbitt, C.A. "Career Development." In F.W. Benton and C.A. Nesbitt (eds), *Prison Personnel Management and Staff Development.* College Park, MD: American Correctional Association and the National Center for Public Productivity, 1988.

Sanchez, C.M. "Attracting and Selecting a Top-Notch Staff, The California Experience." *Corrections Today* 58 (1989): 166.

Sechrest, D.K., and D.A. Josi. "Comprehensive Career Path Report for the California Departments of Corrections and Youth Authority." Riverside, CA: Robert Presley Institute of Corrections Research and Training, 1993.

Shore, L.M., and A. Bloom. "Developing Employees Through Coaching and Career Management." *Personnel* 63, no. 8 (1986): 34–41.

State of California. *Joint Apprentice Committee Master Manual,* pp. 149–150. Sacramento, CA: Department of Corrections, 1988.

Stohr-Gillmore, M., R. Self, and M. Lovrich. "Staff Turnover in New Generation Jails: An Investigation of Its Causes and Prevention." *American Jails* (1991): 47–54.

United States General Accounting Office. "Prison Expansion, Staffing New Facilities Will Be a Challenge for the BOP. Report to the Chairman, Subcommittee on Intellectual Property and Judicial Administration, Committee on the Judiciary House of Representatives." Washington, DC: United States General Accounting Office, 1992.

Wolf, L. "Public Manager Careers." In W. Eddy (ed.), *Handbook of Organization Management.* New York: Marcel Dekker, 1983.

Part III

Management and Organizational Issues

6

Civil Liability

GENERAL OVERVIEW

Legal liability has become an increasing concern for corrections at all levels in the past 25 years. When the President's Commission on Law Enforcement and Administration of Justice *Task Force Report: Corrections* (1967) was written, little was said about the rights of inmates. Most inmate litigation up to that time addressed the responsibility of prison administrators and inmate access to the courts. Since that time, inmate rights have been addressed in many ways by the courts, have been the subject of numerous books and articles, have been captured in national correctional standards, and are a basic part of correctional officer training. Collins's (1997) brief summary of correctional law for correctional officers is now in its second edition. Coupled with training materials from the American Correctional Association and other resource materials on the subject (see Barrineau 1987; Crane 1989), correctional officers and their supervisors are far more aware than ever before of their legal responsibilities to the inmates they supervise. Conversely, officers have found that they, too, have rights in the correctional environment. Many of these issues have been discussed elsewhere in the book; however, they will be summarized here as they relate specifically to the role of the correctional officer. Topics include inmate access to and use of the courts, some of the important cases on prisons, concerns about the use of force, and officers' rights.

As noted earlier, Title 42 Section 1983 of the U.S. Code has been widely used in the filing of almost 34,000 cases between 1970 and 1993 by state prisoners (Ross 1995). Attempts have been made to limit the number of cases filed, and grievance procedures for inmates have been explored as a possible alternative. The success of these cases has not been good. Nationally, prisoner suits make up about 15% of all civil suits filed in the federal courts and 97% are dismissed before trial (Dunn 1994); only 13% resulted in any success for the prisoner, which is one of the worst records of any type of civil suit filed in the Federal courts. Tremendous amounts of time and resources are devoted to these cases, most of which (97%) are filed by state prison inmates. New York State officials estimate that 28,000 inmate cases are now backlogged (Dunn 1994). In California (in 1992) the director of the Department of Corrections found that 95% of the lawsuits filed by the 109,000 inmates had no merit and were dismissed, although the system had to budget $7 million to employ 80 attorneys and 40 support personnel to defend them (Jordan 1992). An assistant attorney general found that lawsuits went from 3 per 1,000 inmates in 1979–1980 to 6 per 1,000 by 1985, leveling off at 5 per 1,000 by 1992. About 1,500–2,000 suits are filed each year, challenging visitation, exercise privileges, food, and access to the law library. Additional suits are in the areas of medical services (about 20%) and the use of force.

Ross (1995), sampling 1,805 prison cases and 718 jail cases over a 20-year period (1973–1993), found that prison officials won in 59% of the prison litigation and jail officials in 42%. Seven major areas were identified: conditions of confinement, administrative liability, physical plant (facility), use of force, Eighth Amendment rights, medical care, and failure to protect. For Section 1983 cases, monetary relief was awarded in 16% of the cases studied, with an average award of $28,101; punitive damages ranged from $100 to $364 million, and nominal damages of $1.00 were used infrequently. Attorney's fees averaged $2,417 (Ross 1995).

There have been several "eras" in the development of correctional institutions. Gill (1982) has documented seven. His sixth era, from 1940 to 1970 (classification, case work, programs of rehabilitation, furloughs, work and educational release) marked the end of what generally is known as the *hands-off* period in prison litigation, which marks the first generation of litigation. Decisions up to this point addressed primarily the responsibilities of prison administrators, such as *Adams* v. *Ellis* (1952): "It is not the function of the Courts to superintend the treatment and discipline of prisoners in penitentiaries, but only to deliver from imprisonment those who are illegally confined." The Supreme Court stated that courts are without power to supervise prison administration or to interfere with the ordinary prison rules or regulations (*Banning* v. *Looney* 1954). They let stand other decisions, stating that the power of promulgating regulations necessary for the safety of the prisons population and the public, as well as for the maintenance and proper functioning of the institution, is vested in corrections officials with expertise in the field and not in the courts. "There can be no question that they [the administrators] must be granted wide discretion in the exercise of such authority" (*Long* v. *Parker* 1968).

The second legal generation is the "hands-on" era, from which most of the cases cited are taken. Depending on the author, this period ran from the middle 1960s through the middle 1980s. In the *Correctional Law Reporter* ("Corrections Court Cases" 1994) survey of the top ten prison and jail cases, half are from this period, half in the third generation, after 1979. The period from 1980 on is referred to by Collins (1997) as the *one-hand-on, one-hand-off period*, because court intervention in prison matters was reduced. We are in this period today, which is referred to as the period of *deference* by Call (1995). The year 1979 was chosen by Call due to the landmark case of *Bell* v. *Wolfish* (99 S.Ct. 1861), in which federal detainees lost on five major issues relating to their confinement. The position of the courts in this period appears to spring from complementary perceptions about the nature of problems and the efficacy—or appropriateness—of judicial intervention in prisons, not unlike the first period. Correctional administrators are responsible for

1. Maintaining internal order and discipline in their institutions;
2. Securing their institutions against unauthorized access or escape;

3. Providing programs (rehabilitation, treatment) for inmates placed in their custody, to the extent that human nature and available resources allow.

DiIulio (1987) would add "amenities," those things required for maintaining a humane prison environment. John Conrad (1965) summed it up by saying that a correctional institution should be lawful, safe, industrious, and hopeful.

Can the courts solve the problems of corrections? For many reasons, courts are ill-equipped to deal with the increasingly urgent problems of prison administration and reform. Judicial recognition of that fact reflects no more than a healthy sense of realism. In several cases, the courts are clear that they will not "second-guess" wardens or administrators or parole boards; that is, those persons who must respond to the immediate problem. The courts, however, will retain their right of oversight and review of their actions, which is all the more reason that corrections professionals must follow good policies and procedures.

INMATE USE OF THE COURTS

Inmates file lawsuits for two reasons (Collins 1997): to challenge the actions of correctional officers or to question general policies on conditions in the institution. Most law relevant to correctional officers is found in agency policies and procedures and related directives, and most departments have legal counsel in-house or readily available to interpret developing case law. As noted previously, the major areas of litigation are medical services, use of force, access to the law library, conditions of confinement (i.e., visitation, programs, exercise privileges, food), First and Eighth Amendment issues, administrative liability (i.e., failure to train, supervise, direct), physical plant (facility), and failure to protect (safety, assaults, suicide prevention).

A recent decision by the Supreme Court appears to have limited inmate access to the courts (*Lewis* v. *Casey* 1996). Whereas the suit affirmed the duty stated in *Bounds* (1977) to provide inmates with assistance in the form of law libraries or persons trained in the law, it places the burden on the inmate to prove actual harm (or "prejudice") that has in some way resulted from inadequate legal resources. If an inmate actually had a suit dismissed due to inadequate resources and could show it, harm could be proven (see Collins 1997).

SPECIFIC AREAS OF CONCERN
FOR THE CORRECTIONAL OFFICER

First Amendment Concerns

The First Amendment can represent challenges for the correctional officer—freedom of religion, speech, and the press. These freedoms cannot be subject to prior restraint in free society, but in a prison the interests of safety and security will often prevail; that is, restrictions are somewhat easier to justify. Collins (1997) observes, however, that the Religious Freedom and Restoration Act (RFRA) passed by Congress in 1993 now places a heavier burden on the correctional staff than the First Amendment and its Court interpretations. We first must consider the old rules and then the tests allowed under the RFRA, although in a historic turn of events in June 1997, the Supreme Court invalidated the RFRA in *Boerne* v. *Flores* (1997). This decision will be discussed later.

In *Turner* v. *Safley* (1987), the Supreme Court held that a prison rule that prohibited inmates from corresponding with inmates in other prisons was constitutional. The Court viewed this regulation as a reasonable way to protect prison security, because the correspondence that was banned could have been used to communicate escape plans or to encourage assaults on other inmates. In *Turner,* the Court made it clear that it was not going to use a heightened scrutiny approach in individual rights cases. In its review of prison regulations prohibiting inmate marriages and inmate correspondence with inmates in other prisons, the Court reviewed all its prisoners rights cases and concluded that these cases had used a "rational basis test." The Court stated emphatically that, "when a prison regulation impinges on inmates' constitutional rights, the regulation is valid if it is reasonably related to legitimate penological interests."

The "rational basis" approach is a much easier standard for the government to satisfy than the heightened scrutiny approach. Under the rational basis test, the burden is shifted to the party whose rights allegedly have been violated to demonstrate that the government had no rational reason for doing what it did or that, if it did have a rational reason, what it did was not reasonably related to it.

In *Turner*, the Court also established four factors that should be considered in assessing the reasonableness of a prison regulation that impinging upon an individual right of an inmate:

1. Whether there is a *rational connection* between the prison regulation and the legitimate governmental interest put forward to justify it;
2. Whether an alternative means of exercising the right exists in spite of what the prison has done;
3. Whether striking down the prisons action would have a significant ripple effect on fellow inmates or staff;
4. Whether there are ready alternatives available to the prison or whether the regulation appears instead to be "exaggerated response" to the problem it is intended to address.

The Court has utilized these four factors in determining the constitutionality of the two regulations at issue in *Turner* and two other key cases.

O'Lone v. *Shabazz* (1987) dealt with the right of inmates to practice their religion. Shabazz was a Muslim who was not permitted to observe Jumu'ah services. Officials did not have to permit Shabazz to return to the prison for the service because that would have created a security risk. Nor did the prison have to allow Shabazz to stay in the prison all day Friday and then let him make up the work on Saturday because that would require additional prison resources. Thus, the prison's actions in denying Shabazz the opportunity to observe Jumu'ah were reasonable in light of the security and resources needs of the prison.

Thornburgh v. *Abbott* (1989) showed a more conservative shift by the court. In *Thornburgh* v. *Abbott*, the Court dealt with the authority of prisons to exclude publications that are mailed to inmates. The rule at issue permitted wardens in federal prisons to exclude publications (although only on an issue-by-issue basis) that they deemed to be "detrimental to the security, good order, or discipline of the institution, or . . . [that] might facilitate criminal activity." Publications could not be excluded because they expressed unpopular views or were religious, political, social, or sexual in nature. The Court found that this regulation was reasonable in light of the prisons' need to maintain security. It distinguished this case from *Procunier* v. *Martinez* (1989), where the Court had struck down a prison censorship regulation as too broad on the basis that *Martinez* dealt with incoming mail and this case dealt with outgoing mail. The Court believed that outgoing mail posed greater threats to prison security.

The regulation in *Shabazz* that prevented Muslim inmates from participating in Jumu'ah and the publishers-only regulation in *Thornburgh* were subject to *Turner* factors, which suggested that prisons should not experience great difficulty in satisfying them. However, the 1993 Religious Freedom Restoration Act now supersedes *Turner* and places a new burden on correctional institutions (Collins 1997, p. 49):

> Under RFRA, if a prison or jail imposes a "substantial burden" on an inmate's exercise of religion, then to justify that burden, the government must show that (1) the restriction or burden "is in furtherance of a compelling governmental interest" and (2) that it is the "least restrictive means" of furthering that interest.

The "substantial burden" test will be difficult apply because the courts are not yet clear about its interpretation. However, as Collins concludes, the courts are still willing to defer to corrections officials when security is seen as a compelling governmental interest, much as they did with the *Turner* test. The most difficult interpretations will hinge on the "least restrictive means" aspect of the law. Collins cites a Wisconsin case of inmates whose religious jewelry was banned (*Sasnett* v. *Sullivan* 1996). Inmates filed lawsuits regarding the wearing of crucifixes. However, the courts could find no mandate in their respective religions requiring the wearing of a crucifix, although each inmate could attest individually to the importance of the crucifix.

In a more recent RFRA case, a Rastafarian inmate was ordered by correctional officers to unbraid his dreadlocks for a search prior to a medical appointment (*May* v. *Baldwin*, 1997). The district court granted summary judgment based on the argument that dreadlocks endanger prison security by affording a hiding place for contraband (Kaufman 1997). The court explained that there was a compelling state interest and the procedures used were the least restrictive means of doing so. In a similar case (*Campos* v. *Coughlin* 1994), a federal district court found in favor of inmates of the Santeria faith wearing multicolored beads. Call and Smarkos (1996) have presented the arguments for and against the RFRA, concluding that more court decisions will be needed to interpret it. Also, the American Correctional Association published a position statement in 1996 supportive of the "reasonableness standard" used in *Turner* and *Shabazz* for validating institutional rules on religious faith and practice (Ingley 1996).

As noted, the RFRA was invalidated in the case of RFRA in *Boerne* v. *Flores* (1997; Associated Press 1997, AP-NY-06-25-97 1046EDT), which may be seen as consistent with these recent interpretations of the RFRA by the lower courts. In a 6–3 decision in June 1997, the Supreme Court said Congress overstepped its authority when it passed the RFRA, which set a much higher standard for religious freedom than a 1990 Court decision that led Congress to pass the RFRA (*Employment Division, Department of Human Resources of Oregon* v. *Smith* 1990). The removal of the "compelling governmental interest/least restrictive means" test raises the question of whether the earlier *Turner* (1987) tests or the *Shabazz* (1987) "security risk" standard, or both, are now again in effect or whether some new standard for judging inmate behavior will be created. These shifts in legal interpretation highlight the importance of in-service training for correctional officers.

Use of Force

Probably the most difficult area for correctional officers is the use of force. Generally, force is justified in cases of self-defense, to protect others or property, to enforce prison rules and discipline, and to prevent a crime, including escapes (see Collins 1997). How much force can be used? Two cases are relevant: *Hudson* v. *McMillian* (1992) and *Whitley* v. *Albers* (1986). McMillian, a Louisiana prison inmate, was the subject of a beating by correctional officers when he was offering no resistance and in handcuffs and shackles. He was badly bruised and had loosened teeth and a cracked dental plate. An observing supervisor apparently told the officers "not to have too much fun." In ordering relief ($800 in damages), the Court found absolutely no need for force and that physical force may constitute cruel and unusual punishment even if the injuries are not serious (see Palmer 1997). The standard used was from *Whitley* v. *Albers* in that the officers acted "maliciously and sadistically to cause harm."

Inmate Albers (*Whitley* v. *Albers* 1986) sued a prison guard who had wounded him in the knee during an inmate uprising, alleging that the shooting was cruel and unusual punishment. The inmate alleged that he had not been involved in the uprising, had assured the prison security chief that he would protect from harm a guard that other inmates had taken hostage, and had made no threatening moves just before being shot. The Court ruled that, in cruel and unusual punishment cases where the government action at issue is not part of the sentence awarded the prisoner, the prisoner must prove that prison officials acted wantonly. In the context of a prison disturbance, that means the inmates must show that officials acted "*maliciously and sadistically* for the very purpose of causing harm." In this case the inmate had failed to allege facts from which such a state of mind could be inferred. These cases demonstrate that correctional officers must at all times remain professional and use good judgment when applying force. Any hint of maliciousness or punitiveness will present a problem.

Searches

One of the most difficult areas after for correctional officers after use of force is searching for contraband. The right of inmates to be free from unreasonable searches and seizures is an individual right that is not affected directly by the now outdated rational basis test but more likely to hinge on "reasonable suspicion" or "reasonable belief" that contraband may be found. The suspicion must be focused on the person searched and facts and inferences drawn from them must be considered (see Collins 1997). The Court has found that the need for prisons to maintain discipline and security often prevails over the privacy interests of prisoners. For example, inmates have no reasonable expectation of privacy in their cells (*Hudson* v. *Palmer* 1984). Inmates who have had contact visits may be subjected to visual body cavity inspections even in the absence of any reason to think that the inspections will turn up evidence (*Bell* v. *Wolfish* 1979), and such inspections can occur for a variety of other reasons, provided the officers are not verbally abusive (*Goff* v. *Nix* 1986; see Collins 1979, p. 61). Also, inmates have no right to observe shakedown searches of their cells (*Block* v. *Rutherford* 1984). It appears that, when prison officials take actions that adversely affect the individual rights of inmates, those actions will be upheld by the Court unless they are clearly unreasonable. This level of suspicion also applies to searches of correctional officers (see *Kennedy* v. *Hardiman* 1980, where reasonable suspicion was found for the search of a correctional officer).

Due Process

Due process was one of the first areas that the Court addressed in the second generation of cases, although the justices have not always spoken clearly. The Due Process Clauses (in the Fifth and Fourteenth Amendments) raise two basic questions: when is a person entitled to due process of law, and when entitled, what process is due? In the prison context, the answer to the first question has arisen in the context of actions taken against an inmate. Such actions include (but are not limited to) disciplinary hearings that may yield a loss of good time credits, placement in segregation (administrative or punitive), transfer to a mental hospital or a less desirable prison, denial of a visitor, and a parole denial or revocation. Because these actions do not deprive an inmate of life or property, the question is whether the inmate has been deprived of a liberty interest in these situations (see Call 1995).

Prisoners acquire liberty interests from the Constitution itself and by creation of state law. The goal of due process is fairness in order to protect the individual from arbitrary actions that may be without factual justification or illegal (Collins 1997). The Court has indicated that not every change in the conditions of confinement having a substantial adverse impact on the prisoner involved is sufficient. Instead, a liberty interest arises when the action taken by the prison is not within the terms of confinement ordinarily contemplated by a prison sentence. Unfortunately, this phrase does not provide a clear definition of when an inmate has a constitutionally protected liberty interest. What is clear is that there are very few such liberty interests. Among the list of unprotected liberty interests are granting of parole (*Greenholtz* v. *Inmates of the Nebraska Penal Complex* 1979), denial of a visit from a particular person

(*Kentucky* v. *Johnson* 1989), transfer to a prison with less favorable conditions of confinement (*Meachum* v. *Fano* 1976), transfer to a prison in another state (*Olim* v. *Wakinekona* 1983), transfer to administrative segregation (*Hewitt* v. *Helms* 1983), and commutation of a life sentence (*Connecticut Board of Pardons* v. *Dumschat* 1981). The only liberty interest protected by the Due Process Clauses and arising directly under the Constitution that the Court has found is that inmates possess an interest in is not being transferred to a mental hospital (*Vitek* v. *Jones* 1980). Inmates also are protected from being involuntarily medicated without a hearing (*Washington* v. *Harper* 1990).

The most basic protections are the right to be informed of the alleged basis for the contemplated action, such as depriving an inmate of good time credits for allegedly stealing from another inmate, and the right to be heard (i.e., to present evidence on one's own behalf). These due process protections are defined in *Wolff* v. *McDonnell* (1974), although Collins (1997) indicates that these requirements may have been lowered in a 1995 decision (*Sandin* v. *Conner* 1995). In a *Wolff* hearing, the inmate has the right to notice, a hearing, and a written statement of the reasons for the action decided on and the evidence relied on in coming to that decision. Even though issues of witnesses testimony, evidence, and use of confidential information have not been decided (Crane 1989), this case was at the top of the CLR survey of prison and jail cases having the most impact on the field.

Protection from Harm

Correctional officers may not show deliberate indifference to inmate medical needs based on the landmark case of *Estelle* v. *Gamble* (1976). The Supreme Court held that "deliberate indifference to a prisoner's serious illness or injury" is proscribed by the Eighth Amendment's ban against cruel and unusual punishment and, therefore, states a valid §1983 action. In looking to the deliberate indifference standard, it is important to underline that deliberate indifference is *not equivalent to mere negligence*. In *Estelle* v. *Gamble*, the Supreme Court stated that "a complaint that a physician has been negligent in diagnosing or treating a medical condition does not state a valid claim of medical mistreatment under the Eighth Amendment." In fact, the inmate (Gamble) was provided adequate medical attention for a back injury.

To state a claim, "a prisoner must allege acts or omissions sufficiently harmful to evidence deliberate indifference to serious medical needs." It is this type of indifference "that can offend 'evolving standards of decency' in violation of the Eighth Amendment." Still, although deliberate indifference is not equivalent to mere negligence, on some occasions, deliberate acts, not involving the intent to injure, if sufficiently harmful, may evidence deliberate indifference to invoke an Eighth Amendment based §1983 claim. Therefore, prisoners will likely look to Eighth Amendment based §1983 litigation to test the Supreme Court's willingness to find instances of deliberate indifference.

As noted, this standard has spread into other areas in addition to medical care. In fact, a "deliberate indifference" standard exists for establishing the "unnecessary and wanton infliction of pain" required for violation. However, it is only one stand-ard, because the Supreme Court in *Whitley* v. *Albers* found that the requirement for proving the unnecessary and wanton infliction of pain should be applied "with due regard for differences in the kind of conduct against which an Eighth Amendment objection is lodged." It is "obduracy and wantonness, not inadvertence or error in good faith, that characterize the conduct prohibited by the cruel and unusual punish-ments clause." In this, the Court appears to have defined an exception of a reduced duty for a correctional agency in the context of institutional security. The Court said that this lowered standard was necessary in this context to balance the competing institutional concerns of the safety of the prison staff or other inmates against the inmate's right to be free from harm.

In *Wilson* v. *Seiter* (1991), the Court used the deliberate indifference standard in an Eighth Amendment case. Prison officials can be found liable for failing to protect an inmate from violence at the hands of other prisons if the officials did not act when they knew there was "substantial risk of harm" and that beatings of a transsexual were the result of officials' "deliberate indifference" to his need for special protection (Greenhouse 1994). Collins (1997) gives the two key factors: conditions must be very bad and the defendants knew of the serious problems and failed to take any sort of meaningful corrective response (i.e., they were deliberately indifferent).

In *Farmer* v. *Brennan* (1994), the Court gave some definition to what it meant by *deliberate indifference*. After stating the fairly obvious, that deliberate indiffer-ence is something more than mere negligence but something less than a specific intent to cause harm to a particular inmate or inmates, the Court concluded that *deliberate indifference* means recklessness. In *Farmer* this meant that "an official must have actual knowledge that an inmate faces substantial risk of serious harm and then must disregard that risk by failing to take reasonable steps to abate it" (Collins 1997, p. 72).

OFFICERS' RIGHTS

With all the concerns about prisoners' rights, the correctional officer also has rights. Many of these rights have been secured through union contracts, which are addressed elsewhere in this book. As Collins (1997) indicates, no clear lines are drawn between what is subject to collective bargaining and what is not. Two legal issues facing correctional officers are urine testing programs and the decision to make a workplace smoke free, neither of which appears to be well addressed at this time. There are laws against discrimination in hiring, assignment, transfer, promotion, training, discipline, termination, compensation, benefits, and many other areas of employee rights.

Employee selection and hiring is a major concern. It is established in law that the employer must demonstrate a clear relation between performance on the selection procedure and performance on the job in order to apply guidelines for employee selection; that is, the selection procedure must be validated, as discussed elsewhere in this book.

Affirmative Action

Equal opportunity and affirmative action are explicit policy in most agencies. However, implementation of these policies raises significant questions:

- When are affirmative action programs required? When are they permitted?
- Does affirmative action constitute some form of reverse discrimination?
- When, if at all, may specific quotas be adopted or ordered?

The Supreme Court has answered several affirmative action questions in a series of 1986 and 1987 decisions. In *Johnson* v. *Transportation Agency, Santa Clara County* (1987), a voluntary affirmative action plan was held not to violate the rights of unprotected groups under Title VII of the Civil Rights Act of 1964, as amended by the Equal Employment Opportunity Act of 1972. The plan that allows sex or race to be considered as one factor in evaluating qualified individuals for jobs in which the protected group is significantly underrepresented.

Johnson, a man, claimed his rights under Title VII were violated when a marginally less-qualified woman was given a job as a county road dispatcher. The woman was the first woman ever hired for such a position in county history. Under an affirmative action plan, which had been voluntarily adopted by the county, sex could be considered as one factor in the hiring process in traditionally segregated job categories. No positions were "set aside" for women. The court approved this flexible plan that was designed to attain, not maintain, a balanced workforce and generally approved of voluntary affirmative action plans that included goals, not quotas.

Outside the context of litigation, an affirmative action plan should be based on evidence of past discrimination and should be narrowly tailored to remedy the prior discrimination. Once the goal is attained, the preference should be dropped. It should be apparent that the area of equal opportunity is one with comprehensive, major implications for any government administrator.

For correctional administrators and officers, the demands of the federal and state equal opportunity statutes and regulations lead inevitably to the conclusion that agencies need specialists to assist in the development and implementation of agency policy and procedures. They must review agency practices to assure their compliance with equal opportunity requirements and other matters relating to personnel, and they must oversee the handling of complaints that may come to the agency through its mechanisms or through complaints made directly to relevant state or federal enforcement agencies.

Sex Discrimination and Harassment

Another area of concern outlawed by Title VII of the Civil Rights Act (42 U.S.C. 2000c) is sexual discrimination. Evaluation of staff performance has become increasingly important as more women have taken jobs as correctional officers. Issues of concern include balancing inmate privacy with equal opportunity for women officers, harassment of women by colleagues, safety on the job, and biased performance evaluations. Collins (1997) notes that female officers continue to win their rights to work in male institutions. Unless a true *bona fide occupational qualification* (BFOQ) exists, discrimination in hiring and deployment of women on the job is illegal.

Outcomes in several other cases are favorable to female officers working in male facilities, with appropriate adjustments for protecting the modesty of the male inmates. Most cases of cross-sex supervision do not prohibit it. In *Michenfelder* v. *Sumner* (1988), a federal appeals court ruled that occasional observation of strip searches by female officers did not violate inmate rights. *Tensley* v. *Alexander* (1993) involved complaints that a female officer was purposely observing an inmate in the shower and on the toilet. The district court ruled these necessary and proper observations. However, in *Torres* v. *Wisconsin Department of Health and Social Services* (1988), an appellate court upheld a policy prohibiting the use of male officers in living units of the state's female institution. The case was not decided on the grounds of privacy, however, but on the issue of rehabilitation. Many of the women on the unit had been physically or sexually abused by men in the past. Collins (1997) discusses male officer supervision of female inmates, finding a limited body of case law, but most is favorable to male officer supervision of female inmates.

Drug Testing

Drug testing of correctional officers is an ongoing issue. Based on a survey of 48 states, Guynes and Coffey (1991) addressed several aspects of the issue, including who is doing it, who can be tested, reasons for testing, procedures and technology, costs, actions taken, and legal issues. They indicate that (as of 1988) the Federal Bureau of Prisons and less than half the states were testing employees or job applicants, that most systems began testing within the preceding four years, and most agencies did not consider drug abuse among staff a major problem. Testing began largely due to concerns about contraband and usually is done only when reasonable suspicion has been established. Few grievances or lawsuits were found, and those cited problems with the testing itself. Of the 15 states with unions, 7 unions have taken no stand, 1 supported it, and 1 opposed it (p. 509).

Issues on the testing of correctional officers' urine for drugs apparently will focus on the right to privacy. A 1987 appeals court case supports random testing of correctional officers only in conditions where they have direct, regular contact (day to day) with inmates in medium to maximum security facilities, and the court was concerned that the testing be truly random (*McDonell* v. *Hunter* 1987). This case is supported by two 1989 cases cited by Collins (1997, p. 137) in which courts "now generally have ruled that random testing of employees whose jobs are particularly concerned with such things a public safety may be required [to be tested] without violating the Fourth Amendment."

There are some limits. A federal district court in Illinois decided against mandatory drug testing for all jail employees without "reasonable suspicion" that the employees tested are drug abusers. It was seen as an unreasonable search, and arguments regarding prevention of smuggling drugs into the facility and maintaining the public's confidence in the integrity of correctional employees were rejected. However, random testing was approved for individuals who are in direct contact with inmates (*Taylor* v. *O'Grady* 1987 and 1989).

In determining the reasonableness of employee drug testing for law enforcement officers, McEwen, Manili, and Conners (1986) indicate that three criteria probably will be used:

1. the justification for the tests, although most can be justified in the "public interest";
2. the likelihood of employee impairment while on the job, which will require the reasonable suspicion . . . of impairment test; and
3. the reliability of the tests and procedural safeguards.

A major issue in all drug testing will be the reliability of the tests themselves. Guynes and Coffey were surprised at the dearth of reported drug testing for job applicants in corrections, noting that 73% of police departments surveyed tested applicants. There also was a shortage of policies and procedures addressing the topic of drug testing. Although not mandating drug testing, American Correctional Association standards for correctional institutions require a drug-free workplace.

SUMMARY

Inmates have come a long way in achieving their rights, but the pendulum has begun to swing back to a more balanced position. As Crane (1989) suggests, the parameters of many of the problems have been well defined and administrators must now find areas where they can comfortably take a stand on issues of sound management of their facilities. Decisions will have varying levels of impact on the correctional officer and his or her role in the institution. The courts apparently will not substitute its judgment in these areas where a "considered choice" must be made by the correctional officer in properly implementing policy and procedures for the safety and security of all individuals in the institution.

REFERENCES

Adams v. Ellis 197 F2nd 483 (5th Cir. 1952).

Associated Press 1997, AP-NY-06-25-97 1046EDT.

Barrineau, H.E., III. *Civil Liability in Criminal Justice*, 2d ed. Cincinnati, OH: Anderson, 1987.

Call, J.E. "The Supreme Court and Prisoner's Rights," *Federal Probation* 59, no. 1 (1995): 36–46.

Call, J.E., and C.T. Samarkos. "RFRA: Which Test Is Best?" *Corrections Today* 58, no. 2 (1996).

Collins, W.R. *Correctional Law for the Correctional Officer*, 2d ed. Lanham, MD: American Correctional Association, 1997.

Conrad, J.P. *Crime and Its Correction: An International Survey of Attitudes and Practices*. Berkeley: University of California Press, 1965.

"Corrections Court Cases with Greatest Impact Identified by CLR Poll." *Correctional Law Reporter* (June 1994): 1–2 and 7–14.

Crane, R. "Correctional Litigation in the 90s," *Corrections Compendium* 14, no. 3 (1989): 1 and 6–9.

DiIulio, J., Jr. *Governing Prisons*. New York: Macmillan, 1987.

Dunn, A. "Flood of Prisoners' Rights Suits Provokes Efforts to Limit Access to Courts." *New York Times* (March 21, 1994), p. 2.

Gill, H.B. "Letters," *Federal Probation* (December 1982): 5.

Greenhouse L. "Prison Officials Can Be Found Liable for Inmate-Against-Inmate Violence," *Court Rules* (June 7, 1994).

Guynes, R., and O. Coffey. "Employee Drug-Testing Policies in Prison Systems." In K.C. Haas and G.P. Alpert (eds.), *The Dilemmas of Corrections, Contemporary Readings*, pp. 508–516. Prospect Heights, IL: Waveland, 1991.

Ingley, G.S. "Position Statements Released." *Corrections Today* 58, no. 2 (1996): 206–208.

Jordan, H. "Cost of Prison Litigation is Linked to Overcrowding," *San Francisco Daily Journal* (December 18, 1992).

Kaufman, L. "In the Courts." *Corrections Journal* (April 22, 1997): 8.

McEwen, T., B. Manili, and E. Connors. "Employee Drug Testing Policies in Police Departments." In *Research in Brief*. Washington, DC: National Institute of Justice, 1986.

Palmer, J.W. *Constitutional Rights of Prisoners*, 5th ed. Cincinnati, OH: Anderson, 1997.

President's Commission on Law Enforcement and Administration of Justice. *Task Force Report: Corrections*. Washington DC: U.S. Government Printing Office, 1967.

Ross, D.L. "A 20-Year Analysis of Section 1983 Litigation in Corrections." *American Jails* 9(1995): 10–16.

Legal Case Citations (in order cited)

Adams v. *Ellis* 197 F.2d 483 (5th Cir. 1952).

Banning v. *Looney* 213 F.2d 771 (10th Cir. 1954), cert. den. 348 U.S. 859, 75 S.Ct. 84, 99 L.Ed. 677 (1954).

Long v. *Parker* 390 F.2d 816 (3d Cir. 1968, Philadelphia).

Bell v. *Wolfish* 441 U.S. 520 (1979).

Lewis v. *Casey* 116 S.Ct. 2184 (1996).

Bounds v. *Smith* 430 U.S. 817 (1977).

Campos v. *Coughlin* 854 F.Supp 194 (S.D.N.Y. 1994).

Boerne v. *Flores* 95 U.S. 2074 (1997).

Turner v. *Safley* 107 S.Ct. 2254 (1987).

O'Lone v. *Shabazz* 107 S.Ct. 2400 (1987).

Thornburgh v. *Abbott* 109 S.Ct. 1874 (1989).

Procunier v. *Martinez* 94 S.Ct. 1800 (1989).

Sasnett v. *Sullivan* 91 F.3d 1018 7th Cir. (1996).

May v. *Baldwin* U.S. Cir. Ct. of App. 9th Cir., No. 95-35860 (1997).

Employment Division, Department of Human Resources of Oregon v. *Smith* 494 U.S. 872 (1990).

Hudson v. *McMillian* 503 U.S. 1 (1992).

Whitley v. *Albers* 475 U.S. 312 (1986).

Hudson v. *Palmer* 468 U.S. 517 (1984).

Goff v. *Nix* 803 F.2d. 358 (8th. Cir. 1986).

Block v. *Rutherford* 468 U.S. 576 (1984).

Kennedy v. *Hardiman* 684 F.Supp. 540 (N.D. Ill., 1980).

Greenholtz v. *Inmates of the Nebraska Penal and Correctional Complex* 442 U.S. 1 (1979).

Kentucky v. *Johnson* 490 U.S. 454 (1989).

Meachum v. *Fano* 427 U.S. 215 (1976).

Olim v. *Wakinekona* 456 U.S. 1005 (1983).

Hewitt v. *Helms* 459 U.S. 460 (1983).

Connecticut Board of Pardons v. *Dumschat* 499 U.S. 898 (1981).

Vitek v. *Jones* 445 U.S. 480 (1980).

Washington v. *Harper* 494 U.S. 210 (1990).

Wolff v. *McDonnell* 418 U.S. 539 (1974).

Sandin v. *Conner* 115 S.Ct. 2293 (1995).

Estelle v. *Gamble* 429 U.S. 97 (1976).

Wilson v. *Seiter* 111 S.Ct. 2321 (1991).

Farmer v. *Brennen* 128 L.Ed. 2d 811 (1994).

Johnson v. *Transportation Agency, Santa Clara County,* 107 S.Ct. 1442 (1987).

Michenfelder v. *Sumner* 860 F.2d 328 (9th Cir. 1988).

Tensley v. *Alexander* U.S. District Court, Michigan (1993).

Torres v. *Wisconsin Department of Health and Social Services* 854 F.2d 1523 (7th Cir. 1988).

McDonell v. *Hunter* 809 F.2d 1302 (8th Cir. 1987).

Taylor v. *O'Grady* 888 F.2d 1189 1987 (7th Cir. 1989).

7

Changing Trends—
Special Populations

Correctional institutions are designed to receive, house, care for, and release the offenders committed to their care. During confinement, maintaining custody is a primary concern. Keeping the institution safe and secure and preventing escapes are the major custodial functions. Quite simply, the first concern of institution staff is custody and security, without which programs of any type are impossible. Although the most appropriate type of treatment is very much subject to debate, security is not considered debatable.

Institutional accommodation and adjustment can be especially challenging for those who are distinct from the majority in some respect. In social situations where most people are of a similar race or ethnicity and generally enjoy good mental as well as physical health, those who do not share such characteristics may encounter difficulties as a result of their status as members of a minority group. In society overall, the majority often is not overly sympathetic to those who lack the benefits of their good fortune. The experience of those under correctional supervision is no exception.

Many important issues face correctional officials as we approach the 21st century, but one particular grouping presents problems that are comparatively new to the correctional environment. These issues are linked to growing numbers of inmates who make up special populations. Roughly categorized, they include inmates with infectious diseases, such as those who are HIV positive or have full-blown AIDS, inmates with mental or physical disabilities, inmates with drug and drug abuse histories, and an increasing number of elderly offenders. Each of the special populations requires correctional institutions to modify procedures and facilities, add new topics for staff training and inmate education, and generally deal with issues that were not raised when inmates in these populations were fewer in number.

If the negative effects of incarceration can be so profound for healthy men, who, within correctional institutions, represent the majority of inmates, the impact can be even more significant for those who differ in some respect from the rest of the inmate population. Although the long-term results may be no less devastating, their concerns, social relationships, and adaptation to imprisonment are somewhat different.

INFECTIOUS DISEASES: HIV AND AIDS

In recent years, a disease that knows no gender, racial, or class boundaries has created a devastating impact on society. Prior to the 1980s, AIDS (acquired immunodeficiency syndrome) was virtually unknown, but in less than two decades, the disease has afflicted society in almost epidemic proportions. Few people do not know someone who has died of AIDS, and it is estimated that between 1 and 1.5 million people are infected with HIV (human immunodeficiency virus), the virus that causes AIDS.

Nor are any social or demographic groups immune. Intravenous (IV) drug users and homosexual or bisexual men remain the largest groups at risk for HIV infection. But the fastest growing populations being affected by the disease are children and women. It should be noted, however, that no particular group of people is inherently at risk, rather high-risk behaviors place people at risk. Many of those being infected today are the inadvertent victims of those who have been involved in such high-risk behaviors as sharing drug needles or engaging in unsafe sexual practices (AIDS can be transmitted through blood, semen, and vaginal fluids).

AIDS in the Corrections System

Like the general population, the corrections system has experienced a substantial increase of inmates who are either HIV-positive or have active cases of AIDS. At the start of the decade, 24% of new AIDS cases in the United States were attributed to IV drug use. The concentration of substance abusers in our nation's state and federal institutions is high. A 1991 national survey of over 700,000 inmates in state correctional facilities found that over 79% acknowledged having used drugs. Twenty-five percent admitted the use of cocaine or crack, and 10% admitted using heroin or other opiates in the month prior to their imprisonment. Another 25% acknowledged IV drug use at some time during their lives (Harlow 1993). A previous survey found that 30% of those reporting IV drug use admitted to sharing needles (Bureau of Justice Statistics [BJS] 1995). The large percentages of inmates admitting IV drug use and the sharing of injection paraphernalia were reflected in the finding of the National Prison Project, where IV drug users represented the majority of inmates with AIDS. By the end of 1994, about 4% of drug offenders in the federal prison system and 15% in state correctional facilities, who had shared needles, were HIV positive (BJS 1995).

Nationally, the state and federal prison population increased from 329,821 in 1980 to over 1.1 million by midyear 1996 (BJS 1996), primarily the result of a nationwide policy of mandatory minimum sentencing for drug offenses, such as the National Drug Control Strategy (NDCS), implemented in 1989. The dramatic impact of such policies is reflected by the AIDS incidence rate in the prison population, rising from 181 per 100,000 in 1990 to 362 per 100,000 in 1992–1993 (Hammett, Harrold, and Epstein 1993). Thus, the ongoing "get tough" policy on drugs with stricter sentencing will have a great impact on American correctional institutions into the 21st century, with a proportional increase in AIDS cases and mortality.

AIDS Epidemiology in American Correctional Institutions

In November 1981, the first confirmed case of AIDS among United States prison inmates appeared in a New York State Department of Correctional Service's facility, just six months after the CDC announced the existence of the disease. By the end of March 1993, the total number of AIDS cases reported by state and federal prison officials was 8,525. Of those, 2,858 inmates have died from AIDS, 39% of which occurred after 1990 (Hammett et al. 1993). In 1989, the percentage of cumulative AIDS cases in United States correctional institutions began to exceed the increases in AIDS cases in the general population (Hammett and Moini 1990). Further seroepidemiological surveys established that HIV infection rates in correctional institutions exceeded the general population by as much as five or six to one (Lurigio, Petraitis, and Johnson 1991). The 1992–1993 National Institute of Justice Center for Communicable Diseases survey reflected an AIDS incidence rate in corrections facilities that was 20 times higher than that of the 1992 U.S. general population (362 cases per 100,000 versus 18 cases per 100,000, respectively) (Hammett et al. 1993).

Some of this difference may be a result of either reduced rates of increase among the population at large or improved reporting and record keeping among correctional systems or both. Nevertheless, correctional institutions and jails confine a population with a higher concentration of individuals who have histories of high-risk behavior, particularly IV drug use. In fact, the National Commission on AIDS points out that "by choosing mass imprisonment as the federal and state governments' response to the use of drugs, we have created a de facto policy of incarcerating more and more individuals with HIV infection. . . clearly, we are thus concentrating the HIV disease problem in our prisons and must take immediate action to deal with it more effectively" (1991, p. 5).

The commission urges the implementation of more educational and drug treatment programs to prevent the spread of HIV infection. In the meantime, data indicate that correctional facilities must accommodate growing numbers of inmates with AIDS. Administrators therefore have an imminent responsibility to meet the needs of active HIV and AIDS cases. But from a broader, longer range point of view, corrections also has a proactive duty to educate all of those under its supervision to the dangers of high-risk behavior. As long as corrections remains the one government agency that intercepts the lives of so many who are at risk, it is essential to seize this opportunity to change their behavior. Given the alarming spread of AIDS, the actions or inaction of correctional departments in this respect will have a profound impact on health and well-being throughout society.

Correctional Responses

Because there is no known cure for AIDS, the vital concern of correctional administrators is to reduce expansion of the disease, particularly within institutional populations. A number of approaches have been implemented in response to this concern, primarily:

- Educating both inmates and staff with regard to how the disease is spread;
- Issuing condoms to protect inmates engaged in homosexual activities from contracting the disease;
- Testing (either voluntary or mandatory) to identify those who are infected;
- Separate housing for inmates in various stages of the disease.

Education and Training

Practically everyone agrees that educational efforts are needed. As one national study found, "[m]ost correctional administrators feel strongly that AIDS education and training are not options but absolute requirements" (Hammett and Moini 1990, p. 4), and virtually all correctional institutions and jails reported offering or developing AIDS training or educational materials. Such programs are essential to provide facts concerning how the disease is transmitted, thereby, it is hoped, changing high-risk behaviors. In addition, they can help to eliminate the myths surrounding casual transmission that can lead to overreaction and unwarranted discrimination.

Ideally, programs should be offered for both inmates and staff members in a proactive manner, well before widespread concern promotes panic. Among inmates, for example, at least one study has found that not only is there considerable confusion about the manner in which AIDS can be transmitted, but lower levels of knowledge also were associated with higher perceptions of the risk of contracting AIDS while incarcerated (Zimmerman, Martin, and Vlahov 1991). In other words, the less inmates knew about objective facts concerning AIDS transmission, the more fearful they were of acquiring the virus while incarcerated. Nor is there any reason to believe that similar lack of knowledge on the part of institutional personnel is any less influential. AIDS training for staff members can diminish such unfounded fears while encouraging basic precautionary measures.

Condom Distribution

Although support for AIDS education is widespread, one particular policy of some facilities is another matter entirely—the distribution of condoms. On the one hand, this practice has been widely criticized as giving official sanction to unauthorized sexual activities. On the other hand, advocates maintain that, because it is virtually impossible to prevent inmates from engaging in homosexual behavior, it is better to provide them with protection than to risk spreading the disease throughout the institution.

HIV Testing

Like the condom issue, testing inmates for HIV has both supporters and critics. Recent advances in HIV treatment that delay the onset of AIDS underscore the need for early detection and intervention. In light of this medical incentive, more people in the general population are undergoing diagnostic tests. But, of course, they are doing so of their own free will. Within corrections facilities, few would argue against providing tests and follow-up medical services on a voluntary basis for those requesting such help, as evidenced by data showing that 75% of correctional institutions and 90% of jails make testing available on request (Hammett and Moini 1990, p. 6). But the mandatory testing of everyone creates a divergence of opinion.

This involuntary means of identifying HIV-positive inmates increasingly has come under fire from both sides of the issue. On the one hand, some inmates have demanded mandatory mass testing for everyone's protection. In opposition, others have challenged such practices as an invasion of their right to privacy. Thus far, the courts have neither uniformly upheld nor denied either side.

The courts have been relatively consistent in upholding the constitutionality of state laws permitting mandatory testing. At the same time, they have supported the right of correctional administrators to refuse to implement mandatory testing. Therefore, current judicial reasoning appears to be that testing is not constitutionally required under the Eighth Amendment (which prohibits cruel and unusual punishment), but neither is it prohibited under the Fourth Amendment (which protects privacy).

As a compromise between the extremes of mandatory and voluntary screening, some state correctional agencies target AIDS testing toward high-risk groups (such as IV drug users, homosexual men, and prostitutes). In fact, mandatory mass screening has been conducted primarily in small states with few inmate AIDS cases, making it a costly practice in comparison to the benefits derived. Some jurisdictions have discontinued the practice for reasons ranging from funding shortages to the realization that it was creating more problems than it was intended to solve. It is notable that the American Correctional Health Services Association has gone on record as opposing mandatory testing, based on the concern that it is "costly and serves no useful public health function" (American Jails 1992, p. 87).

Separate Housing

Regardless of whether inmates are screened on arrival or submit to testing voluntarily, once AIDS is detected, the issue becomes what actions are appropriate to take. As the National Commission on AIDS has observed, "[t]here is certainly no point in screening without a clear notion of what is to be done with information uncovered in the screening process" (1991, p. 22). From a humanitarian point of view, obviously it is essential to provide appropriate medical care (although meeting this obligation can create serious financial difficulties, particularly as the number of cases escalates). Moreover, because of the overwhelming emotional impact of AIDS, most would agree that counseling and other supportive services are equally critical. But it is the most controversial question concerns where to locate inmates who have tested positive.

As Collins (1997) points out, the leading case on segregation of inmates who are HIV-positive is *Harris* v. *Thigpen* (1991), which concluded that a policy of segregating all inmates known to be HIV-positive did not violate the constitutional rights of the segregated inmates. The same case also approved a policy of testing all inmates to determine if they were HIV-positive. However, corrections officials must be clear as to the health or security interests furthered by the testing policy, and many courts have remained neutral on some AIDS issues. The question of segregation of HIV-positive inmates is further confused with respect to federal law on the provision of rehabilitation programs and the status of HIV-positive as a disability that disallows discrimination in programming (see Collins 1997, p. 142). As with mandatory and voluntary testing, correctional administrators again are caught between two contradictory arguments. On the one hand, inmates free of AIDS have raised Eighth Amendment challenges, maintaining that it is "cruel and unusual punishment" to be unprotected from others with this communicable disease. But at least one court has held that prisoners must specifically show how the conditions of confinement they are challenging put them at risk of contracting AIDS (Anderson 1989, p. 21). In a similar case, inmates demanded mandatory screening and housing segregation of those who test positive. The judge rejected their arguments, ruling that the state had taken reasonable precautions to minimize the risk that inmates would contract the virus (p. 2).

At the same time, HIV-positive inmates have questioned whether it is a violation of their rights to be housed separately from the general population. In this respect, one court has declared that inmates shall not be segregated solely because they are HIV-positive, although they may be isolated on a case-by-case basis according to security or medical needs (National Commission on AIDS 1991, p. 22). But, in another case, the court supported the argument of correctional administrators that "the segregation of infected prisoners was mandated to protect both the AIDS victims and other prisoners from tensions and harm that could result from fears of other inmates" (Olivero 1990, p. 114). Even though most judicial rulings have upheld the constitutionality of separate housing, as with testing, "the courts have concluded that the Constitution neither requires nor prohibits segregation" (Belbot and del Carmen 1991, p. 147).

Legal Implications

Litigation concerning HIV and AIDS issues in correctional facilities began to appear in the nation's courts in the middle to late 1980s. The majority of cases were initiated by inmates, questioning the constitutionality of AIDS policies in state correctional systems. As these cases reflect, such disputes have raised a number of legal issues. In fact, along with mandatory screening, measures aimed at the segregated housing of those with HIV represent the major types of AIDS-related cases filed by inmates (see *Harris* v. *Thigpen* 1991).

An immediate legal implication of a separate housing assignment policy is that it readily identifies those with HIV, thereby compromising the confidentiality of AIDS testing. State laws and court rulings vary in terms of how strictly they protect the confidentiality and anonymity of those tested for HIV. States with such protections generally limit notification to the inmate and attending physician. Only a few jurisdictions have official policies of notifying correctional officers. Staff members, however, are not always satisfied with these confidentiality provisions. In response, it has been pointed out that educational programs can reduce concerns about the transmission of AIDS (which is often what prompts demands for disclosure). Moreover, disclosures, in fact, may lull correctional officers into a false sense of security, leading them to believe that all infected prisoners have been identified.

In addition to revealing the confidentiality of their health status, separately housing those who are HIV-positive can have further repercussions. The National Commission on AIDS (1991) notes that not only is there "no legitimate public health basis for segregating prisoners with HIV disease," but also, those who are so isolated:

- Often lose access to religious services, work programs, visitation rights, libraries, educational and recreational programs, and drug/alcohol treatment;
- Serve in virtually solitary confinement within small prisons, and in larger institutions, are often grouped together indiscriminately, regardless of their security classification (p. 3).

It therefore is not surprising that such practices have represented a sizable proportion of the lawsuits related to AIDS. Undoubtedly, these cases have generated some of the impetus toward the current trend away from segregation—toward "mainstreaming" HIV-positive inmates with the rest of the general population. But, beyond the threat of legal action, this change in housing policy has resulted from a combination of additional factors, including increased costs, less fear, more compassionate attitudes, and the rising numbers of inmates with HIV infection or AIDS, which is making segregation both impractical and unfeasible (Hammett and Moini 1990, p. 8).

A realistic compromise between the extremes of complete integration and total segregation has been recommended that would take into account both high-risk behavior and HIV or AIDS infection (Lawrence and Van Zwisohn 1991). This approach would classify the person according to a continuum reflecting institutional behavior as well as the health status of those who are HIV-positive. Housing and supervision would then be designed to both reduce opportunities for high-risk activities and provide for the medical needs of those who are becoming progressively ill.

There are no clear-cut guidelines on how corrections facilities should respond to the threat of AIDS. As a result, some administrators have experimented with preventive measures, ranging from providing condoms to promoting education. Identification approaches likewise have varied from requiring mandatory mass testing, to selectively screening high-risk groups, to simply making tests available on a voluntary basis. In reaction to the results, some agencies have implemented housing segregation policies. Others have explored compromises, such as increasing segregation on the basis of how far the disease has progressed. Many have either continued or returned to "mainstreaming" those who are HIV-positive with the rest of the population. The only thing sure about AIDS is that, until there is a cure, the issues surrounding this disease undoubtedly will continue to create further conflict, confusion, and court cases.

INMATES WITH MENTAL OR PHYSICAL DISABILITIES

It has become increasingly apparent that people with mental and physical disabilities face a number of social and psychological difficulties. These problems include stigmatization of the disabled and social barriers to friendship and intimacy. Traditionally, individuals with disabilities were excluded from the mainstream of society in education, employment, and social activities. These problems could be overwhelming, particularly when combined with other conditions. Professionals in a variety of agencies have become concerned with the problems of the disabled. There is little research, however, concerning individuals with disabilities in correctional institutions.

Mentally Disabled Offenders

Throughout history, society has reacted to those who have mental disorders with a mixture of fear, mistrust, and repulsion. In the Middle Ages, they were thought to be possessed by evil spirits, and if fortunate enough to escape burning at the stake, they faced banishment from society. In later years, ashamed families would secrete mentally disordered relatives in basements or attics. When society began to assume more public responsibility for their care, they again were secluded, in large remote institutions closed off from public scrutiny. Eventually, concerns were voiced about both the conditions in which they were being confined and the types of disorders for which they were being held. Mental institutions were criticized as dumping grounds where the elderly, handicapped, mentally retarded, and other undesirables virtually were imprisoned. Even among those with legitimate mental problems, it was determined that many suffered from conditions that could be treated as effectively on an outpatient basis.

Much of this criticism came to a climax during the civil rights movement of the 1960s, when widespread support was generated for protecting the interests of the disenfranchised, including the mentally ill and retarded. Coupled with the development of better psychotropic drugs, the deinstitutionalization of large mental hospitals began with various forms of community mental health legislation in the 1970s. However, in the process of replacing institutional confinement with community-based treatment, society ran out of money or interest or both. Wandering aimlessly in the community, psychotic much of the time, and unable to manage their internal control systems (these chronically homeless, previously institutionalized mentally ill people) found the criminal justice system was an asylum of the last resort (Belcher 1988).

As with alcoholics and drug addicts, those whom society cannot or will not care for effectively often become correctional clients. In that respect, public attitudes toward the mentally ill have not changed dramatically over the years, still reflecting a combination of suspicion and aversion. But, according to a report by the National Commission on the Causes and Prevention on Violence (1969), despite fears of being victimized by a violent criminal psychopath, "generally, persons identified as mentally ill represent no greater risk of committing violent crimes than the population as a whole" (p. 444).

Admittedly, to speak of mentally disordered offenders (MDOs) encompasses a wide range of behaviors, from the mildly disoriented or neurotic to those who are severely psychotic and completely out of touch with reality. This umbrella term is used broadly to relate to mental conditions that differ from what is considered "normal." It is important to make a clear distinction between the developmentally disabled and the mentally ill. According to the Americans With Disabilities Act (ADA), a mental disability is any "mental or psychological disorder, such as retardation, or-

ganic brain syndrome, emotional or mental illness, or specific learning disability."
The ADA distinguishes between mental illness and developmental disability (retardation). *Mental illness* is defined as "a group of disorders causing severe disturbances
in thinking, feeling, and relating. They result in substantially diminished capacity for
coping with ordinary demands of life. . . . A mental illness can have varying levels
of seriousness" (Rubin and McCampbell 1995).

Developmental Disability (Mental Retardation)

Previously known by such terms as *mentally defective* or *feebleminded* and more
recently as *developmentally disabled*, mental retardation is a clinical classification
resulting from an abnormally low IQ (usually in the area of 70 or below). There is
not necessarily any relationship between retardation and criminal behavior. However,
the limited intelligence of the developmentally disabled severely restricts their employment opportunities, which can lead to stealing for survival. It also tends to make
them susceptible to being led into crime by others. And, when they do break the law,
they often do not have the mental capacity to do so without being detected.

Because of their nominal intelligence, when such persons do engage in crime,
they may be found incompetent to stand trial. Or they may not be held accountable
for their actions in a court of law, just as a small child would not be held criminally
responsible due to the lack of an ability to distinguish right from wrong. As a result,
it is not surprising to find that their proportion of the institutional population in corrections is quite small. Moreover, because of their limited numbers, programs for
them are very scarce. Although there is no "cure" for mental retardation, with special
assistance, some can be helped to improve the level of their development toward
achieving greater social independence.

But a far greater danger for them than lack of treatment is their potential for
being victimized while incarcerated. Not only are they subject to verbal ridicule and
physical abuse by other inmates, but to conceal their deficiencies, they rarely participate in rehabilitation programs. In addition, they are slower to adjust to routine and
have more difficulty in learning regulations (Santamour and Brown 1985). Often,
they simply do not understand what is expected of them. Correctional officers who
are not sensitive to the developmentally disabled therefore can mistakenly assume
that an inmate is being defiant when, actually, the person may not comprehend the
officer's instructions.

Correctional officers who are not trained to recognize the behavioral characteristics of the developmentally disabled may assume that the inmate has a normal
ability to grasp instructions. This is a particular problem for these offenders, because
many of them are skillful at hiding their disability in an effort to appear "normal."
As a result, they tend to accumulate more disciplinary interactions and are more likely
to be denied parole, serving on average two to three years longer than others with
the same offense (Santamour and Brown 1985).

To prevent such difficulties some departments have established procedures for
identifying developmentally disabled offenders and placing them in special units
where they can receive appropriate care, equitable discipline, and life skills training
that will help them become more independent on release. Unfortunately, they are

more likely to be either unrecognized or included in the general population and supervised by personnel who are not aware of their special condition.

Mental Illness

Unlike the simplicity of identifying mental retardation by one's score on an IQ test, the complexities of mental illnesses defy easy classification. In terms of seriousness, mental illness can range from harmless senility to violent-prone psychosis. The term *criminally insane* was used at one time to classify severely mentally ill offenders, but now they more often are included within broader categories such as mentally ill or mentally disordered. In fact, legal and medical definitions of various mental conditions still can differ significantly. At least in part because of such confusions in terms of definitions, an accurate number of the mentally ill who are incarcerated is virtually impossible to obtain. We use the term *insanity* to differentiate such offenders from those with varieties of less severe conditions that also could be encompassed under the term *mental illness*.

It has become common to hear of defendants entering pleas of "not guilty by reason of insanity" at the trial stage, particularly when well-publicized cases employ this defense successfully. Indeed, "madness" has been a criminal defense since the 13th century. Although it obviously has a medical interpretation, in the criminal justice system, insanity is a legal term: a status that is decided by the court, taking into consideration the opinions of medical experts. The criminally insane, then, are those who have been declared so by the court.

In the past, defendants ruled incompetent to stand trial or declared legally insane during trial could be confined in a mental health institution for an indeterminate period of time. But a 1977 Supreme Court ruling (*Jackson* v. *Indiana*) held that those found incompetent for trial cannot be held indefinitely and established that any such commitment must be justified by treatment progress. However, even if released under criminal law, the patient may be recommitted under civil law. If at some point the mentally insane are determined by medical staff to be "cured," there may well be nothing to prevent their release, because technically, they were not "convicted" in a court of law. In an effort to prevent untimely releases from mental health institutions of those who otherwise could be held in a correctional institution, Michigan passed the first Guilty but Mentally Ill legislation in 1972. Several other states have followed suit. Although these statutes vary, the basic intent is to establish factual guilt or innocence in a court of law (regardless of the insanity outcome), which therefore would enable a correctional sentence to be imposed, thus preventing the offender who is declared mentally insane from escaping criminal responsibility.

In addition to mental health institutions, the criminally insane may be confined in a special forensic hospital (i.e., a psychiatric hospital that is also a secure correctional institution). In smaller states and localities, a separate psychiatric unit may be set up within an existing institution to accommodate them. Contrary to past practices, the legally insane no longer are confined indiscriminately with the general population.

This certainly does not mean that no mentally ill inmates are among the general population. An inmate may suffer from any number of mental disturbances without being declared legally insane. Aside from the relatively few who are so designated, many others with varying forms of mental disorders are confined within correctional facilities. No valid statistics document exactly how many mentally ill offenders are behind bars, although in 1978 Santamour estimated that nearly 30% of the nations 500,000 prison or jail inmates were mentally ill or retarded (Santamour 1989; see also Santamour and Brown 1985). According to the National Commission on the Causes and Prevention of Violence, "the popular idea that the mentally ill are over-represented in the population of violent criminals is not suggested by research evidence" (1969, p. 44). On the other hand, a summary of the psychiatric evaluations of inmates over an almost 50-year period found that nearly half (49%) needed psychiatric attention (Bennett, Rosenbaum, and McCullough 1978). Treatment for this special group is both essential from a compassionate point of view and a practical management necessity.

It might seem that an obvious solution would be to transfer such cases to a state mental health hospital, which is better equipped for their care. But, since the deinstitutionalization movement, that is far more easily said than done. Before accepting an inmate, state mental health laws now often require that, in addition to being legitimately mentally ill, "clear objective evidence must also exist that the inmate is a real and immediate danger to himself or herself or to others; or that the inmate is unable to attend to his or her basic needs . . . this standard, when rigidly applied effectively precludes the transfer of many inmates . . . to mental institutions" (Kalinich, Embert, and Senese 1991, p. 81). Moreover, without a sizable complement of psychiatric staff, it may be difficult to determine just who is mentally ill, because manipulative inmates may feign symptoms to get attention or a different housing assignment. These concerns speak to the importance having correctional officers trained to recognize the signs and symptoms of mental illness so that they may be prepared to manage these individuals.

Physically Challenged Offenders

Every correctional system has physically challenged (e.g., disabled or handicapped) inmates and must be prepared to accommodate them regardless of their disability. Although the need to provide for this special category of inmates is not new, it is becoming more critical. Perhaps the most significant event in the integration into the mainstream culture by inmates with disabilities was the passage of the American With Disabilities Act (ADA) in 1990. It is generally conceded that the ADA is probably the most sweeping civil rights legislation passed since the enactment of the Civil Rights Act of 1964 (Rubin 1993). According to the American Civil Liberties Union, legal issues involving disabled and elderly inmates will be a major source of civil litigation by the turn of century.

A number of issues are being addressed by corrections officials to accommodate the physically disabled. These include revised policies and procedures for custody and security, personal safety, disciplinary actions, programs, food and medical service, and housing. The implementation of these revised policies and procedures will require better trained and educated correctional officers.

Custody and Security

Custody staff members will have to respond differently to this population and with different equipment than is normally required. Training must be provided to increase sensitivity to the physically challenged inmates' special needs. Correctional officers should be taught how to properly search a wheelchair-bound paraplegic, disassemble wheelchairs and prostheses, and otherwise conduct a complete strip search of a physically disabled inmate.

Security concerns inevitably lead to questions about the use of restraints. Correctional administrators and institution policy will determine the amount of flexibility allowed. Questions will arise concerning requirements for leg cuffs on paraplegics, waist chains across colostomy bags and even handcuffs for those on crutches. Medical personnel should be consulted when making these decisions.

Transportation also requires special equipment and training. Handicapped-accessible vans or buses will be needed to lift and safely transport wheelchair-bound inmates. In some cases, a van equipped with gurneys or ambulance services may be necessary for inmates unable to use the institution's normal transportation system.

Personal Safety

The need to protect physically challenged inmates from exploitation leads directly to safety issues. First, disabled inmates need to be protected from other inmates; this may require additional training to increase officer sensitivity and awareness. Second, disabled inmates need to be protected in case of fire or natural disaster. Building evacuation planning and emergency response must include special consideration for the disabled. Wheelchairs and crutches can block exits, leading to panic and unnecessary injury. Overall planning should include a safe evacuation route and procedures to safely handle this special population without unduly slowing the evacuation of the other inmates.

Disciplinary Measures

Correctional staff members may find that physically disabled inmates are more prone to emotional behavior change than other inmates. Their reaction well may determine whether a minor dispute becomes a major disciplinary incident. Proper control of disabled inmates requires a facility's segregation space be handicapped accessible. Disabled inmates housed in segregation may need more monitoring and medical attention than nondisabled inmates. As with any inmate, many potential disciplinary incidents can be avoided by skilled officer intervention.

Programs

Institutional programs should include the needs and special limitations of the physically disabled inmate. Program staff members may find that considerable effort must be spent helping disabled inmates cope with being handicapped and incarcerated. A particular concern is with the movement of these inmates to programs in the institution (e.g., visiting, school, work, recreation), which must be managed or supervised by correctional officers. Officers must be capable of assisting medical staff as well as physical, occupational, or vocational therapists.

A major challenge for all staff is providing the disabled inmate with meaningful work, study, and recreational opportunities. It is difficult to find institutional jobs for disabled inmates that provide an opportunity to earn sentence reduction credits. However, these inmates generally prove to be excellent workers.

Education and recreation activities should also be tailored for these inmates' needs and interests. Relatively passive recreation activities such as ceramics, leather work, and recorded books are excellent choices. For the most severely handicapped, handheld computer games can help preserve hand-eye coordination. For units with off-site recreation and education activities, transportation needs and access to the facilities should be considered.

Food and Medical Service

At least as important as programming concerns for this special group are food and medical service. Food service issues to consider include whether disabled inmates can eat with the general population, including appropriate access to the dining hall, and whether they get a special diet. The question of how disabled inmates eat their meals may be complicated in the case of the severely handicapped. If inmates must be fed in their housing areas or need special utensils, sanitation, food transportation and safety need to be addressed. If they are unable to feed themselves, administrators must decide whether other inmates or staff will assist.

A number of medical concerns should be considered when housing disabled inmates. Foremost among these concerns is having a adequate nursing staff to provide the extra care needed. Nursing responsibilities include patient assessment and nursing care as well as patient and officer education. Many inmates will need special instruction in self-care.

A major issue is helping with activities of daily living. These include dressing, bathing, feeding, and transporting inmates to other areas such as programs and recreation. Ideally, medical staff such as nurses' aides are available to provide assistance. However, in the real world of limited budgets and insufficient staff, inmates, volunteers, and trained aides are frequently used for these activities.

Housing

As in other areas of the institution, housing requires many special accommodations for the disabled inmate. It must be handicapped accessible, but today that means a great deal more than it used to. Simply putting up handrails in the showers no longer is adequate. Handrails, showers, toilets, sinks, and water fountains often must be redesigned to meet state and federal standards. The Architectural and Transportation Barriers Compliance Board Accessibility Guidelines used by the U.S. Department of Justice are discussed in some detail by Atlas (1994).

The square footage requirement for handicapped inmates is greater than for the normal institutional population. Lockers must be low enough to be reached from a wheelchair and writing tables must be high enough to accommodate the height of a wheelchair. Although most inmates clean their own living areas, some disabled inmates need to have that done for them.

In large states, centralized housing may result in visitation problems for disabled inmates' families. Therefore, despite extensive modifications to accommodate them in specially designed facilities, some physically disabled inmates may prefer to live in a less supportive environment due to its location. Correctional administrators will be tempted to transfer unhappy inmates to institutions closer to home. However, even if the transfer is made with the best of intentions, the system exposes itself to civil lawsuit liability if the unit is not equipped to handle the special needs of the inmate.

Like all special populations in the state and federal correctional institutions, managing physically disabled inmates presents an ongoing challenge for corrections officials. Although the numbers are few and their needs great, the system must be prepared to accommodate this unique group. Their management will require better trained and educated correctional officers. As Morton and Anderson (1996) point out, not everyone is suited to working with offenders with disabilities. Careful staff selection and specialized training and equipment may be required, and they suggest that state and local assistance should be made available in the development of specialized programs (i.e., visually or hearing impaired, elderly, mentally retarded).

AMERICANS WITH DISABILITIES ACT

In addition to attention by the courts to physical and mental needs of inmates, the legislative branch has also addressed this issue. The 1990 Americans With Disabilities Act has been an especially important influence on correctional procedures and facilities. The ADA was designed to grant full citizenship to Americans with disabilities and to entitle them to equal opportunity and access to mainstream America (Rubin and McCampbell 1995).

The ADA was based on the belief that people with disabilities traditionally have been isolated and segregated. For purposes of the law, a person has a disability if he or she suffers from a physical or mental impairment that substantially limits a major life activity like seeing, hearing, walking, breathing, or learning. The only time a government entity can exclude a disabled person from a program, service, or activity is in a situation where the person would not "otherwise be qualified." As such, Title II of the ADA (effective since 1992) applies directly to correctional facilities housing inmates with disabilities. It prohibits discrimination in the services, programs, and activities provided by state and local government entities on the basis of disability. For example, if the only requirement for participation in an institution's drug counseling program is that the offender has a history of drug abuse, then disabled inmates with a history of drug abuse cannot be excluded just because they are disabled. On the other hand, if the institution provides vocational training for inmates who have completed certain basic education classes, those with learning disabilities who have previously been excluded are not being discriminated against. The key is that disabled inmates who otherwise would be qualified for a program, service, or activity cannot be excluded merely on the basis of their disability.

The literature examining the prevalence of disabilities among inmates in correctional systems in the Untied States indicates that there are some disabled inmates, but precise counts are not available. A case therefore can be made for more systematic screening and evaluation and improved computerized information systems, so that inmates with disabilities can be more accurately identified and treated. As previously mentioned, security concerns, such as exploitation and victimization of these potentially more vulnerable inmates, also could be avoided if more accurate data were available.

With respect to program services, studies indicate that, at the present time, correctional facilities provide few mechanisms for screening, flagging, and treating disabled inmates. Although a variety of evaluation services and programs are available to at least some inmates in the majority of states, it appears that services that specifically address the problems faced by disabled inmates are found in only a small number of states. In a few jurisdictions, some program services are not provided to any inmates.

For California, it was found that 1,375 of the state's 142,000 inmates, or just under 1%, were disabled (Morain 1996). Of those, 650 needed canes or other devices to walk, 350 were in wheelchairs, 219 were blind or nearly blind, and 141 were deaf or severely hearing impaired. Housed in 15 of 32 institutions, it is expected that these numbers will rise as the prison population ages. A recent court order ruled that California must implement the ADA, which is estimated to cost $50 million (in a system with an annual budget of $4 billion), although lawyers for the Prison Law Office, which brought the case, say it will cost less. Concerns were expressed that disabled inmates often lose good time credits because they cannot be placed in prisons with limited accessibility. Training for correctional officers will be required, as will televisions equipped with caption devices for the deaf as well as signs and books in Braille or large type.

Regarding training for correctional peace officers, the California State Commission on Peace Officer Standards and Training has a 54-page training package designed for police officers who must manage the developmentally disabled or mentally ill. It includes units on understanding the problem, responding with understanding, recognizing individuals with these problems, the rights of these individuals, the proper procedures for getting these individuals to available community services, and developing sensitivity to persons with developmental disabilities or mental illness. It is not known whether any correctional training program currently includes such a module.

In summary, inmates with disabilities have special security and treatment needs. Exact numbers are not known; quite often they are counted as part of the medical population, as are the elderly. In addition, the reliability of the data is in question because of differences in the definition of disabilities and differences in the screening and evaluation of disabilities. Research indicates that disabled inmates are not singled out for treatment and that little is known about the scope of their difficulties, during or after the time they spend incarcerated. A variety of programs appear to be offered in the majority of correctional systems, but not necessarily in a consistent fashion. There appears to be a need to systematize evaluation and treatment of inmates with disabilities, given the difficulties they are likely to encounter while incarcerated and after release.

According to Collins (1997), the ADA is not without its problems, and some courts have begun to question the degree to which the act protects inmates, if at all. An example is the use of HIV-positive inmates in the kitchen, where the fear was not transmission of the disease but that it might incite disturbances among other inmates. Federal case law has upheld this position (*Gates* v. *Rowland* 1994). Thus, legitimate security needs may allow exceptions to the law.

The ADA does not apply only to inmates; it also applies to the recruitment and training of staff members with disabilities. Perhaps the best discussion of these issues is presented by Rubin (1993), who provides definitions (e.g., pregnancy is not an impairment) and guidance on how to implement the law for hiring. She notes that the ADA is not designed to guarantee jobs to the disabled nor provide preferences in hiring for this group. However, employers must reevaluate their employment selection processes to ensure that they do not adversely affect persons with disabilities, either intentionally or unintentionally. Hiring must be based on meeting established prerequisites of the position (e.g., education and experience) and whether the individual can perform the job. One article (Van Sickle 1994) provides a photo of a wheelchair handicapped correctional officer working in a jail. Reasonable accommodations are required, but they are not a duty "unless the accommodation will enable the employee to perform the essential functions of the position" (Rubin 1993, p. 3). Such decisions can be made on a case-by-case basis; however, the employer is not required to endure an "undue hardship" (i.e., significant difficulty or expense) in meeting this requirement.

An important aspect of making decisions about employing disabled individuals is the assessment of the essential tasks of the correctional officer. Todd (1996) did such a study for a regional jail in West Virginia, using time and motion techniques. The activities of correctional officers were studied to include reading, lifting, hearing, seeing, walking, climbing, speaking, sprinting, bending, squatting, counting, and standing for three basic officer assignments: central control, rover, and tower. The data provided the regional jail authority with the criteria needed to develop hiring procedures and policies that meet ADA requirements.

OTHER SPECIAL OFFENDER POPULATIONS

Beyond those who are afflicted with infectious diseases and the mental or physically challenged are any number of inmates with special needs in the correctional setting. It is apparent that discussion of the extensive treatment requirements of many such offenders is well beyond the scope of this book. However, several special groups are addressed briefly throughout the remainder of this chapter, including those with sustained histories of drug or alcohol abuse, sex offenders, and the elderly.

Some (such as those who are addicted to alcohol or drugs) have been included because of the sizable proportion of the correctional population they represent. Others merit attention because either they often have been overlooked as a result of their limited numbers (e.g., the sex offender) or their growing numbers are causing increasing concern (e.g., the elderly). The groups focused on certainly do not exhaust all categories of special offenders, but they do illustrate the scope of unique problems with which correctional officers must cope.

Drug Abusers

Unquestionably, IV drug use with unsanitary needles is a major transmitter of AIDS. It goes without saying that drug abuse hardly is limited to this group. Not only have arrests for drug violations increased 61% between 1985 and 1994 (BJS 1995), there is little doubt that any number of additional property crimes are linked to the need for ready cash to support drug habits. Because of drug-related crime and the nation's "war on drugs" during the past two decades, increasing numbers of drug users have been coming to the attention of the criminal justice system. This has been demonstrated by the Drug Use Forecasting (DUF) program, sponsored by the National Institute of Justice, which routinely conducts urinalyses among arrestees. DUF reports indicate that as many as 60% test positive for cocaine and up to 80% in some cities test positive for at least one illicit drug (Wish 1991). Furthermore, it has been reported that perhaps two-thirds of those entering state and federal correctional institutions have histories of substance abuse (Leukefeld and Timms 1992).

Treatment Programs

Given the increasing number of drug offenders coming into this nation's state and federal correctional institutions, the need for treatment programs has never been greater. Although they may not be widely available, a number of innovative drug rehabilitation efforts are being provided within correctional institutions. In terms of focus, they range widely—from group counseling, intensive therapy, and self-help groups to the use of acupuncture. One of the most prominent comprehensive programs is the therapeutic community (TC) technique. Typically, this treatment model is based on the concepts of Synanon (a program developed in California in the late 1960s by a recovering alcoholic). The TC model requires involvement by institutional staff (see Kassebaum, Ward, and Wilner 1971), and correctional officer involvement can range from nearly full participation to various forms of management. Lipton (1996) provides a good definition of the therapeutic community and an analysis of the success of such treatment efforts, noting that they are based on group participation and self-help principles. He does not discuss the role of the correctional officer in the TC environment, although the necessity for increased "receptivity" of these programs by correctional officials is discussed.

Treatment Results

Although such efforts to treat drug abuse undoubtedly are commendable, their long-term effectiveness is another matter entirely. In this respect, programs offered in correctional institutions probably are not much different from those provided in the community. For example, one 20-year follow-up of an inpatient hospital treatment program found only 10% of those released abstaining from drugs for five or more consecutive years (Valiant 1973). Within correctional institutions, the numbers of those incarcerated who already have undergone treatment is indicative of unimpressive results, where 30% of all state and federal inmates report having participated in a drug treatment program at some point—12% more than once (National Institute of Justice 1990).

That drug-related behavior was not changed while incarcerated is further demonstrated by figures indicating that two-thirds of drug offenders fail to complete their parole successfully. This does not necessarily mean that they have returned to drug use. But to the extent that drugs were the source of their involvement with the criminal justice system, it is reasonable to conclude that they have probably resumed former habits. On the other hand, corrections often tend to focus exclusively on its failures (perhaps because there seem to be so many of them), overlooking the admittedly fewer but nevertheless significant successes.

Nevertheless, although some individuals undoubtedly are helped back into a productive lifestyle, many are not. In part, these mixed results and limited availability of drug treatment reflect changing ideologies from the medical model to the justice model. Current correctional strategies do not reward rehabilitation, rather they reward quiet control and trouble-free days. To realign the system, correctional institutions must create credible opportunities for inmates to improve their lives, sustaining that opportunity in the community after release, and for achieving significant reductions in recidivism and parole revocation.

In other words, reducing drug use among criminal offenders cannot be accomplished in the absence of a rehabilitative orientation. That does not mean that treatment is the only component of drug rehabilitation, however. Careful screening and appropriate intervention must be followed by close supervision, including both continued support and surveillance on release. In fact, it has been noted that a major weakness of many drug rehabilitation efforts in corrections is that they operate without the benefit of follow-up treatment and continuing care (Josi 1996).

Support must be practical as well as emotional. It will do little good to send an abuser home drug free and presumably "cured" with no prospect of employment. Incarceration can compel abstinence from drugs and address withdrawal symptoms. But it is unlikely that long-term effectiveness will be achieved if the underlying social and psychological causes of physically addictive behavior are not confronted—or if interventions end with one's institutional sentence.

Substance abuse within the facility is a major concern for correctional officers. It cannot be assumed that confinement will insulate offenders from drug use, as reflected by the fact that inmates are now being tested for drugs in almost all state and federal correctional institutions. Drug screening in correctional institutions likely underestimates the actual prevalence of drug and alcohol use. Because of the institutional grapevine, there are few secrets inside the walls of the institution and word of an impending drug test spreads rapidly.

Needless to say, illegal substances are popular contraband items within correctional facilities, and they are not all brought in from the outside. To the contrary, drug abuse within institutional walls has extended to the misuse and abuse of prescription medications dispensed by institution infirmaries. Many of the inmates who had been drug abusers on the street find themselves undergoing the pain of withdrawal while incarcerated, during which "they will attempt to obtain anything and everything possible from the hospital in the hopes of relieving the tension, anxiety, and other unwanted symptoms they're experiencing" (Pierini 1991, p. 32).

Regardless of the source, addicted inmates can be expected to make concerted efforts to continue their drug use while incarcerated, just as would be expected if they were forced to undergo involuntary abstinence in the community. In that regard, correctional facilities are plagued by the same difficulties as drug control agencies on the outside.

Alcohol Abusers

Among the many unfortunate by-products resulting from the nation's epidemic of drug abuse is that it has diverted attention away from a number of other significant social issues, such as the poverty and neglect that can create inducements for drug experimentation. But even more directly related is a long-standing problem that has plagued society well before the current "war" on illegal drugs was waged. Of course, we are refer to the abuse of or addiction to a legal drug—alcohol. Because it is so widely, inexpensively, and legally available (at least for adults), alcohol in some ways actually may be a greater threat. This does not mean that many people do not consume alcohol in a socially responsible manner. It becomes a problem when the overuse of this drug begins to damage health, deteriorate family relationships, affect employment, and generate crime.

Like illicit drugs, the use of beer, wine, or hard liquor often begins at young ages, even though alcoholic beverages are legally restricted for those under 21 in all states. But illegality does not prevent consumption. Of all noncriminal (status) offenses, liquor violations represent the greatest number of cases processed by juvenile courts (Allen and Simonsen 1995). As with illegal drugs, all use of alcohol does not necessarily lead to addiction. But, among those who are particularly susceptible as a result of personality maladjustment or even inherited physical tendencies, abuse can lead to addiction.

Institutional Profile

In comparison to those who use illegal drugs, it appears that alcohol abusers may be even more heavily concentrated in some correctional institutions. Of all inmates in state correctional facilities, 37% report being under the influence of alcohol when they committed their most recent crime. The combination of alcohol with other drugs (polyabuse) also is appearing more frequently among correctional populations, as well as the public at large.

Of course, being "under the influence" during the commission of a crime does not inherently mean that the person is an alcoholic. It may indicate only that the offender becomes more susceptible to criminal suggestions or cannot control behavior when drinking. On the other hand, some alcoholics are completely convinced of their ability to "handle" increasingly large amounts of liquor, managing to function without detection in society and not seeking help until alcoholism has begun to destroy their lives. As a result, alcoholism is to a great extent a hidden disease, with no accurate measures of its prevalence within either corrections facilities or the outside community.

Treatment Programs

Many inmates with an alcohol problem have participated in some kind of treatment. According to Green (1996), about 60% of drinking inmates have been in at least one alcohol-abuse program during their lifetimes, and about 20% join alcohol treatment groups while they are institutionalized.

Inmate alcohol treatment programs differ from other programs in several respects. First, correctional programs seek to prepare inmates to stay sober once they leave the institution; outside programs seek to focus on the present. Second, inmates are not supposed to have access to alcohol, although they do have opportunities to drink their own "home brew," made from bread, juice, and scraps of fresh produce, alcoholic beverages smuggled in from outside, and over-the-counter products such as mouthwash and hair tonic. Alcoholics outside the of the institution are not denied access to alcohol. Third, participation in an alcohol program outside of the institution is voluntary (except as a condition of parole or probation), whereas inmate alcohol programs often are perceived by inmates as necessary to gain early release. Thus, although program participation is supposedly voluntary, correctional administrators indirectly coerce many inmates (through promise for parole) into programs in which they otherwise would not participate. Such participation is known as *programming out*; and it is done for the wrong reason, getting out of the institution rather than self-help.

As with drug intervention, treatment approaches range from psychotherapy to special diets designed to counteract vitamin deficiencies. The most prevalent institutional program is Alcoholics Anonymous (AA). AA was founded in 1935 by "Dr. Bob" and "Bill W." By 1933, there were more than 1,800 such groups in correctional facilities throughout the United States and Canada. Each has a local arrangement with an AA chapter outside the institution. According to a recent survey by AA, institutions participating in AA have an average of 1.25 groups per facility; some facilities have as many as 10 groups (Green 1996).

The core of AA is its famous "12 steps." With the help of a higher force that is individually interpreted by each participant, the steps move from confronting the problem through changes in behavior and to restitution to those previously harmed. The steps culminate in a spiritual awakening and continuing personal introspection that keeps one sober. Some incarcerated alcohol abusers also have participated as paraprofessionals in youth counseling programs, with the prisoners speaking about the problems associated with drugs and alcohol.

Sex Offenders

Like the confusion surrounding classification of various forms of mental illness, states have differing definitions of sexual crimes (e.g., "lewd and lascivious behavior," "carnal knowledge," "unnatural acts"). As with special offender populations in general, this discussion could include an extremely wide variety of behaviors, but will be limited to the most common sexually oriented offenders in the correctional system: prostitutes, child molesters, and rapists. Although each category of offender represents a type of problem, sex offenders often represent special management problems for correctional officers, especially child molesters and some rapists who may be the targets of inmate hostility.

Prostitutes

A major difference between prostitution and other sex crimes is that it is an offense committed for financial gain. Particularly among young juvenile runaways, drug addicts, alcoholics, and others who have minimal legitimate employment opportunities, selling one's body offers a desperate means of survival. Social attitudes toward prostitution vary throughout the world and even within different states in the United States. Some areas legalize and regulate the trade, whereas others strictly prohibit it. Most jurisdictions vacillate between these two extremes, officially outlawing prostitution but not vigorously enforcing it.

In part, these differences reflect the consideration of prostitution as a "victimless" crime; that is, a crime committed by two consenting parties. But this does not mean that prostitution does not generate victims. Customers can become robbery victims. Prostitutes themselves can be abused by either customers or their "pimps." And, with the spread of AIDS and other infectious diseases, both are subject to an even greater threat today. Moreover, prostitutes infected with the HIV virus and/or other infectious diseases pose several serious and unique challenges to correctional administrators. According to Vlahov et al. (1991), incarcerated women have higher rates of HIV seroprevalence than do men (2.5 to 14.7% versus 2.1 to 7.6%) due to higher rates of intravenous drug use and an overall increase in incarceration rates for drug crimes and/or prostitution.

Although the rate of imprisonment for males is about 16 times higher than that of females, the number of women serving time has increased considerably in recent years. Since 1985 the annual rate of growth of female inmates has averaged 11.2% (compared to 7.9% for males). By 1996 women accounted for 6.3% of all prisoners nationwide, up from 4.6% in 1985 (BJS 1997). As correctional officials build new facilities to house this increasing population they must keep in mind the necessary requirements for the HIV-afflicted female inmate. Among the special needs of this group is access to drug treatment, especially for the female prostitute who is often also an intravenous drug user.

Child Molesters

In contrast to its ambivalence toward prostitution, society holds clear attitudes toward the molesters of innocent children: that they are despicable. Among inmates, these offenders are at the bottom of the social hierarchy—rejected, scorned, and threatened by other inmates. As the public has become increasingly concerned with taking action against such violators, more vigorous efforts have been made to report, prosecute, and punish their actions. Despite these efforts, however, many cases remain hidden by fear and shame.

Perhaps the most tragic element in the sexual abuse of children is that many of its victims grow up to perpetuate the crime, becoming abusers themselves. This, of course, does not mean that all of those who are abused will become molesters, but it has been estimated that the vast majority of such offenders were former victims (Ellis and Brancale 1956). Many of these offenders victimize children in an attempt to resolve their own abusive experiences.

Some correctional facilities may separate child molesters from the general population for their own protection. But, unless they are identified as having some other problem that would give them a higher priority for treatment (such as drug addiction or mental illness), often little is offered to them in terms of therapy. Even when programs are available, it has been found that, to be effective, they must be accompanied by a change in attitudes and perceptions of both inmates and staff.

Quite often in correctional institutions the fear of reprisal from other inmates and the perception of ridicule, or worse, from staff, forces the "child molester" to deny their status and refuse to take part in sex offender programs. The lack of participation in these programs may increase their risk of reoffending upon release. Attitudes and perceptions of correctional officers toward these inmates can be conditioned through education and training, as they have been for mentally ill, elderly, and AIDS-infected inmates. Some officers may not respond to these efforts, however, and it may be more effective to concentrate agency resources by providing specialized training to officers who work in programs with these inmates. The problems and prospects for efforts to train and condition correctional officers to specialized programs are described in Chapter 8 "Organization-related Role Conflicts," and in particular, the case study of the Amity RighTurn substance abuse program at a California correctional facility.

Rapists

For many years, rape was considered a sexually oriented offense, which (like the myths about child molestation) was associated with excessive sexual drives. There is increasing recognition that heterosexual rape also is committed more for the desire to control and dominate the victim than for sexual gratification. As one former prosecutor has phrased it, "people who think rape is about sex confuse the weapon with the motivation" (Vachss 1993).

Forcible rape is classified as a crime of violence involving aggressive, hostile behavior directed toward degrading and dominating another person. It is a crime more closely related to assault than to other forms of sexual misconduct and now is referred to officially as *sexual assault*. Not only are the majority of rape victims injured, but more than almost any other violent offenders, rapists are likely to have had prior criminal charges against them (BJS 1996).

During the 1930s, most states adopted criminal sexual psychopath laws to identify chronic rape offenders and commit them to state hospitals for treatment. However, because these laws generally defined *sexual psychopaths* as those who have a "mental derangement," coupled with a propensity toward committing "sex offenses," the most serious and dangerous rapists sometimes were not covered by the law. Rather, minor sex offenders (such as voyeurs or "peeping Toms" and exhibitionists) were more likely to be targeted in many cases. Moreover, because of medical and legal variations, accurately determining sexual psychopathy is quite difficult. In recent years, a number of states have replaced the *sexual psychopath* term with *mentally disordered sex offender* (MDSO) or *dangerous sex offender*. Whatever they are designated, chronic rapists, by their very definition, can be expected to continue criminal behavior if appropriate treatment is not provided, and they can represent special management problems for facility staff.

Treatment Considerations

When considering treatment effectiveness within correctional institutions, it is difficult to form conclusions based on institutional behavior and treatment responsiveness. According to French (1992), "treatment, especially within a correctional setting, can compound the issue by masking environmental stimuli that may contribute to the sexual behaviors" (p. 1195). We now realize that it is a mistake to judge treatment success solely on behavioral appearances of how clients respond to talk therapy, their perception of women or children, or some other associated feature such as church or AA attendance. Silverman and Vega (1996) summarize the literature on the role of the inmate as the good "therapee" who could con the institutional and treatment staff, as well as the parole board, into believing he or she was cured (pp. 146–147).

Another treatment consideration, according to French, is that of sex as an associated clinical feature that may surface, for the first time, as a result of the phenomenon of incarceration: "In these situations stressors associated with the phenomenon of incarceration tend to exacerbate sex-related clinical features linked to untreated mentally ill inmates" (1992, p. 1197). The link here seems to exist between sex-stress features of incarceration and a number of major clinical syndromes including posttraumatic stress as a reaction to institution rape or sexual adaptations and adjustment disorders, especially those with a depressive-anxiety mix. Impulsive sexual aggression is not an uncommon means for venting these frustrations of incarceration. Institutional stress also can exacerbate certain associated features of psychotic inmates, notably hypersexuality. This is a common feature of acute schizophrenia, schizoaffective disorders, atypical psychosis, and manic-depressive disorders. The last feature has been a serious problem within incarcerated populations within the past 30 years, with the deinstitutionalization of mental hospitals and facilities for the mentally retarded. As previously mentioned, those who are not afforded community-based treatment, often end up being treated within the criminal justice system.

A unique treatment for the dangerous (fixated) male sexual offender, regardless of whether he is a rapist or molester, is the use of the synthetic female hormone progesterone. DeproProvera and Provera influence the sex drive by decreasing the male libido through suppression of testosterone and luteinizing (fantasy hormone) hormones. According to Berlin and Krout (1986), this form of chemical castration is superior to surgical castration not only because it is reversible but also because surgical castration does not lower the effects of luteinizing hormones, which, for the most part, are the root of deviant sexual fantasies. It must be realized that chemical castration is not the answer for all dangerous sexual offenders. Moreover, it is not a cure in itself, even for those sexual offenders who respond well to treatment.

What is the ideal treatment formula of MDSOs? According to French (1992), a treatment program for sexual offenders within correctional environments needs to have three interrelated components: clinical psychopharmacological interventions, psychotherapy that addresses the sexual offense, and lifelong monitoring once the offender is released from custody. On the legal front, all convicted sexual offenders need to be entered into a national network in which court schools, churches, children's organizations, an police departments can check the background of employees or potential employees.

The Elderly Inmate

Crime traditionally is considered a young man's game, but even though that appears accurate, correctional institutions in the United States are housing a growing number of older inmates. According to the U.S. Bureau of Justice Statistics, the number of inmates aged 55 and older more than doubled from 1981 to 1990. In a study conducted by the Federal Bureau of Prisons, it was predicted that the federal system, which houses the largest number of older inmates, will have a population increase in those aged 50 and older of from 11.7% in 1988 to 16% by the year 2005 (Morton 1996). Between 1979 and 1986, the percentage of state correctional institution inmates over the age of 25 increased from 64% to 73%. Such collective statistics do not appear to be very startling. However, figures for individual states more clearly reflect aging trends, particularly in areas of the country with large percentages of the elderly in their population.

There are several factors influencing the number of older people in correctional institutions. First, there are more older people in the general population, and they are living longer. According to the U.S. Census Bureau, those aged 65 and older make up the fastest growing population group in the United States, and in the last 60 years, the average life expectancy has increased from 54 years to over 75 years. At the same time, society's heightened concern about crime and violence has resulted in longer sentences and mandatory incarceration to include life without parole for an increasing number of offenses. Several jurisdictions, including the federal government, have abolished parole and limited probation as a sentencing option.

As the elderly become a larger percentage of inmates, correctional administrators will be faced with unique challenges to address their needs. If aging inmates are simply placed with the overall population, they will he vulnerable to being preyed upon by younger, healthier inmates. They also are less likely to be able to participate physically in the recreational and vocational programs that are traditionally offered in correctional facilities. Nor, in many cases, can they eat the same foods as other inmates, because aging often is accompanied by more restrictive diets. Meeting the housing, recreational, rehabilitative, and even dietary needs of geriatric inmates presents issues that correctional agencies will be confronting in the years ahead.

Perhaps most significant in terms of costs, as more and more older offenders are confined behind bars, long-term health care will become an increasingly greater concern, just as it already is within the general population in free society. According to Kelsey (1986), "nearly every geriatric inmate has some long-term chronic debilitation that requires frequent medical attention" (p. 56). In 1988, the Federal Bureau of Prisons found that older inmates had higher rates of chronic illness, including cardiac and hypertension disorders, than their younger counterparts. Meeting such needs is costly: the bureau predicted that, by the year 2005, those two illnesses alone will cost more than $93 million to treat (Morton 1996). In 1989, it was estimated that the average expense of medical care and maintenance for inmates over 55 was $69,000 a year, about three times the norm (Carroll 1989).

Some might advocate that early release should be extended to the elderly, for financial if not humanitarian reasons. In that regard, at least one agency has implemented a "compassionate release program" for terminally ill inmates who are no longer a risk to society, giving them an opportunity to live out their remaining days in relative dignity. But many older prisoners have outlived their relatives and used up their savings. With no prospect of employment, where are they to go? For these types of cases, others have proposed that secure nursing homes and electronic monitoring would be more suitable alternatives (Fox and Stinchcomb 1994).

SUMMARY

Correctional officers must manage a variety of offenders within the general population of their institutions. These include inmates with AIDS and HIV infection, mentally ill and retarded, disabled, elderly, substance abusers, and sex offenders. Even though these types of offenders have been in institutions since their inception, shrinking resources, fewer programs, and crowded conditions make it imperative that correctional officers be better trained to handle these individuals on a day-to-day basis. Because of their "minority" group status in prison populations, the needs of many of these inmates have not often been addressed. The increasing numbers of AIDS cases coming into jails and prisons, coupled with increasing numbers of disabled and elderly and a potentially more violent group of inmates with lengthy mandatory sentences have forced correctional managers to better prepare staff members to manage these populations.

With the spread of AIDS throughout society, it is not surprising to find that this disease is on the increase among inmates, particularly since those convicted of drug offenses are likely to be sentenced to prison or jail terms. Although IV drug users and homosexual or bisexual men are the largest groups at risk of HIV infection, it is spreading rapidly among women and children as a result of secondary infection. Correctional responses to reducing the transmission of HIV have included educational programs, issuing condoms, HIV testing, and separate housing. Legal challenges have focused primarily on mandatory testing and the segregation of HIV-positive inmates. Thus far, the courts have ruled that mandatory testing is neither required under the Eighth Amendment nor prohibited under the Fourth Amendment. Similar judicial findings have resulted from cases challenging the segregation of HIV-positive inmates. Again, the courts have held that it is neither required nor prohibited.

In contrast, the criminally insane are those so designated by the courts, using legal criteria related to one's capacity to distinguish right from wrong. Those determined to be criminally insane may be confined in mental health facilities, forensic hospitals, or the separate psychiatric ward of a correctional institution. But many others may be incarcerated who are not legally designated "insane" but suffer from various forms of mental illnesses. In recent years, it has become more difficult to transfer such inmates to a mental health hospital, but correctional facilities generally are ill-equipped to meet their needs.

Mentally disordered offenders (MDOs) represent a sizable component of correctional populations, especially since the deinstitutionalization of mental health services. The developmentally disabled differ from the mentally ill in that their mental capacity has been retarded at an early stage of development. They usually are identified by an IQ of less than 70, which renders them easily susceptible to apprehension when they engage in crime. Within correctional institutions, the developmentally disabled represent special problems, since they are slower in adjusting and learning what is expected of them. Their behavior can also be misinterpreted as defiance.

In the past, the corrections field, like the general public, has been slow to respond to the needs of the physically impaired. Following implementation of the Americans With Disabilities Act in 1990, both public agencies and private employers are legally prohibited from discriminating against the disabled. The direct impact this legislation will have on the inmate population still is uncertain, but it has generated widespread publicity, calling attention to the special needs of the disabled throughout society.

Drug abusers represent another component of correctional clientele that is growing at alarming rates, particularly among minority group members. Drug treatment programs are available in most correctional facilities, but they reach a relatively small percentage of inmates and the punitive emphasis of the justice model does not encourage participation. Even though the long-term success of such programs is not always impressive, it is important to note that treatment is not the only component of drug rehabilitation. Careful screening and appropriate intervention must be followed by close supervision, including both supportive assistance and continued monitoring.

Despite current concerns with the abuse of illicit drugs, alcohol historically has been the most abused substance and remains the "drug of choice" among young people. Although many are able to use alcohol in a socially responsible manner, others become addicted to it. Treatment programs for this disease generally emphasize strengthening the patient psychologically so that alcohol is no longer a convenient "crutch" for solving problems or relieving tensions.

Like the mentally ill, sex offenders defy simple classification. They encompass conduct ranging from prostitution to rape or child molestation. Prostitution differs from other sexually oriented crimes in that it is committed for financial gain. Because both parties engage in this offense voluntarily, it often receives a low priority within all components of the criminal justice system. On the other hand, child molesters have become an increasing public concern. Many cases nevertheless remain hidden by fear and shame. Effective correctional treatment programs for molesters must be accompanied by a change in institution norms, which traditionally force them to conceal their offense out of fear of victimization. Like myths about child molestation, rape was considered a sexually oriented crime in the past. Now there is greater realization that rape is a violent offense, committed more from a desire to control and dominate the victim than for sexual gratification. Without treatment, chronic rapists can be expected to continue their behavior. But identifying the proper intervention is difficult, because all sex offenders do not necessarily need the same type, intensity, or duration of treatment.

Like drug abusers, the elderly represent a rapidly expanding correctional inmate group. Along with the overall aging of the population in general, longer prison sentences are resulting in greater numbers of older inmates. As this trend continues, corrections facilities will be faced with meeting their unique requirements in terms of everything from housing assignments to dietary restrictions, recreational provisions, and rehabilitative programs. Moreover, the long-term health care of geriatric inmates will become increasingly costly. In fact, meeting the special needs of all groups of offenders discussed in this chapter presents a significant challenge for correctional programs and facilities that are already hard-pressed to meet even the basic needs of more "traditional" offenders.

REFERENCES

Allen, H. E., and C.E. Simonsen. *Corrections in America: An Introduction*, 7th ed. New York: Macmillan, 1995.

American Correctional Association. *Correctional Officer Resource Guide*, 3d ed. Lanham, MD: American Correctional Association, 1997.

Anderson, A.F. "AIDS and Prisoners' Rights Law: Deciphering the Administrative Guideposts." *Prison Journal* 69, no. 1 (1989): 18–29.

Atlas, R.I. "ADA-Interim Final Regulations for Courthouses, Jails and Prisons," *American Jails* (1994): 65–67.

Belbot, B.A., and R.V. del Carmen. "AIDS in Prison: Legal Issues." *Crime and Delinquency* 37, no. 1 (1991): 134–152.

Belcher, J.R. "Are Jails Replacing the Mental Health System for Homeless Mentally Ill?" *Community Mental Health Journal* 24, no. 3 (1988): 190–214.

Bennett, L.A, T.S. Rosenbaum, and W.R. McCullough. *Counseling in Correctional Environments*. New York: Human Services Press, 1978.

Berlin, F.S., and E.K. Krout. "Pedophilia: Diagnostic Concepts, Treatment and Ethical Considerations." *American Journal of Forensic Psychiatry* 7 (1986): 13–30.

Bureau of Justice Statistics. *Drugs and Crime Facts, 1994*. Washington, DC: U.S. Government Printing Office, 1995.

Bureau of Justice Statistics. *Prisoners in 1996*. Washington, DC: U.S. Government Printing Office, 1997.

Bureau of Justice Statistics. *Sourcebook of Criminal Justice Statistics, 1994*. Washington DC: U.S. Government Printing Office, 1995.

Bureau of Justice Statistics. *Sourcebook of Criminal Justice Statistics, 1995*. Washington, DC: U.S. Government Printing Office, 1996.

Carroll, G. "Growing Old Behind Bars." *Newsweek* (November 20, 1989): 20.

Collins, W.C. *Correctional Law for the Correctional Officer*, pp. 198 and 220. Lanham, MD: American Correctional Association, 1997.

Ellis, A., and R. Brancal. *The Psychology of Sex Offenders*. Springfield, IL: Charles C Thomas, 1956.

Fox, V.B., and J.B. Stinchcomb. *Introduction to Corrections*, 4th ed. Englewood Cliffs, NJ: Prentice-Hall, 1994.

French, L. "Characteristics of Sexuality Within Correctional Environments." *Corrective and Social Psychiatry* 38 (1992): 1195–1218.

Green, G.S. "Alcohol Treatment Programs in Prison." In M. McShane and F.P. Williams III (eds.), *Encyclopedia of American Prisons*, pp. 24–27. New York: Garland, 1996.

Hammett, T.M., L. Harrold, and J. Epstein. *1992 Update: AIDS in Correctional Facilities: Issues and Options.* Washington, DC: U.S. Department of Justice, 1993.

Hammett, T.M., and S. Moini. *1989 Update: AIDS in Correctional Facilities: Issues and Options.* Washington, DC: U.S. Department of Justice, 1990.

Harlow, C.W. "HIV in U.S. Prisons and Jails," Bureau of Justice Statistics special report. Washington, DC: U.S. Department of Justice, 1993.

"Inmate HIV Testing." *American Jails* 6(5): 87. 1992.

Josi, D.A. "Lifeskills '95: A Pragmatic Alternative for Juvenile Parole; the Evaluation of a Community Reintegration Program for Youthful Offenders." Doctoral dissertation, University of California, Irvine, 1996.

Kalinich, D., P. Embert, and J. Senese. "Mental Health Services for Jail Inmates: Imprecise Standards, Traditional Philosophies, and the Need for Change." In J.A. Thompson and G.L. Mays (eds.), *American Jails: Pubic Policy Issues*, p. 81. Chicago: Nelson-Hall, 1991.

Kassebaum, G.W., D.A. Ward, and D.M. Wilner. *Prison Treatment and Parole Survival: An Empirical Assessment.* New York: John Wiley and Sons, 1971.

Kelsey, O.W. "Elderly Inmates: Providing Safe and Humane Care." *Corrections Today* 48, no. 3 (1986): 56.

Lawrence, J.E., and Van Zwisohn. "AIDS in Jail," pp. 122–124. In J.A. Thompson and G.L. Mays (eds.), *American Jails: Public Policy Issues.* Chicago: Nelson-Hall, 1991.

Lipton, D.S. "Prison-Based Therapeutic Communities: Their Success with Drug-Abusing Offenders." *National Institute of Justice Journal* (1996): 12–20.

Lukefield, C.G., and F.M. Tims. *Drug Abuse Treatment in Prisons and Jails.* Rockville, MD: National Institute on Drug Abuse, 1992.

Lurigio, A.J., J. Petraitis, and B. Johnson. "HIV Education for Probation Officers: An Implementation and Evaluative Program." *Crime and Delinquency* 37 (1991): 125–134.

Morain, D. *State's Prisons Told to Follow Disabilities Act*, p. A1. Sacramento: State of California Commission on Peace Officer Standards and Training, 1996.

Morton, J.B. "Elderly Inmates." In M. McShane and F. P. Williams III (eds.), *Encyclopedia of American Prisons*, pp. 190–194. New York: Garland, 1996.

Morton, J.B., and J.C. Anderson. "Implementing the Americans With Disabilities Act for Inmates." *Corrections Today* (1996): 86, 88–89, and 140.

National Commission on Acquired Immune Deficiency Syndrome. *National Commission on AIDS Report: HIV Disease in Correctional Facilities*, pp. 193, 197, 199, and 200–201. Washington, DC: 1991.

National Commission on the Causes and Prevention of Violence. *Crimes of Violence.* Washington, DC: U.S. Government Printing Office, 1969.

National Institute of Justice. *Drug Use Forecasting: 1988 Drug Use Forecasting Annual Report.* Washington, DC: U.S. Department of Justice, 1990.

Olivero, M. J. "The Treatment of AIDS Behind the Walls of Correctional Facilities." *Social Justice* 17, no. 1 (1990): 110–134.

Pierini, L. "Biting the Hand That Feeds Them: The 'Other' Prison Drug Problem." *Police* (1991): 32–36.

Rubin, P.N. *The Americans With Disabilities Act and Criminal Justice: An Overview, Research in Action*, pp. 211 and 221. Washington, DC: National Institute of Justice, 1993.

Rubin, P.N., and S.W. McCampbell. *The Americans With Disabilities Act and Criminal Justice: Mental Disabilities and Corrections*, pp. 205 and 217. Washington, DC: National Institute of Justice, 1995.

Santamour, M.B. *The Mentally Retarded Offender and Corrections*. Lanham, MD: American Correctional Association, 1989.

Santamour, M.B., and R.C. Brown. *Sourcebook on the Mentally Disordered Prisoner*, pp. 207–208. Washington, DC: U.S. Department of Justice, 1985.

Silverman, I.J., and M. Vega. *Corrections, a Comprehensive View*. New York: West, 1996.

Todd, T. "ADA and Hiring Practices at West Virginia Regional Jails." *American Jails* (1996): 59–60.

Vachss, A. "Rapists Are Single-Minded Sociopathic Beasts . . . That Cannot Be Tamed with Understanding." *Parade Magazine* (June 27, 1993), p. 5.

Valliant, G.E. "A 20-Year Follow-up of New York Narcotic Addicts." *Archives of General Psychiatry* 29 (1973): 237–241.

Van Sickle, D. "Title II of the Americans With Disabilities Act and Correctional Facility Responsibilities." *Corrections Compendium* 19, no. 12 (1994): 1–3 and 8.

Vlahov, D., T.F. Brewer, and K.G. Castro, et al. "Prevalence of Antibody to HIV-1 Among Entrants to U.S. Correctional Facilities." *Journal of the American Medical Association* 265:1129–32. 1991.

Wish, E.D. "Drug Testing and the Identification of Drug Abusing Criminals." In J.A. Inciardi (ed.). *Handbook of Drug Control in the United States*. Westport, CN: Greenwood, 1991.

Zimmerman, S.E., R. Martin, and D. Vlahov. "AIDS Knowledge and Risk Perceptions Among Pennsylvania Prisoners." *Journal of Criminal Justice* 19, no. 3 (1991): 239–256.

Legal Case Citations (in order cited)

Harris v. *Thigpen*, 941 F.2d 1495 (11th Cir. 1991).
Jackson v. *Indiana*, 92 S.Ct. 1845 (1977).
Gates v. *Rowland*, 39 F.3d 1439 (9th Cir. 1994).

8

Organization-Related Role Conflicts

A number of the task-related roles of correctional officers assigned to correctional facilities frequently are characterized by conflict. Role conflict, according to Shamir and Drory (1982), involves two or more sets of pressures, requiring different reactions or behavior. Conflict in correctional institutions is created by tension among correctional officers and inmates, between officers with different job assignments, and officers and administrators. Many officers who face complex and difficult tasks requiring interpersonal and leadership skills may feel helpless and develop a sense of failure. The effect of these role conflicts on individual officers contribute to stress and the related phenomenon of burnout. It is critical that corrections professionals understand the impact of the corrections environment on their mental and physical health and well-being.

This section identifies and discusses three organizational factors that are major contributors to personal role conflict for the corrections professional. The first, institutional crowding, may have serious effects on the health and well-being of correctional officers and create extreme emotional stress. Correctional institutions always have had internal problems with inmates and correctional staff. However, recent studies have shown that crowding may increase the number of disciplinary infractions, rates of criminal behavior, violence, inmate-on-staff assaults, and heighten tempers and staff aggression in crowded institutions (McShane 1996).

Second, role conflicts among staff factions are a major contributor to the stressful nature of the work environment within the institutional setting. For example, security staff and treatment staff often perceive each other as interfering with their ability to perform their duties effectively. The traditional "custodial" goal of correctional institutions often is seen as antithetical to the rehabilitative "treatment" goal of inmate programs.

Finally, the law enforcement and corrections community in recent years has sought to mirror the community that they serve. Large numbers of women and members of minority groups have joined the workforce of both professions. This often has led to a change in attitudes and practices in the correctional institution. In addition, past research has documented how correctional officers are predominately white and from rural areas. Many inmates, on the other hand, are members of a minority class, often have low levels of education, and come from predominately urban areas. It is not difficult, therefore, to understand how conflict can arise in the institutional context between correctional officers and inmates. If the correctional workforce does not reflect that diversity, it will have difficulty communicating, relating, assessing values, and predicting behavior.

INSTITUTIONAL CROWDING

During the past two decades, both federal and state correctional institution populations throughout the United States soared as never before. Moreover, mandatory sentencing guidelines, tougher parole policies, and longer sentences continue to keep more criminals in prison for longer periods of time. During the 12 months that ended June 30, 1995, the number of prison inmates grew by 89,707, the largest annual increase in U.S. history (Bureau of Justice Statistics 1996). In addition, many feel the nation's prison populations will continue to increase dramatically well into the 21st century. A 1995 study on prison population published in *Corrections Compendium*, forecast a 51% overall increase in U.S. prison population by the 2000 (Wunder 1995).

Most institutions have been hit hard by the overwhelming increase in inmate population. By the end of 1995, 39 states, the District of Columbia, and the federal prison system reported operating at 100% or more of their capacity. According to a report released by BJS, by year-end the federal system was operating at 26% over capacity; state systems, on average, were operating at 114% of their highest capacity and 125% of their lowest capacity (BJS 1996).

Breaking It Down

According to the BJS, there were 1,127,132 state and federal inmates in the United States by year-end 1995. The total incarceration rate of state and federal inmates sentenced to more than a year reached 409 per 100,000 residents during the same time period, an increase of 6.3% over the previous year. Since 1985, the total number of inmates in the custody of state and federal correctional institutions has more than doubled—violent criminals accounted for 40% of this growth. During this same period, the proportion of federal inmates sentenced for drug violations rose from 25% to 61%. The increase in drug offenders accounted for nearly three-quarters of the total growth in federal prison population.

State and federal prisons are not the only institutions to have felt the impact of the population boom. By midyear 1995, the number of persons held in local jail facilities grew at an annual rate of 4.2% to 507,044 (BJS 1996). Since 1985, the nation's jail population has nearly doubled on a per capita basis. During this period the number of jail inmates per 100,000 residents rose from 108 to 193 (BJS 1996).

In addition, recent "two" and "three strikes" laws have created a backlog of inmates in many county jail systems. In California, for example, few defendants who face long prison terms or life sentences actually accept plea bargains—they want a jury trial. Under California's "three strikes" law, most counties set bail for second-strike defendants at twice the usual amount and refuse bail for third-strike defendants (Shichor and Sechrest 1996). According to a report by the California state Legislative Analyst's Office (LAO), Los Angeles County estimated that it was housing more than 1,000 "three strikes" defendants awaiting trial (LAO 1995).

Effects of Overcrowding

The results of overcrowding are serious deprivations in the quality of life for everyone in a correctional institution. Even though we have built hundreds of new prisons and expanded existing facilities during the last decade, the average amount of space per inmate has decreased by over 10% (McShane 1996). Throughout the system, high inmate to staff ratios lead to poor supervision and scheduling difficulties, which result in less inmate activity and greater safety risks for both correctional officers and inmates.

The nature of a crowded environment creates serious problems for correctional officers as well as for the inmates and may be responsible for a number of stress related afflictions. Philliber (1987) identified a number of stress related factors common to corrections work in overcrowded conditions (such as danger and lack of predictability). Other studies have shown that crowding may increase the number of disciplinary infractions per inmate. Correctional staff members are unable to exert as much managerial control over the population of excessively crowded facilities. According to Blumstein,

> As the numbers prisoners increase, the space normally used for recreation or education is diverted to dormitory use. Incidents of violence between prisoners increase, and control of the institution gradually slips to the most aggressive groups. . . . The exhaustion of services and the limitation on recreational activities further lead to tension, boredom, and conflict. . . . Eventually, there is a degradation of morale among the staff, greater staff turnover, and a vicious cycle of diminished control. (p. 1)

The courts have also been identified as a stressor in the correctional arena, "as correctional officers are often said to be affected by issues surrounding overcrowding, and officers often feel handcuffed in dealing with inmates—afraid that they might violate an offender's civil rights and face legal repercussions" (Slate 1993, p. 129).

Making decisions can be stressful, but the level at which the decisions are made and the potential harm from bad decisions increase the potential for stress. The stakes are higher when one has responsibility for people rather than things.

Solutions to Institutional Crowding

Reactions to prison crowding have included three basic strategies. One involves a front-end reduction in the number of people going into prisons; another, a back-end increase in the number of inmates released (neither of which have been vigorously pursued). The third and most utilized strategy includes both the expansion of existing facilities and the construction of new institutions.

Front-End Reduction

The intent of front-end solutions is to limit the number of people entering prison, through the use of selective incapacitation and community-based alternatives. Selective incapacitation is based on the premise that a few serious offenders are responsible for a majority of the crimes. Therefore, it would be most economical and practical to allocate the limited bed space to those high-rate, chronic offenders. The primary problem with selective incapacitation is that of prediction. Many criminologists assert that it is too difficult to ascertain who is a serious offender and therefore needs to be incarcerated. For many theorists, the use of risk-assessment tools to predict who should be released is dangerous and potentially unfair.

Along with selecting only certain offenders for incarceration is the idea of selecting others for community-based alternatives. Probation and shock probation can greatly reduce prison populations. Alternative sentences also could include community service, restitution, day fines, education and treatment programs, and electronic monitoring. Certain groups of offenders may be most appropriate for diversion, such as drug offenders and alcohol offenders, who may be directed to therapy centers.

Backdoor Solutions

Backdoor approaches also have been employed to reduce overcrowding. These approaches are designed to release more of those already confined, through such options as time off for good behavior, parole, weekend confinement, and other forms of early or temporary release. On occasion, emergency release mechanisms have been employed to reduce crowding by a specific number of prisoners as a one-time event. This occurs when judges issue orders to reduce crowding immediately or face fines, the installment of population caps, or the closing of the facility.

Still other approaches include sending inmates with outstanding warrants or pending charges back to places where those charges originated once they are eligible for parole. This even may mean sending incarcerated illegal aliens into the custody of the Immigration and Naturalization Service (INS) for deportation hearings.

New Construction

Most correctional systems have been building new facilities and expanding existing ones to ease the pressure of crowding and keep up with the rise in convictions. In fiscal year 1995, state and federal governments allocated $5.1 billion for the construction of new prison space.

Increasing available institutional housing through renovation or new construction is controversial. Proponents argue that incarceration, as punishment, is here to stay. Because there is public support for prisons, we have a responsibility to build adequate facilities. Opponents, on the other hand, argue that if we continue to build we will just continue to fill up any space that is created. In other words, some believe that availability alone drives up incarceration rates—overcrowding today is simply a result of an attempt to warehouse all of our social problems. Moreover, reliance on increasing physical capacity not only has been costly, but also criticized by those who maintain that "expanding a failure will only create a more expensive failure" (Travis, Schwartz, and Clear 1980, p. 60).

Despite the enthusiasm of state legislatures for building new prisons, overcrowding is enormous and growing. Perhaps enthusiasm for building is counterbalanced by an equal enthusiasm for harsher legislation.

ROLE CONFLICT

Correctional officers routinely assume numerous essential yet sometimes contradictory roles (e.g., counselor, diplomat, caretaker, disciplinarian, supervisor, crisis manager), often under stressful and dangerous work conditions. Overwhelming evidence suggests that stress is an important contributor to the abnormal incidence of health problems among correctional personnel (Cheek and Miller 1983; Stinchcomb 1986).

Moreover, the diversity of tasks correctional officers must perform can prove problematic; role conflict may be difficult if not impossible to avoid. Stinchcomb (1986) found that pressure from administrators and problems with coworkers were the strongest predictors of physical problems among this occupational group.

Treatment versus Security

The divergent and often incompatible goals of treatment and custody within correctional institutions frequently result in ambiguous role expectations and role conflict among correctional officers. Although a hierarchical, quasi-military authority structure probably is indispensable for the efficient operation of correctional institutions, it can sometimes inhibit communication among staff and present barriers to effective problem solving. The role conflict faced by many correctional officers has a direct influence on the image projected. Many feel they are security enforcement officers, not social workers; they did not create nor can they alleviate an inmates physical and mental problems.

Correctional institutions are designed to receive, house, care for, and release offenders committed to their care. During confinement, maintaining custody is a primary concern. Keeping the institution safe and secure and preventing escapes are the major custodial functions. Quite simply, the institution cannot treat inmates if it does not have them in custody. Although the most appropriate type of treatment is very much subject to debate, security is not considered debatable.

Traditional security involves well-known, routine practices, such as counting, controlling movement, conducting searches, staffing tower observation points, regulating contact with the outside, and managing inmate behavior. Some inherent restrictions are built into the physical plant itself. Others result from custodial procedures implemented by staff. All emphasize maintaining compliance with the rules and regulations of the institution. When such compliance is not achieved, the results can be disastrous: escapes, violence, riots, and other disturbances that jeopardize the safety and security of inmates, staff, and the facility. But these custodial features represent only one aspect of maintaining institutional control. Often overlooked are the more informal, noncoercive controls emerging from the relationship established between correctional officers and the inmate population.

The nature of that relationship has changed considerably over time. Prior to the 1960s, the role of those "guarding" inmates had changed little since its origin in the Auburn Penitentiary. Primary attention was focused on enforcing institutional regulations and supervising custodial procedures. Given the limited scope of their duties and what was expected of them, operational staff were commonly referred to as *guards* or *turnkeys*. But, during the height of the medical model, it became apparent that line correctional personnel could play an important role beyond custodial supervision.

Until this point, the significant potential of those dealing directly with the inmates for achieving a positive impact on their behavior was largely overlooked. But it has now become clear that operational staff perhaps are even more influential than treatment staff because of their continuous interaction through day-to-day contact with those incarcerated. Like the teachers a child encounters at school, treatment personnel play a major role in shaping values and attitudes. But teachers cannot completely replace the impact of the family, with whom the child interacts more intimately on a daily basis. In a correctional institution, the operational staff are to some extent the inmate's surrogate "family," whose empathy and understanding can go far toward making time in a correctional institution more tolerable and treatment more effective.

This recognition of a broader role for line staff began the translation from the punitive, rule-enforcement "guard" to the modern concept of a "correctional officer," whose responsibilities extend beyond custody toward establishing a genuine relationship based on mutual respect. This does not mean, however, that enforcing traditional security measures is overlooked in an effort to avoid destroying relationships. Inmate respect is not earned by "looking the other way" when rules are violated. On the other hand, officers who demonstrate a caring concern and empathetic understanding are more likely to obtain a level of voluntary compliance that can reduce the need to rely exclusively on coercive techniques. With even the most efficient custodial procedures, it is difficult to control those who do not voluntarily consent to be controlled. Therefore, in the long term, developing effective working relationships not only promotes treatment but serves security objectives as well. This combination of conventional controls and informal influence through relationship building best enables an institution to achieve its custodial mandate.

Functions of Custody

Every prison has custody at its central core. The primary function of custody is to provide external controls for those who lack sufficient internal controls to function effectively in a free society. Ideally, custody should provide only that amount of external control that is immediately necessary. For this reason, correctional institutions function at various levels of security, from minimum to maximum. Even for those who initially are assigned to a high level of security, the system is designed to reduce the level of control gradually for those who increasingly demonstrate the ability to function on their own as they better internalize self-control.

Although correctional facilities represent the ultimate form of control, less restrictive social controls also are maintained by many other institutions in society: the family, schools, churches, civic organizations, and so on. Through these institutions we learn morals, values, and socially acceptable behavior. Only when the socializing influences of these other institutions have failed with a particular person does correctional control take over. Custody in corrections, of course, is more direct and better organized, because it deals with people in a closed environment, where behavior must be more strictly controlled to prevent inmates from disturbing others or harming themselves.

Purposes of Custody

Custodial procedures in correctional facilities are designed to control individual behavior for the well-being of the total institution. More specifically, the immediate operational objectives of custody are to

- Prevent escape;
- Maintain order and safety;
- Promote the efficient functioning of the overall institution.

In the long term, the types of behavioral restraints involved in maintaining custody also are designed to shape the offender's behavior in a manner that better enables reentry into society as a contributing, law-abiding citizen (or at least, not a dangerous one). Undoubtedly, other programs offered during the period of confinement—counseling, vocational training, work release, and the like—contribute significantly to this long-term goal. But custody permits such programs to function.

Custody-Treatment Relationships

It is difficult, if not impossible, to develop meaningful programs when work schedules are "frequently interrupted by violence" or classrooms become "battlegrounds." If one constantly is concerned about self-protection and institutional disruption, the appropriate environment for working, learning, or changing behavior is simply lacking. There is a correlation between good security and good inmate programming, and blending the two creates a system responsive to the needs of both inmates and staff. In other words, custody and treatment go hand in hand. Most program staff members realize that effective programs cannot exist in a disorderly, dangerous institution. Most correctional staff members understand that offering a variety of institutional programs actually helps them manage the institution more effectively. In short, these two main segments of the institutional community need each other.

Even under the best of conditions, correctional institutions are far from the ideal environment for the implementation of meaningful treatment programs. But in those facilities where basic control is absent, treatment faces a formidable obstacle. On the other hand, the most secure institution might be one that keeps the inmates in their cells at all times. But it would be next to impossible to provide education, training, or any other programs under those conditions. Nor does such restriction prepare the inmate for the interaction with others that inevitably is encountered on release. Consequently, the institution is faced with finding the appropriate balance between program operations and security needs.

Security Techniques

Different correctional institutions seek to achieve this balance in different ways. In part, the extent to which service versus custody is emphasized will depend on the security classification of the institution. Certainly, more freedom and opportunity for program participation are available in minimum security facilities. However, that does not mean that services must be sacrificed to achieve custody. Quite the contrary, custody is a necessary condition for treatment.

Maintaining custody is achieved in part through the architectural features and security hardware of the physical plant itself. But even the most architecturally sound institution designed for the highest level of security also requires such control procedures as separation, restricted movement, counts, searches, and the regulation of everything from visiting and correspondence to tools and property.

CULTURAL DIVERSITY

Correctional institutions in recent years have recognized the need to mirror the communities they serve. Expanding the employment of women and members of minority groups in corrections is beginning to produce a workforce more reflective of the public being serviced. Meeting the needs of our diverse society for the next century, however, will require additional planning, education, and understanding of the needs and values of the members of society. As the U.S. population changes, so does its workforce. The population is aging because of improved health care and the deluge of baby boomers born between 1946 and 1964. The passage of the Americans With Disabilities Act in 1990 drew attention to the needs of the disabled population. The number of individuals with disabilities in the workforce is expected to increase.

Diversity and change have not always been easy to adjust to within correctional agencies. In addition to having to accommodate to a "new breed" of employee in terms of race, gender, or ethnicity, many of those beginning correctional work today have limitations that would have previously excluded them from correctional employment. The combination of an increasingly more diverse workforce has created challenges for correctional administrators. Previously, correctional officers were considerably more homogeneous, sharing similar job-related values and attitudes. This was obviously disadvantageous in terms of generating change or meeting the needs of diverse clientele. But it was advantageous in terms of managing, supervising, and accommodating like-minded employees. Along with the benefits of a more varied workforce, corrections is now faced with the challenge of adapting to the differences they represent.

Women in Corrections

According to the American Correctional Association (ACA), 80% of all correctional officers in state institutions are men, 70% are white, and 95% are non-Hispanic (ACA 1995). But despite their fewer numbers, interesting and informative research has been conducted in recent years on women correctional officers.

The first correctional officers were called many things, but ma'am was not one of them. The earliest prisoners, both male and female, were guarded by men. At times the male guards expanded their activities to include physical abuse and sexual exploitation of women prisoners.

The process of replacing male guards with female matrons began in the 1820s but did not move very quickly. The first female prison guard was hired in 1832, after Auburn Prison opened a separate wing for women prisoners. In the late 19th and early 20th centuries, as states built facilities specifically for women offenders, some legislatures required the institutions to be administered and staffed entirely by women. Later much of that legislation was repealed (a shortage of qualified women managers and a lack of faith by male legislators in the administrative abilities of women), thus allowing men to assume administrative positions in facilities for women (Zupan 1992).

The situation began improving in the 1970s, when women began more forcefully asserting their rights to job and advancement opportunities (see Chapter 6, "Civil Liability"). In 1972, Congress amended the 1964 Civil Rights Act to prohibit sex-based employment discrimination by public employers at state, county, and local levels. The courts also have supported and generally upheld a woman's right to employment. Today, in state correctional systems, about 20% of the correctional officers are women; in the federal system, about 12% are women (Camp and Camp 1997). These numbers remain deficient, but they are improvements over the previous situation. Of course, a more telling percentage is for the women correctional officers assigned to all-male institutions. Zupan (1992) notes that by 1981 all but four correctional systems (Alaska, Pennsylvania, Texas, and Utah) employed women as correctional officers in all-male state institutions.

Recent studies reported by the ACA and Criminal and Juvenile Justice International (1996) indicate an increased complement of female officers assigned to male institutions has a positive influence on both inmate behavior and male officer management of inmates. According to the CJJI report, female correctional officers were "assaulted only 27.6% as often as were male officers" (p. 2). And, across seven states that averaged more than 20% female officers (compared to 12% nationally), the CJJI researchers found a "47% reduction in assaults on female officers . . . [and] a 41% reduction in assaults on male officers" (p. 2) when compared to the national average.

No doubt, as we approach the 21st century the increased number women working in correctional institutions will continue. In addition, the push for employer-sponsored or -supported child care, flexible benefits, and flexible work hours is likely to continue. As with older workers, more women in the labor force also may lead to more part-time workers.

Minority Group Members in Corrections

Multiculturalism is the U.S. workforce is most noteworthy when it comes to members of minority groups. Ethnicity in the workplace is increasing and intensifying as new immigrants, predominately from Asia and Latin America, find it difficult to blend into the mainstream. As a result, many Americans must interact with people who are culturally different from themselves.

By the year 2000, the African-American workforce will increase by an estimated 29%, the Hispanic workforce by 74%, and other races by 70% (Johnson and Packer 1987). According to *Workforce 2000*, by the year 2000, 85% of the growth in the U.S. workforce will be represented by women and members of minority groups. Demographers estimate that, if birth rates and immigration patterns continue, those groups of Americans who are now thought of as minority will be the majority by 2030.

Managing and working in a culturally diverse workplace will be the norm for more and more correctional officers. The implications are tremendous. The inmate population is multicultural. If the correctional workforce does not reflect that diversity, it will have difficulty communicating, relating, assessing values, and predicting behavior.

Encouraging Diversity

Title VII of the Civil Rights Act of 1964 (as amended), the Age Discrimination in Employment Act, the Americans With Disabilities Act, and a host of local equal employment opportunity statutes make race-, sex-, national origin-, age-, religion-, and disability-based discrimination in the workplace illegal. The legal penalties for noncompliance are serious and have increased with the Civil Rights Act of 1991. In addition, many correctional agencies' employment processes have been subject to scrutiny federal courts and judges because of statute violations. It is not just good business anymore—it's the law!

CASE STUDY: TREATMENT VERSUS SECURITY— ADVERSARIAL RELATIONSHIP BETWEEN TREATMENT FACILITATORS AND CORRECTIONAL OFFICERS[1]

The goals of a modern correctional institution are twofold: custody and treatment. The custodial goal is the obligation to the community to ensure that inmates are constrained within acceptable, and frequently specified, behavioral guidelines. The treatment goal requires doing something positive to ensure that, upon release, the offender has a legitimate opportunity to become a productive, noncriminal member of society. Quite often, the methods to achieve these goals are viewed as conflicting and may result in friction among institutional personnel (Lombardo 1982).

Custodial staff and treatment staff often perceive each other as interfering with each others abilities to perform their duties effectively. This type of occupational conflict between staff factions is a key determinant of stress among correctional officers (Long, Skouksmith, Voges, and Roache 1986).

The ideological mandates of custody and rehabilitative treatment do not have to be mutually exclusive. The relationship between security officers and treatment facilitators can be a source of stress, or it can be a significant factor in dealing with stress effectively. Conflict between them may be an artificially contrived perception, without one the other is impossible to achieve (Vito 1994). To successfully offer to inmates a wide range of educational and other programs, it is first necessary to establish and maintain safety and security. The opportunity for meaningful treatment intervention can only be pursued in an orderly environment (Vito 1994). The very nature of "treatment versus security" represents a duality of purpose that is indivisible and incapable of separation, two different agendas with satisfactory if not always compatible results.

The correctional officer, in particular, is recognized as "the keystone to the success or failure of any kind of treatment program" (Allen and Simonsen 1992, p. 496). The correctional officer can be the single most important person in terms of influencing the inmate and having the potential for enhancing or minimizing, through his or her actions, the effectiveness of the various treatment programs (Glaser 1964; Teske and Williamson 1979; Wicks 1980).

This perspective has been the cornerstone of change in the design of treatment programs like therapeutic community and functional or unit team management; programs which incorporate the correctional officer into the treatment milieu. With treatment and correctional staff working together at the same location, "[t]he physical division that is traditionally established in the prison setting is eliminated" (Vito 1994, p. 4). Quite simply, in order to maintain effective security and at the same time provide meaningful treatment, the custodial and treatment staff must cooperate.

[1] An earlier version of this paper was published as D.A. Josi and D.K. Sechrest, "Treatment versus Security: Adversarial Relationship Between Treatment Facilitators and Correctional Officers," *The Journal of Offender Rehabilitation* 23, nos. 1–2 (1996): 167–184. Copyright © The Haworth Press Inc. Reprinted with permission of the publisher.

A series of interviews with the correctional officers and the treatment staff of a promising substance abuse treatment program located at a Southern California State Corrections facility suggests that the differing goals and individual backgrounds of the two factions can facilitate an adversarial "we versus them" attitude, a situation that has historically been a problem in correctional facilities. Despite the competitive nature of their relationship, staff members from both organizations expressed a guarded optimism in their ability to resolve areas of disagreement. A number of recommendations aimed at improving inter-group communication cooperation and understanding, most of which were suggested by the participants, are presented at the end of the paper.

Amity "RighTurn"

The Amity RighTurn Substance Abuse Treatment Program is operated for the California Department of Corrections by Amity Corporation, a private non-profit organization based in Tucson, Arizona. It operates a program at the R. J. Donovan Correctional Center near San Diego, California. As described in program materials and interviews with treatment staff, the Amity RighTurn program brings to the Donovan facility a model based on building relationships within a community that stresses honesty and the development of a non-substance using, non-criminal lifestyle. The uniqueness of the Amity program finds further expression in the composition of its treatment staff, their background and training, and their definitions of the treatment process.

Amity RighTurn is a 9 to 12 month intensive therapeutic community "in-prison" substance abuse program for 200 male inmates, with continuation services for up to 60 inmates paroling to San Diego County (Lowe 1992). The program began in November of 1990 and reached its maximum capacity in March 1991. A key requisite to effective treatment for illicit drug addiction is the willingness of the subject to admit they have a problem. Historically, the long-term success rate of individuals who attend mandatory drug treatment programs have not been very promising. Therefore, inmate participation in the Amity RighTurn program is strictly voluntary.

Inmates accepted into the program are housed in their own living and program units, segregated from the general prison population (Lowe 1992). Two portable trailers adjacent to their living unit provide classroom and meeting space for the RighTurn program. Inmate participants receive 20 hours of intensive programming per week. Their therapy schedule consists of group sessions (including psychodrama exercises), individual counseling, educational seminars, intensive workshops, and video replay. Inmates also participate in regular institutional education and employment programming (Lowe 1992).

Successful drug treatment for the incarcerated abuser include several significant dimensions: sufficient intensity and duration of program efforts, life skills acquisition and self-help components, adequate aftercare, administrative and material support, and a motivated and caring staff who have had life experiences similar to their own (Gandossy 1980; Elliott, Huizinga, and Ageton 1985; Chaiken and Johnson 1988;

Wexler, Falkin, and Lipton 1990). Although the RighTurn program is based on the successful therapeutic community model[2] some level of dissonance and distrust was found between the treatment facilitators and the correctional staff. Left unresolved, any level of mistrust and conflict between these two factions could affect the treatment process.

Evaluating Staff Relations

In 1992, research personnel from California State University, San Bernardino, conducted an evaluative study of drug treatment programs in California. The purpose was to find a specific program or individual program components that might contribute to a "model" drug treatment approach for confined adult and juvenile offenders (Sechrest and Josi 1992). Of those studied, only the Amity "RighTurn" Substance Abuse Program included interviews with both security and treatment personnel.

The overall goal of the visit to the program at R.J. Donovan Correctional Facility was to conduct a comprehensive evaluation. However, in 1992, not enough participants had completed the RJD/Amity program to warrant an outcome study. As an alternative, it was decided, in conjunction with the California Department of Corrections Office of Substance Abuse Programs, to augment their ongoing process evaluation through staff interviews. During a two day period in May, 1992, project staff interviewed twelve of the Amity/RighTurn treatment staff and 15 correctional staff assigned to the treatment program in several areas of interest.

Amity Treatment Staff

At the time of the initial visit, Amity employed 13 full-time and 8 part-time treatment counselors in the program. Ethnic and cultural demographics of the staff members were similar to the inmate population; nearly half were ethnic minorities, 11 of the 13 counselors had a history of substance abuse and considered themselves in recovery. The length of recovery ranged from 5 to 25 years, with the majority in excess of 15 years of abstinence. It was not determined whether their abuse histories were similar to those of the inmates (e.g., alcohol, cocaine, heroin, polyabuse).

The majority of the treatment staff had received some type of certification through either Amity, college courses, or through previous work experience. Four indicated prior experience dealing with youths at risk; two others had worked as

---

[2] Adapted from the successful therapeutic model first developed by Synanon in the early 1960s, the institution-based therapeutic community treatment modality has been shown to be very effective both in the treatment of incarcerated abusers for their drug addiction and more specifically in the reduction of offender recidivism rates. Wexler, Falkin, and Lipton (1990) conducted an evaluation research study on the nation's largest institution-based therapeutic community, the Stay'N Out program operated by the State of New York. The Stay'N Out program was designed for adult offenders and has operated for over 14 years. According to Wexler et al., "This is the first large-scale study ($N = 1500$) that provides convincing evidence that prison-based TC treatment can produce significant reductions in recidivism rates for males and females" (Wexler et al. 1990, p. 71). R.J. Donovan's RighTurn Substance Abuse Treatment Program is a prototype of the Stay'N Out program.

employment counselors for either public (municipal) or private organizations. Length of experience in treatment programs ranged from ten months to 22 years. Half of the staff had a minimum of 3 to 5 years job-related experience, and the rest averaged more than 13 years experience in the treatment field. Ten of the 12 full-time counselors had been in drug treatment programs, including Amity and Synanon; over half of those who had prior treatment were involved in a therapeutic community. Only one had ever received private, one-on-one therapy. The Amity training program is central to the development of the counseling staff. Four of the staff interviewed were Amity graduates, with others in the process of completing the mandatory requirements.

Each member was first interviewed separately, using a series of open-ended questions. Although not part of the original plan, all 13 were eventually re-interviewed as a group. The purpose of the follow-up interview session was to discuss possible solutions to the problems mentioned during the "one-on-one" interviews. The interviewers found the Amity staff to be a highly motivated group of dedicated professionals who were not at all hesitant to discuss their prior substance abuse history. In addition, each openly discussed the ongoing program in an honest, forthright manner, without the usual "scripted" dialogue often associated with contract service organizations.

California Department of Corrections Staff

During a two day period in May, 1992, interviews were conducted with 15 members of the correctional staff assigned to the Amity RightTurn program. Ten correctional officers, one Lieutenant, one Sergeant, and the three correctional counselors (correctional officers who have received additional substance abuse counseling to assist the Amity treatment facilitators) were interviewed. Five of the 15 correctional staff interviewed had been to a 40 hour training session at the Amity Ranch in January, 1991; three correctional officers were no longer involved with the Amity RightTurn program. Questions were asked concerning training, circumstances leading to program involvement, comparisons between working with this treatment program and a more routine assignment, and relations with Amity RighTurn treatment staff and other correctional staff.

Officers who started with the program came to it in different ways. Those presently assigned to the treatment unit arrived there on a purely rotational basis. None requested assignment to the Amity living quarters, and none was interviewed about a possible interest in the program prior to their assignment. All of the officers currently working in the unit stated that they liked working with the Amity participants and had no intention of attempting to transfer before the normal rotation.

The 10 correctional officers were interviewed individually using a list of pre-approved open-ended questions. Initially a bit hesitant, by the end of the interview all were quite candid and open with their individual feelings about the treatment program, the Amity personnel, and the corrections department in general. Overall the interview team was confident of the officer's sincerity and honesty. Middle management personnel (Sergeant and Lieutenant) were interviewed together. The three correctional counselors were first interviewed individually and eventually together as team members. Counselors were candid and forthright in their answers. However, the two management personnel were "guarded" in certain responses. This was not unexpected due to their apparent need to present answers consistent with CDC guidelines.

Interview Outcomes

Treatment Staff

Interviews with treatment facilitators found evidence of a highly motivated staff, composed primarily of former substance abusers, who bring to the program a level of commitment and dedication necessary to successful treatment outcome. When asked to describe their interactions and relations with non-Amity prison staff members, most felt a majority of the correctional staff did not support the treatment program and would like to see them fail. The staffs' perception of correctional officer disapproval appeared to revolve around their previous use and abuse of drugs, even though the average length of abstinence was 15 years. Although comfortable with their backgrounds and proud of their accomplishments, a majority of the treatment facilitators felt as though the correctional staff treated them like "second class citizens," and in some cases "little better than the inmates."

The issue of ex-addict success with the incarcerated abuser is not without controversy (Flaherty 1992). According to Amity personnel, the employment of ex-substance abusers as therapeutic counselors is a crucial aspect in gaining participant trust; the declaration of one's past history demonstrates the effects of program participation and helps establish trust and honesty. What the facilitators refer to as the "story" provides a model of present and future behavior which affects participants in two ways. First, as inmates learn the treatment process, they develop their own skills of personal disclosure and become comfortable with telling their own stories. Second, and perhaps more importantly, the treatment staff "stories" allow participants to see staff members as role models—well-adjusted individuals who have managed to "clean up their act." According to Amity personnel, this "show" of staff success provides participants with a hopeful image of their own future.

Most researchers agree that long-term substance abuse is not easily "cured." Treatment is an ongoing process that must be continually reinforced through focused support counseling by qualified professionals. A principal with the Amity Corporation noted, "once drug dependence has developed, it can persist as a chronic condition, and relapse is often the rule" (Anglin and Hser 1990). Some argue the high relapse potential of addicts is reason enough not to use ex-addicts as treatment counselors. According to Flaherty (1992), ". . . former addicts who become drug therapists often relapse themselves and therefore cannot always be considered positive role models" (p. 21).

Treatment Staff Recommendations   In general, members the treatment staff felt these issues and other minor problems could be reduced if not completely resolved through direct interaction with members of the correctional staff. Problem resolution fell into two general areas. First, they supported an examination and review of what appeared to many as the "adversarial" nature of the interaction process between the correctional officers, including the administrative staff, and the treatment staff. Many expressed the belief that dissension between the two factions could be eliminated through increased dialogue about each faction's particular objectives. Solutions involved training of correctional staff in the Amity model, and the establishment of some structured interaction among those who share responsibility for this population.

The second recommendation concerns continued attention to treatment staff burnout. Although no evidence of such burnout was discovered through the interview process, and the training program appeared to address this problem more than adequately, this recommendation emphasized the need to monitor treatment staff job-related stress and employee burnout levels.

Correctional Staff

From all indications, the warden and his executive staff were completely supportive of this innovative treatment program, but cooperation and support from correctional line staff were somewhat mixed. It was not altogether surprising that a majority of the officers interviewed appeared wary and suspicious of the treatment program. Many felt the treatment facilitators had little regard for security regulations and the general policies of the institution. More than half felt a "we versus them" attitude existed between the Amity treatment counselors and the correctional officers. Central to this perception was an overall consensus by a majority of officers that the Amity staff "blatantly" and "willfully" violated institution security procedures. According to one officer, ". . . their willful disregard for institutional security procedures is going to get someone seriously hurt or killed. We have repeatedly warned them about minor violations and how they can escalate into major problems within the walls. It is almost as though they violate the rules on purpose."

Comments such as "ex-dopers treating inmates is like the blind leading the blind" and "they [treatment staff] care more about the inmates comfort and well being than they do about following the rules" or "they [treatment staff] purposely violate the regulations against prisoner contraband to turn the inmates against us" were the sentiments expressed by a majority of the correctional officers.

The correctional officers indicated that security issues were a continuing problem and stated that they had often had, and continue to have, problems with Amity staff on security matters. Many of their concerns centered around security violations in the trailers. The consensus was that either treatment staff did not realize they were violating security procedures or were purposefully ignoring them. The majority felt Amity staff should write incident reports for violations such as chewing gum (contraband), viewing unauthorized movies (in the program trailers), and swearing at visitors. In addition, correctional supervisors voiced the same concerns over contraband (gum, movies, etc.) as the line officers. The supervisors felt as though Amity RighTurn staff thought the trailers were off limits to them for purposes of security and safety.

Scheduling was a problem, in that officers felt the Amity staff should maintain and not deviate from their previously approved schedules. According to the officers, safety within an institution requires predictability and consistency. Many felt as though the treatment staff were either unaware, did not understand, or just did not care about their concerns. A few of the correctional officers suggested that the treatment staff went out of their way to "sabotage" the officers efforts to reinforce inmate regulations.

The correctional staff also expressed their concern over what the majority perceive as "favoritism" shown to program inmates by the treatment staff. Although a few officers did mention the Amity staff was helpful in solving problems on the unit, most complained of the "less formal" attitude of the Amity inmates toward them as a result of inadequate supervision by Amity staff. "The Amity inmates are more verbal than inmates from other units," and thus the officers had to listen to them more closely and more often.

The officers felt the inmates were trying to work out problems and oftentimes needed someone to listen to them. However, all of the officers felt like the Amity RighTurn inmates expected more privileges than other inmates. Many stated that the inmates were "in and out" of the building more often than normal. Approximately one third of the officers interviewed felt that the inmates behaved quite differently in diverse situations. As one officer suggested, "When they are in the trailers, they act concerned and serious about improving their lives. When they are on the yard, they act like all the other inmates. When they are in Building 15, they act like spoiled children who want more care and attention than the normal inmate."

The correctional counselors also criticized Amity staff for the "adversarial" nature of their relationship to correctional staff. According to one counselor, working conditions would improve "if the 'we versus them' mentality of the Amity RighTurn staff towards the correctional officers could be alleviated." In addition, the correctional counselors felt that relationships between the two staffs would improve dramatically if the treatment staff would pay more attention to security concerns. As one counselor stated, "Amity counselors need to pay attention to the rules, instead of acting like dope fiends."

There was an expressed concern by the correctional counselors that the program started too quickly and without enough preparation by Amity staff and CDC personnel. In time the situation improved, but problems still remain. For example, correctional supervisors voiced their concern over the lack of any discernible difference in the number of disciplinary reports (115s) filed and positive urine tests found as compared to the non-program living units. These respondents felt that by virtue of being enrolled in the Amity RighTurn program both of these numbers should be considerably lower than those of the general population.

The three correctional officers who had Amity training rated the treatment staff higher than the seven who had not had this training. Effective communication and cooperation between members of both factions were mentioned by all three of these officers as necessary elements to increased understanding. If the individual respondent felt as though the member(s) of the treatment staff communicated and was cooperative, his impression was usually positive. The lack of communication and cooperation only reinforced an officers negative perceptions about members of the Amity staff. This was true of the correctional supervisors as well. The correctional counselors felt their relationships with treatment staff were from "fair" to "very good." All were communicating daily with some members of the staff, but were prevented from getting more personally involved by their significant workload.

Concern was also expressed about the lack of "team building" with treatment staff. Also officers wanted timely information about program activities. Officers mentioned that they did not feel like an integral part of the treatment team. As one respondent stated, "Not being part of the treatment team, we don't know enough about the program to get into deep discussions with Amity staff." Over half of the correctional officers felt like a "them versus us" relationship existed between treatment and correctional staff. Because the inmates acted differently in the program as opposed to the yard or their housing unit, officers often had to handle problems generated in the trailers without knowing all the details of the incident. Another correctional officer felt that the group process was a source of problems in stating that "Amity staff makes the inmate angry in group and then they cut them off, and they are still angry. Then the inmates are sent back over to the building [Building 15], and we have to deal with this anger." The consensus among the correctional officers was that the Amity staff treated them as an enemy instead of a teammate. The correctional counselors also commented on a perceived lack of cooperation between treatment and correctional staff.

Correctional Staff Recommendations   When asked for suggestions to improve this interaction between corrections and treatment personnel, all the correctional officers emphasized the need for improved communication. The majority of the officers indicated that they wanted information to make the program work but were not invited to come and find out about the program by either the Amity staff or CDC supervisors. The officers overwhelmingly supported the inclusion of more mandatory staff meetings (involving officers, supervisors, counselors, and treatment staff), if held during the normal workday. As one officer remarked, "We need time to set aside to go to staff group and be better informed." However, none of the correctional officers were willing to go to group meetings on their own time. They felt it was CDC's responsibility to set aside time and resources for them to attend staff group.

When asked how working with the Amity RighTurn program affected their relations with other correctional staff, most of the correctional officers indicated it had little effect. One, however, stated he felt "like I have to defend myself a lot to friends who are totally against the program." The correctional counselors did indicate some friction with other correctional staff and other counselors, based on their involvement with the treatment program.

The correctional counselors felt that both treatment staff and correctional staff needed additional training. They suggested that correctional officers be given training at the Ranch in Tucson, feeling that Ranch attendance was a integral part of the future of the Amity RighTurn program.

Conflicts over scheduling and security concerns point to a marked need to bring the separate missions of treatment and custody together. Simply put, the treatment staff must begin to contribute to security measures and the correctional staff must become more aware and informed of treatment issues. The skills used to provide services to the inmate residents (e.g., seminars, workshops, and groups) can be used to bring the important components of treatment and security together to contribute to the common goal of reducing drug use and producing productive citizens.

In an article by the warden and treatment staff of the facility, the problems cited in this study were not mentioned. In fact, Warden Ratelle indicated that there had been "really . . . no downside to the Amity program during the past six years" (Mullen, Ratelle, Abraham, and Boyle 1996, p. 121). Moreover, they cite findings of an independent study showing that just under half (46.2%) of the Amity graduates are reincarcerated as compared to 63% of those receiving no treatment, and only 26.2% of the Amity graduates who completed their residential program recidivated. Apparently the problems of correctional officers and treatment staff have been re-solved, at least to some degree. As Warden Ratelle indicates, "We have an excellent staff here at RJD—and they are getting better each year" (p. 121). The methods used to overcome some of these problems and create the "buy-in by correctional staff," which they mention as a key factor in program success, should be documented in a follow-up study.

Discussion

Successful substance abuse treatment within a penal setting is dependent upon the level of cooperation between treatment and custody. Intra-group conflict however, is a barrier to program success. A series of interviews with correctional personnel and the treatment staff of a substance abuse treatment program for incarcerated male inmates revealed a level of distrust and suspicion between the two factions. It was determined that their perception of goal differences (treatment versus security) and their failure to communicate with each other was a major contributor to their mutual distrust. While conflict between these two factions is not unusual, as thoroughly documented in prison treatment literature, the problem must be acknowledged and addressed (Hepburn and Albonetti 1980).

It is not unusual for correctional employees to suffer from occupational related stress syndrome and job burnout due to unresolved conflict issues; both of which are well-documented among correctional workers and treatment providers (Johnson 1977; Kahn 1978; Teske and Williamson 1979; Bartol 1979; Poole and Regoli 1980, 1983; Hepburn 1985; Crouch 1986; Cullen, Link, Cullen, and Wolfe 1990; Patterson 1992). The Amity/RighTurn program presents a double challenge because their staff occupy both roles. In addition, workers within the correctional environment may also be susceptible to certain forms of cynicism and authoritarianism just as the police are, perhaps for many of the same reasons.

There are certainly other factors that influence the onset of job stress that may well increase occupational burnout within the correctional setting. Among these would be the danger, fear, and isolation first identified by Skolnick (1966). The situations institutional personnel have to deal with are sometimes complicated and explosive, and the proper reaction to them requires a thorough understanding of dyadic and group relations of human and personal behavior, an understanding of what makes prisoners act as they do, and an appreciation of the impact that their actions will have upon others.

According to Vito (1994), support for treatment programs among correctional officers has been underestimated. In addition, officers tend to underestimate the degree to which others share their belief in rehabilitation. They often feel that their peers are alienated and are more custody-oriented than they are (Vito 1994). A number of studies have found that officers support treatment as a legitimate goal (Duffee 1986; Williamson 1990, among others). Yet, they also underestimate the proportion of their fellow officers who were sympathetic toward inmates and treatment.

Individual officers believe in rehabilitation, yet they also feel that their fellow officers do not. Therefore, custodial staff generally support treatment programs, but that support is often unexpressed. The paradoxical nature of this phenomena was evident in a number of the correctional officer interviews. When interviewed as a group, most denounced the efficacy of inmate treatment programs, however, when re-interviewed in private, many expressed their personal belief in treatment and rehabilitation efforts for the incarcerated substance abuser.

Communication between the "RighTurn" custody staff and the treatment staff was somewhat ineffective, which often resulted in poor working relationships. A leading indicator of the communication deficit was the level of distrust between the two staff factions. Statements received from the correctional officers suggests a general distrust of the Amity staff is, in part, due to the individual's (treatment staff) personal background and substance abuse history. Ex-addict/offenders are viewed as deviant/deviants by a number of correctional officers. In this era of "professionalization," they are not seen as "professionals."

Central to the proverbial "line in the sand" perception of their relationship (or lack thereof) with members of the treatment staff, were numerous references to "an overall lack of communication and cooperation" from all parties, not just the Amity personnel. Officers with positive experiences were those who interacted and communicated with the Amity staff on a regular basis. Not unexpectedly, those with limited contact were the most suspicious and distrusting of the treatment staff. The lack of communication and interaction between the two factions reinforced their negative opinions.

The correctional officers' dogmatic position only fuels an existing paradox for the Amity staff. If, or as, the treatment facilitators become "more professional" they will be accepted by the correctional staff. Professionalization would mean greater *distance* from the addict/offender population. However, according to the Amity staff, their strength is their closeness to the addict/offender personality. Can this paradox be resolved? Probably not. The correctional staff can be trained to work with the Amity staff, but they *must* retain their distance from ex-offenders to preserve their job identity. The existing line between correctional officers and offenders is already dangerously thin. Oddly, the treatment facilitators seek professional status to shed the ex-addict identity so they can deal with the correctional officers/organization better. Unfortunately, as they build trust with the corrections staff, they risk losing the trust of the inmate/addicts—they will be seen as defectors to the administrative organization. Treatment facilitators must preserve the "we-them" notion in order to be effective, yet find a successful resolution to the existing communications gap.

The resolution of the paradox has been sought in unit management where it is okay for the correctional officer to be involved as a treatment facilitator with the inmates. However, it is the correctional officer who does it, "others" still will be outsiders. Perhaps the barriers to the correctional staff are lower, trust greater. How can we know for sure?

Implementation of the types of recommendations suggested by both factions should improve relations between the correctional officer staff and the treatment staff. While it is doubtful that these barriers will ever be completely removed, there are indications that properly trained and involved correctional officers can be an asset to a treatment program. In fact, as is well documented, their participation is critical to success.

Further development of these types of recommendations might be applicable to *all* staff interactions in correctional facilities. Education, medical, library, recreation, and related program staff also experience these problems. The reduction of barriers to interaction by staff will serve to improve programs and present a consistent and unified message to inmates regarding expectations of them by all staff.

REFERENCES

Allen, H.E., and C.E. Simonsen. *Corrections in America: An Introduction.* New York: Macmillan, 1992.

American Correctional Association. *Directory of Juvenile and Adult Correctional Departments, Institutions, Agencies and Paroling Authorities.* Laurel, MD: American Correctional Association, 1995.

American Correctional Association. "Who Is Safer in Male Maximum Security Prisons?" *Corrections Today* (April 1996).

Anglin, M.D., Hser Y. "Treatment of Drug Abuse." In M. Tonry and J.Q. Wilson (eds.), *Drugs and Crime*, pp. 393–460. Chicago: University of Chicago Press, 1990.

Bartol, K.M. "Professionalization as a Predictor of Organizational Commitment, Role Stress, and Turnover." *Academy of Management Journal* 22, no. 4 (1979): 815–821.

Blumstein, A. "Prison Crowding." In *National Institute of Justice: Crime File Study Guide.* Washington, DC: U.S. Department of Justice.

Bureau of Justice Statistics. *Prison and Jail Inmates, 1995.* Washington, DC: U.S. Department of Justice, 1996.

Camp, C.G., and G.M. Camp. *The Corrections Yearbook 1997.* Criminal Justice Institute, Inc. New York, 1997.

Chaiken, J., and B.D. Johnson. *Characteristics of Different Types of Drug-Involved Offenders.* Washington, DC: National Institute of Justice, 1988.

Cheek, G.E., and M.S. Miller. "The Experience of Stress for Correction Officers: A Double-Bind Theory of Correctional Staff." *Journal of Criminal Justice* 11, no. 2 (1983): 105–120.

Crouch, B.M. "Prison Guards on the Line." In K.C. Haas and G.P. Alpert (eds.), *The Dilemmas of Punishment*, pp. 177–206. Prospect Heights, IL: Waveland, 1986.

Cullen, F., B.G. Link, J.B. Cullen, and N.T. Wolfe. "How Satisfying Is Prison Work? A Comparative Occupational Approach." *Journal of Offender Counseling, Services and Rehabilitation* 14, no. 2 (1990): 89–108.

Duffee, D. *Correctional Management: Change and Control in Correctional Organizations.* Prospect Heights, IL: Waveland, 1986.

Elliott, D.S., D. Huizinga, and S.S. Ageton. *Explaining Delinquency and Drug Use.* Newbury, CA: Sage, 1985.

Flaherty, T.J. "You Need Not Be an Ex-Addict to Help Addicted Offenders." *Corrections Today* 54 (1992): 20–22.

Gandossy, R.P. *Drugs and Crime: A Survey and Analysis of the Literature.* Washington, DC: National Institute of Justice, 1980.

Glaser, D. *The Effectiveness of a Prison and Parole System.* Indianapolis: Bobbs-Merrill, 1964.

Hepburn, J.R. "The Exercise of Power in Coercive Organizations: A Study of Prison Guards." *Criminology* 23, no. 1 (1985): 145–164.

Hepburn, J.R., and C. Albonetti. "Role Conflict in Correctional Institutions: An Empirical Examination of the Treatment-Custody Dilemma Among Correctional Staff." *Criminology* 17, no. 4 (1980): 45–459.

Johnson, R. "Ameliorating Prison Stress: Some Helping Roles for Custodial Officers." *International Journal of Criminology and Penology* 5 (1977): 263–273.

Johnson, W.B., and A.E. Packer. *Workforce 2000: Work and Workers for the 21st Century.* Indianapolis: Hudson Institute, 1987.

Kahn, R.L. "Job Burnout: Prevention and Remedies." *Public Welfare* 30 (1978): 61–63.

Legislative Analyst Office. *Crime in California.* Sacramento, CA: Legislative Analyst Office, 1995.

Lombardo, L.X. *Guards Imprisoned: Correctional Officers at Work.* New York: Elsevier, 1982.

Long, N., G. Skouksmith, K. Voges, and S. Roache. "Stress in Prison Staff: An Occupational Study." *Criminology* 24 (1986): 331–345.

Lowe, L.L. *A Process Evaluation of the R. J. Donovan Correctional Facility Amity Corporation Substance Abuse Program.* Sacramento: California Department of Corrections Office of Substance Abuse Programs, 1992.

McShane, M.D. "Institutional Crowding." In M.D. McShane and F.P. Williams III (eds.), *Encyclopedia of American Prisons*, pp. 134–137. New York: Garland, 1996.

Mullen, R., J. Ratelle, E. Abraham, and J. Boyle. "California Program Reduces Recidivism and Saves Tax Dollars." *Corrections Today* (August 1996): 118–123.

Patterson, B.L. "Job Experience and Perceived Job Stress Among Police, Correctional, and Probation/Parole Officers." *Criminal Justice and Behavior* 19, no. 3 (1992): 260–285.

Philliber, S. "Thy Brother's Keeper: A Review of the Literature on Correctional Officers." *Justice Quarterly* 4 (1987): 9–37.

Poole, E.D., and R.M. Regoli. "Role Stress, Custody Orientation, and Disciplinary Actions." *Criminology* 18, no. 3 (1980): 215–226.

Poole, E.D., and R. Regoli. "Professionalism, Role Conflict, Work Alienation and Anomia: A Look at Prison Management." *The Social Science Journal* 20 (1983): 63–70.

Rowan, J.R. *More Female Correctional Officers Mean Fewer Assaults Overall—Another Myth Debunked.* Roseville, MN: Criminal and Juvenile Justice International, 1997.

Sechrest, D.K., and D.A. Josi. *Substance Abuse Programs for Incarcerated Offenders in Four Settings.* Riverside, CA: Robert Presley Institute for Corrections Research and Training, 1992.

Shamir, B., and A. Drory. "Some Correlates of Prison Guards' Beliefs." *Criminal Justice and Behavior* 8 (1982): 233–249.

Shichor, D., and D.K. Sechrest. *Three Strikes and You're Out: Vengeance as Public Policy.* Newbury, CA: Sage, 1996.

Skolnick, J. *Justice Without Trial.* New York: Wiley, 1966.

Slate, R.N. *Stress Levels and Thoughts of Quitting of Correctional Personnel: Do Perceptions of Participatory Management Make a Difference?* Ann Arbor, MI: University Microfilms, 1993.

Stinchcomb, J.B. "Correctional Officer Stress: Is Training Missing the Target?" In B. Wolford and P. Lawrenz (eds.), *Issues in Correctional Training and Casework*, pp. 19–23. New York: Psychilit Abstracts, 1986.

Teske, R., and H. Williamson. "Correctional Officers' Attitudes Toward Selected Treatment Programs." *Criminal Justice and Behavior* 6, no. 1 (1979): 59–66.

Travis, L.F., M.D. Schwartz, and T.R. Clear. *Corrections: An Issues Approach*, 2d ed. Cincinnati, OH: Anderson, 1980.

Vito, G.F. "Treatment and Custody: Two Sides of the Correctional Coin." Paper presented at the meeting of the 124th Congress of Correction of the American Correctional Association, St. Louis, 1994.

Wexler, H.K., G.P. Falkin, and D.S. Lipton. "Outcome Evaluation of a Prison Therapeutic Community for Substance Abuse Treatment." *Criminal Justice and Behavior* 17 (1990): 71–92.

Wicks, R.J. *Guard! Society's Professional Prisoner.* Houston, TX: Gulf, 1980.

Williamson, H.E. *The Corrections Profession.* Newbury Park, CA: Sage, 1990.

Wunder, A. "Corrections Systems Must Bear the Burden of New Legislation." *Corrections Compendium* 20, no. 8 (1995): 7.

Zupan, L.L. "The Progress of Women Correctional Officers in All-Male Prisons." In I. Moyer (ed.), *The Changing Role of Women in the Criminal Justice System*, 2d ed., pp. 323–343. Prospect Heights, IL: Waveland, 1992.

9

Technological Change

The technology available to correctional officers has escalated greatly in the past ten years, essentially since the development of the personal computer and related technologies. The correctional officer has not developed or introduced most of the technology he or she must use, although officers and other users should have some input into the choices made for new technologies. Whether this input occurs or not, it is important that the modern correctional officer be familiar with new technologies, with the most important being computer applications. ACA standards (1990) on information systems and research specifies policy and procedures for information storage and retrieval, master indexes, and daily reports.

The term *technology* includes a wide range of devices, from the simple to the very complex. It includes personal computers, video surveillance cameras, communications equipment (e.g., cell phones, body alarms), metal detection devices, security fences, restraint devices, identification aids, inmate purchasing systems (i.e., "swiping" credit cards for purchases), drug detection devices, fire safety equipment, and video arraignments in jails. Computers can be of use in classification and disciplinary proceedings. Weapons such as stun guns, or the "electric disabler" (ACA standard 3-4191) also are important new technologies, although their use may fall into the "malicious" or "sadistic" use of punishment under the wrong conditions (see Chapter 6, "Civil Liability"). A California court restricted the use of rubber-pellet stun guns (technically a 37mm grenade launcher) on violent or agitated mentally disturbed inmates ("Court Upholds Limit" 1995). A psychiatrist had to consent to its use, which drastically reduced the use of the guns. ACA (1990) standards provide specific criteria for weapons use.

The officer is a computer "end user" who must maintain an operational focus: how can technology support security and safety concerns in the facility? Can computers help keep track of inmates, and can they improve staff performance? Traditional texts in criminal justice say little about technology, but a quick tour of the vendor booths at any of the national association meetings will make anyone aware of the possibilities. And all of the new applications require some degree of training to familiarize staff members with their usefulness. Stories are told of expensive electronic bracelets to track released offenders that are not used because staff members are not trained in their use.

COMPUTERS IN CORRECTIONS

There was life before computers, especially in correctional institutions, where implementation has often lagged behind the free world. This is not an attempt to teach the use of computers but to provide an awareness of the possibilities and realities presented to the correctional officer for improving performance. Computers have become very accessible in the past five to ten years; and this accessibility often accrues to inmates, where security breaches can occur. What could be done only on a mainframe computer maintained by a central office can now be done on a personal computer (formerly a microcomputer) located in the facility.

It is sufficient for our purposes to note that all management processes now share one common characteristic: operational success is dependent on the collection, analysis, storage, and retrieval of information. There is an increasing dependence on information. Therefore, the personal computer has become both a survival tool and a problem. As noted, computers around inmates can present serious problems of security, and several jurisdictions have had to learn how to restrict inmate access to this new technology.

Because computer technology, particularly the personal computer, has revolutionized communication and is in most institutions, information processing and computer literacy has become critical, if for no other reason than to see that inmates do not gain control of this technology and use it to their advantage. For example, everyone has read a story about a jail inmate who has broken into the inmate database and arranged for his release. Inmates have also used on-line services to conduct businesses, even arranging to have checks sent to them illegally. On the other hand, secure computer terminals on living units can be used to appraise inmates of their current legal status, especially in jails. This application can relieve tension and anxiety over court dates and inaccurate information that may lead to problems.

Information Systems

An "information system" includes the concepts, personnel, and supporting technology for the collection, organization, and delivery of information for administrative use. Information falls into two main categories:

1. *Standard information* is the data required for operational control. The daily count at a prison, payroll data in a personnel office, and caseload levels in a probation agency are obvious examples of standard information. This information is often called *point in time* information because it is available for immediate access, on demand.
2. In addition, an information system must be capable of supplying *demand information*. A manager does not need to know immediately how many prisoners will be eligible for release during the next 12 months by offense, length of term, and month of release, but an information system must be capable of generating such a report when required. These generally are called *periodic reports*.

Shugoll and Dempsey (1983) prefer the terms (1) *operational data*, case information used in daily decision making, and (2) *statistical data*, aggregate data compiled for reports and statistical summaries. Whatever terminology is used, it follows that an information system should be capable of collecting data for statistical use and providing itemized listings for operational or administrative action. Correctional officers are not only users of these data but they often are the individuals who enter these data into the system or supervise its entry. In this sense, they require basic training in computer language and technology.

Supervisors and correctional officers will want to know the following types of information on a regular basis:

1. Summary of offender events and results of events, such as transfers to alternate control, hearings and actions by the board, and releases to parole;
2. Personnel summaries, including appointments, assignments, relief from assignments, and separations;
3. Event summaries by population characteristics;
4. Event summaries by personnel characteristics;
5. Fiscal events summarized by programs, such as expenditures for facilities and equipment and personnel.

A system capable of routine period-in-time reports of these kinds also will be capable of a wide variety of demand information.

Federal Bureau of Prisons

Probably one of the most sophisticated management information systems is the key indicators system (KI/SSS) maintained by the Federal Bureau of Prisons (Sechrest, McShane, and Haefeli 1994). The system is a major part of their strategic planning and operates across nine areas: administration; health services; industries, education, and vocational training; program review; information, policy, and public affairs; correctional programs; human resource management; community corrections and detention; and the Office of the General Counsel and Review. Key indicators is a database of 2,000 data elements and offender or institutional characteristics, readily accessible by the CEO (warden), regional director, or executive staff.

To stay current with changing management needs, KI/SSS is monitored and continually updated to capture new information. KI/SSS provides current information on a specific area or discipline, like any MIS system, and provides the longitudinal or trend data needed for comparative analysis. Other than the mainframe applications that feed KI/SSS, several local PC-based applications (e.g., dBase) are used to collect and enter data on operations and significant incidents, including use of force, assaults, and urinalysis. Data are collected from each institution through a standard electronic form and transmitted to the appropriate division via an electronic mail system. Each month data from the various mainframe computer systems are combined with data from the bureau's local PC-based and institutional self-reporting applications and downloaded to a compact disk (CD-ROM). The CDs are distributed to each institutional warden, regional director, executive staff, and to selected branch chiefs, updating last month's CD. Currently, more than 120 PC locations throughout the bureau are on the monthly CD distribution list. Even though the KI/SSS system continually is undergoing improvements, it represents a very sophisticated approach to information management.

Two state systems that were studied (Sechrest et al. 1994) provide a view of the types of applications the correctional officer may encounter. The Illinois DOC management information system has 15 components that are used to track operations. These generally are grouped by the operations they support: a budgetary accounting reporting system (BARS) and an automated roster management system (ARMS), which may have the greatest application for correctional officers.

The ARMS maintains security posts and produces reports for each institution. It provides a daily roster, master roster, seniority lists, and training reports. Additions, changes, and deletions for post and employee data can be done on-line. Computer files include two databases, each containing 7,500 records. Systems have been established for affirmative action reporting, auditing, and monitoring the hiring process. Systems are in place within the Illinois central management services (CMS) computer system, as part of the payroll system, that are designed to monitor the hiring process and to track affirmative action hiring. The system also maintains an automated trust fund system to monitor canteen purchases and an automated property control system.

An offender tracking system (OTS) allows tracking offenders in the system. Incident and crime reporting also are automated. The OTS system admits inmates into the system and is used to determine their security classification and reclassification levels. It oversees transfers of records, housing placement, program and assignments changes, tracking of scheduled institutional movements, and writs, bonds, detainers, warrants, and furlough documents. Population counts are maintained by tracking cell house changes and movements. Health and dental information is kept in this system. Parole preparation information is kept in the system, which also tracks discharge dates (sentence calculation). More than 130 reports are available to users.

The New Jersey Department of Corrections (NJ DOC) has two primary computer systems for processing critical inmate and administrative computerized functions. Thirteen applications are run at each of the department's 15 institutional sites:

- *Inmate information* tracks data required by the correctional staff for terminal display, regular reports, and ad hoc reports. These reports include release date, conviction data, demographic data, work programs, educational programs, aliases, and disciplinary information. The system has interfaces with the inmate banking, health care, and pharmacy applications.
- *Inmate banking* records inmates' monetary transactions, separating personal money from earnings resulting from work-release assignment. It produces monthly statements for each inmate and reports for internal affairs identifying

potential patterns for contraband transactions. This application has a close interface with the canteen application.

- *Canteen and commissary* tracks inmate requests for canteen purchases. It automatically rejects items that exceed quantity restrictions, location restrictions, and items that cause a negative balance in the inmate's account. It maintains a canteen inventory, automatically debits the inmate's account, and provides a list of items purchased by an inmate that are restricted due to dietary assignments.
- *Custody officer scheduling* provides a complete working roster of all custody officers, including their shift, division, days off, job assignment, and leave schedules. It tracks seven overtime lists to ensure fairness of overtime call-ins according to union contract agreements. This application has interfaces with the personnel and time and attendance applications.
- *Personnel information* tracks all data the department requires to produce personnel reports, such as leave balance reports, late record listings, absence listings, and service award listings. It automatically updates employee records for annual leave accruals and percentage cost-of-living adjustments.
- *Time and attendance* integrates data from the custody officer scheduling system and the personnel information application to produce time and attendance reports and exception reports for payroll purposes. On a biweekly basis, it provides all time worked and leave statistics to institutional timekeepers for payroll processing.
- *Fixed assets* tracks departmental assets over $300 and meets the requirements of the NJ Treasury Department's directives for each state agency to maintain records of such assets.
- *Pharmacy* tracks inmate prescription orders, provides prescription labels, provides drug contraindication data, and maintains inventory control.
- *Health* tracks inmate visits with doctors or nurses, symptoms, diagnosis, prescribed treatment, and appointment control.
- *Financial management* provides accounting control over appropriated accounts, purchase orders, and accounts payable.
- *Materials management* maintains inventory controls for all institutional goods, products, and supplies.
- *Training history* provides firearms training records, qualification and requalification status, and an automated reschedule notification function. This module is integrated with the officer scheduling module.
- *Networking*, working through the central office, automatically transfers the computerized record of inmates and employees transferred or reassigned from one facility to another.

Systems such as these provide a basis for understanding the capabilities of information systems in corrections. Whatever system is being used, correctional officers must be trained in it initially and receive periodic updates, whether through regular training or through informal contact with system representatives.

ADDITIONAL TECHNOLOGIES

Security

Communications equipment (e.g., cell phones, body alarms) are becoming more sophisticated, as are metal detection devices, to include metal scanners and drug "sniffing" devices. Security fences have become a matter of greater concern as electrified fences are being developed. The liability implications of these types of fences is yet to be determined. The potentially lethal device is installed between perimeter fences. The electrified wires are charged with 5,100 volts and various safety features are provided, including warning signs. It is acclaimed in California as a cost savings of $2 million annually in a typical prison because it eliminates some perimeter towers (*Electrified Fences* c. 1995). More conventional "sensor" fences with computerized tracking (which electric fences also have) also require knowledge of computers.

Improved body alarms and protective devices that help ensure officer safety will require continual assessment and testing. Even key control has the potential to be automated, and inmate identification now includes the possibility of scanning retinas. Drug detection technologies are improving every day, and although these are mostly in the hands of medical personnel, officers must understand when to use them and how results are to be interpreted. Correctional officers should maintain a healthy skepticism regarding these devices until they are fully tested. Again, nothing substitutes for good training in inmate management.

Even though the use of video cameras can be useful in security, they can present problems. Based on both professional standards and court decrees, reliance on audio or video monitors does not constitute adequate supervision, and they do not substitute for staff supervision and personal contact. American Correctional Association (1990) standards recommend the use of such equipment primarily in hallways, elevators, corridors, or at points on the security perimeter, such as entrances and exits.

Video Arraignments

A new procedure in many jurisdictions is the use of video cameras for arraignments. These systems provide much greater efficiency in the use of both judges' time and staff time. Transportation costs are cut and security breaches reduced by keeping inmates in the jail facility and having them interact with the judge over television monitors. Several jurisdictions now use video arraignments. Dade County (Miami) Florida had the system installed in 1982 at a cost of $40,000. The system is a reported success from the standpoint of both judges and defendants (Terry and Surette 1985).

CONCLUSIONS

Technology has become an increasingly important part of the work of the correctional officer, especially as management sees its potential for more efficient and less costly operation of facilities. Much of the technology must be learned on the job; however, basic training and education are required to introduce these innovations and prepare individuals to use them. Further training more likely will be provided at educational institutions, especially computer applications, or through specific vendors, in the case of hardware. Also, computer learning systems for correctional officers are one route to continued training in general subjects as well as specific topic areas, such as new technical applications. It is possible that private sector operators who have a stake in reducing personnel costs will be the major users and innovators in making technological applications in the future.

REFERENCES

American Correctional Association. *ACA Standards for Adult Correctional Institutions.* Lanham, MD: American Correctional Association, 1990.

"Court Upholds Limit on Use of Stun Guns on Prisoners." *Riverside* [CA] *Press-Enterprise* (June 10, 1995), p. A5.

Electrified Fences. A New Concept in Prison Security. Brochure used at the American Correctional Association, c. 1995.

Sechrest, D.K. , M.D. McShane, and L. . Haefeli. *Program Review and Internal Audit in Corrections.* Washington, DC: U.S. Department of Justice, National Institute of Corrections, 1994.

Shugoll, M., and J. Dempsey. "The Availability, Accessibility, and Level of Computerization of Criminal Justice Data: An Interstate Comparison." *Journal of Criminal Justice* 11(1983): 429–446.

Terry, C.W., III, and R. Surette. "Video in the Misdemeanor Court: The South Florida Experience," *Judicature* 69 (June–July 1985): 13–19.

10

Future Concerns

PRIVATIZATION

The privatization of correctional services at all levels is a hot topic in the field, one that may represent a direct threat to the jobs of correctional officers. The California Correctional Peace Officers Association (CCPOA) is attempting to pass legislation to forbid privatization of state facilities. Several questions are raised regarding privatization, especially relating to costs and the hiring criteria and training of the correctional officers operating privately run facilities.

The major arguments for privatization in the current era are economic and administrative. It is repeatedly stated that the private sector can operate prisons cheaper by providing at least the same quality of service as the public sector and demonstrating more flexibility in terms of anticipating needs and devising ways to meet them. The number of beds in private facilities is said to have increased from 3,100 in 1987 to 85,000 in 1996 in the United States, with far more beds projected for the future. In several articles, Sechrest and Shichor (1993, 1996, 1997; Shichor and Sechrest 1995, 1996) question whether private organizations have proven that they can hold inmates cheaper and more effectively than public sector agencies. Among the major questions are the following. Do private firms rely on public agencies for some services? Do they "lowball" to get in and then raise costs later? Does their workforce receive less in pay, benefits, and other employment conditions? How are officers certified and trained? Can, or should, such officers operate maximum security facilities? In the final analysis, is it unfair to criticize public facilities for doing a poor job when they are underfunded, then go to a private organization with more money and not expect them to do a better job? A major concern is with contracting with and monitoring such facilities: can public sector agents do it and do it well?

Costs of Privatization

In their study of private facilities, Sechrest and Shichor found major problems in the area of uncovered costs related to the administration of private facilities. These included dual administration, which requires a state (or county) presence at facilities no matter who runs them; administrative costs to public agencies, such as monitoring, budgets, and approvals; and medical and emergency (fire, disturbances) costs passed on to public agencies. At a 400-bed community correctional facility in California in March 1997, local police and the local state correctional facility emergency squad had to quell a riot. Shared services (e.g., administrative, fire, riot response) may not be as readily available to private operators. The public sector may have to make these services available to the private sector to entice it to operate in areas traditionally belonging to government.

These concerns must be placed in the context of possible efficiencies. For example, can private firms cut red tape in purchasing and even constructing facilities? Or, can this lead to the purchase of poorer quality goods and services? Private corporations offer "budget certainty"; that is, the public administrator gets a "fixed price" that is known in advance and, one hopes, *with no surprises*; however, any needed service that exceeds contract specifications will be charged to the public contracting agency. It is desirable for private contractors to reduce their risk as much as possible, and they may do so at a cost to the public sector, even putting such clauses into their contacts.

With these issues in mind, what do we know about the viability of privatization? A U.S. General Accounting Office (GAO) report (1996) said, "we could not conclude from these studies that privatization of correctional facilities will *not* save money. . . . However, these studies do not offer substantial evidence that savings have occurred. . . . Regarding quality of service, of the two studies that made the most detailed comparative assessments, one . . . reported equivocal findings, and the other . . . reported no difference between the compared private and public facilities."

Privately operated facilities in California routinely were sending serious medical cases to state-operated facilities, and the medical expenses could not be tracked and applied to the overall costs of the private facility. In this sense, the public sector has subsidized the private sector, and this may be especially true in crisis situations. Who will manage the private facility if the officers strike or if the facility goes bankrupt, which has happened in Pennsylvania (*Public Employee* 1986).

Management Concerns

One reason the federal Bureau of Prisons (BOP) decided against further privatization of its facilities was riots in two facilities operated by private contractors. The BOP detention center in Eloy, Arizona, which held criminal aliens prior to deportation, was operated by Concept, Inc., a Louisville-based company with contracts to operate several other prisons. Two *major disturbances* occurred in the facility only a few months after it opened in 1994. It was found that many "guards" were being paid only $5.87 per hour and that staff turnover was nearly 40% during the first five months of operation (Matlock 1995). Concept, Inc., says it has solved the problems and has a showcase facility. In June 1996, an immigration and naturalization service detention center in Elizabeth, New Jersey, operated by Esmor Correctional Services, Inc., had a similar disturbance (Matlock 1995). Concerns about the hiring of high-quality staff members also are found in the communities in which they are placed. The change of a federal facility from public to private in a small southern California town caused considerable concern by local citizens that private sector employees would be paid less and hence contribute less to the local economy (Teves 1996). This raises the question of the big fish and the little fish. Are the big private companies the only ones who can do the job more efficiently and at less cost? Should all private facility contractors be required to meet minimal performance criteria in several areas? And to what extent would this drive up their costs?

For most public agencies, control is a major issue. Clearly, turning over a local jail facility to a private operator takes control away from the sheriff or correctional administrator over jail operations. Who will make the decision to take away that control to privatize and for what reasons? When the decision to privatize is made, which public official is responsible? And, who in local government is responsible for monitoring the performance of the private contractor, including making contract adjustments? Should the sheriff take the added responsibility for monitoring the performance of the private vendor? It is hard to imagine the sheriff becoming an objective monitor for a facility that was seen as needing private sector management.

Personnel and Punishment

Privatization can present some other serious consequences. For example, public agencies are more likely to be bound by laws regarding hiring practices (screening, selection, affirmative action), training, promotion, and retention. Who will provide the oversight necessary to see that these things are done for private sector employees, consistent with local laws and regulations? Whatever arrangements are made, there is a consensus among legal experts that the ultimate responsibility for what happens in the facility will remain with government authorities. A serious question remains as to whether the determination of punishment (sentencing), which is undoubtedly a government function, can be separated from the administration of punishment, as the advocates of privatization claim.

Liability issues are of great concern. Who will be responsible for the use of deadly force? It generally is agreed that full responsibility remains with the sheriff and the county (see Walla 1995). It is maintained, especially by labor unions, that the state cannot contract out its police powers. For example, the CCPOA (union) pointed out that state contracting agencies retain full liability for the actions of private contractors, and the union lobbied successfully to kill legislation to authorize contracts for private prison facilities (Thompson 1995). Another question is whether private contractors will be able to obtain sufficient insurance to cover potential claims. How will public agencies doing the contracting be able to judge the levels of liability needed? In any case, the counties involved are likely to be sued jointly with the private contractor because they have "deeper pockets" in lawsuits.

Conclusions

The issue of privatization of correctional facilities remains unsettled. Logan's comparison of state and private prisons concluded that there is "a pattern of superior achievement on management-related performance measures when the private operation of [the prison] was compared to its previous operation by the state itself' (1996,

p. 83). In doing so, he cites several characteristics that appeared to be improvements made by private prison operators. He concludes by stating that the service provider—private or public—is irrelevant to the issue of who can deliver the best performance (p. 84, quoting an unpublished manuscript by Charles W. Thomas).

We suggest that there are some critical issues remain to be resolved in private contracting for correctional facility operation. These include the issues of punishment, maintaining authority, sound contracting, actual costs, liability, use of force, delegation of power, monitoring private operations, locating a high-quality staff, unionization of private sector personnel, and maintaining public relations in the face of challenges to traditional practices. A serious question remains as to whether the determination of punishment (sentencing), which is undoubtedly a government function, can be separated from the administration of punishment, as the advocates of privatization claim.

The extent of liability and actual cost savings by the private sector are not fully established. It is conceivable, although not certain, that unions eventually will find their way into private facility operations, which can drive up costs. Very little track record is available pertaining to the operation of private detention facilities in particular, and in some cases it has not worked. On the other hand, indications suggest that local governments can be inventive and outperform private companies both in service and cost effectiveness (Osborne and Gaebler 1992). It seems to be a positive development that the public sector shows a major interest in improving its performance and a readiness to become competitive with the private sector. This trend is demonstrated by the recent introduction of attempts to increase individual performance among public workers (see Lane and Wolf 1990) and improve management techniques (Osborne and Gaebler 1992). In this sense, competition from the private sector, as suggested by Logan and Thomas, may have a positive impact on public facility operations. However, several questions remain as to what areas and to what extent the private sector should be involved in correctional facility operation. For the correctional officer, it matters a great deal who is operating these facilities, especially as it relates to job permanency, salaries, and benefits over the long term.

UNIONS, ASSOCIATIONS, AND THE CORRECTIONAL OFFICER

Unions have altered the context of employee-management relations, and political interest often dominates over practical correctional goals. As the union movement has come into the corrections field, it faces an increasingly aware public, which knows more about the criminal justice system than ever before. Accountability is demanded on all issues, large and small. Employees must work faster and smarter than in the past, and they must be tougher mentally to face the challenges of the field. Unions may help reduce attrition and improve working conditions, but they also are subject to criticism. In California, for example, the California Correctional Peace Officers Association has been challenged on several fronts: political influence, driving up system costs, and protecting poor performance.

Most correctional facilities are operated on the "military" model of organization. This model is designed to distribute commands from the top down to achieve immediate results with little or no discussion. Safe and efficient facility operation often requires immediate, unquestioned response, especially when emergencies arise. Although less true than in the past, many correctional officers have retired from the military, and the military model of organizational behavior is understandable and comfortable for them. There even is evidence from the military, however, that it is becoming increasingly involved in participatory management. Much of this involvement comes through participation in unions.

Attrition, or loss of staff, is a major concern in corrections facilities, as in any organization. Little research has been done on correctional officers. Allen and Simonsen (1995) report turnover rates of 12%, although it can run as high as 50% in some systems. Benton and Rosen (1982) found five factors associated with staff attrition: benefits and perceived benefits, supervisory style, management practices, job content, and unionization. Lower staff losses were associated with higher salaries, greater participation in decision making, more programs for inmates in the facility, and belonging to a union.

Closely related to both performance measurement and salaries is the need to reward staff members for satisfactory performance. Studies show that higher starting salaries for correctional officers are associated with lower levels of attrition. Benton and Rosen found that institutions paying less than $10,000 in 1978–1979 had total attrition rates of 31%, whereas rates were 21% for those paying more than $10,000 (1982, p. 4). This was true for supervisory officers as well. Because promotions may be limited, salary scales must allow for "step" increases based on merit, and cost of living adjustments must be included in annual budgets. Nonmonetary rewards or meritorious service awards also may be effective in rewarding performance, particularly if they are tied into the annual performance evaluation system. All these efforts by management are important, but by far the biggest factor in improving the job of correctional officer has been their participation in unions.

Professional Associations and the Rise of Unions

Unionization of corrections is not a well-research or much-discussed topic. In years since World War II, the union movement spread from the private sector to public agencies such as police and fire departments. As this occurred, correctional officers began to take notice. During this time, most correctional officers belonged to various types of state employee associations or national associations that represented their interests. The most notable national association is the International Association of Correctional Officers (IACO). The IACO ("1996 Annual Correction Officer/Supervisor Year" 1996) gives the Correctional Officer and Supervisor of the Year awards and sponsors National Correctional Officer Week and a memorial for officers killed on duty. The IACO initiated the legislative effort to double the death benefit paid to officers killed on duty, which was successfully lobbied through Congress (IACO 1996). IACO has established a Correctional Officer's Creed. It has recently established a certification program for correctional officers. The first certification of an academic program was at Winona State University in Minnesota in 1995 ("First Certification" 1996).

Several other associations are critical to the work of the correctional officer and to the upgrading of the entire field. The American Jail Association is a significant participant in the effort to upgrade correctional officers. It holds several training sessions each year that are well attended. It recently instituted a certification program for jail managers through its Jail Manager Certification Commission. The American Correctional Association publishes national standards that provide guidance for correctional officers in the performance of their duties. Accreditation of correctional facilities is offered through its Commission on Accreditation for Corrections, and it provides a significant opportunity for correctional officers to demonstrate their commitment to excellence in the operation of their facilities. All these organizations work together to ensure improvements in the field and to develop professionally.

Unions and Their Goals: The California Case

California Correctional Peace Officers Association represents over 23,000 correctional peace officers in California. In 1980, it had 2,000 members and the average salary was $21,000 a year. By 1994 starting pay was $23,316 a year with a top pay of $44,676 a year and physical fitness pay, a bilingual bonus, and special pay for less desirable duty posts. It has become a very strong union, with 23,000 members (Hurst 1994). It contributed a total of $525,000 toward the reelection of Governor Wilson in 1994, which is seen as one of the largest such contributions for a gubernatorial candidate in modern times (Weintraub 1994). The same union spent nearly $1 million in an independent advertising campaign on the governor's behalf in 1990 (Weintraub 1994). Only the California Medical Association spent more than the CCPOA on political candidates in 1992 (Hurst 1994). From Wilson's election in 1991 to 1994 correctional officer's salaries increased 10%. The CCPOA claims to support other candidates for public office.

The union benefits handbook proclaims that the union is "one of the most powerful and effective bargaining units in California" (CCPOA 1995). Since 1982, when the CCPOA began negotiating for the peace officers, they have become among the highest paid peace officers in the state. A peace officer is "expected to enforce State and Federal laws while providing service to the public by confiding and supervising convicted felons" (California Department of Corrections 1996). The minimum educational requirement for employment is education equivalent to completion of the 12th grade (a General Education Development [GED] certificate). Beginning officers have a six-week academy and a two-year apprenticeship program requiring a minimum of 3,600 hours (450 days) of experience in their designated work category. They are expected to be "mature, physically fit and emotionally stable [with] good leadership and motivational skills, good personal and social adjustment; and the ability to deal with others consistently and fairly" (California Department of Corrections 1996). The minimum annual salary for the first two years of employment is $28,260.

The CCPOA defends members from job-related legal actions and claims to contest more State Personnel Board actions than any of the other 20 units in state government, with 12% of the state workforce and more than 40% of the board's caseload (CCPOA 1996). The organization works to pass legislation that will improve professionalism, enhance officer safety, and increase pay and benefits, all in the interests of public safety. The CCPOA lists 23 separate member benefits, including the system of "post and bid," which allows senior officers to selected job positions and shifts; various types of incentive pay and benefits (e.g., a 5% pay increase at 20 years, shift differentials, more vacation time, retirement inflation protection); and various other benefits, such as legal representation.

Criticism of Correctional Officer Unions

Allen and Simonsen (1995, p. 523) note that organization and collective action have brought many benefits to correctional officers, but that "they will get little sympathy from the administrators and the public until they show concern for the overall mission of the institution as well as their personal needs." The question is raised as to how responsible a union must be in working for the public. In a 1995 budget debate over prison spending in California, it was found that some correctional officers were making $100,000 per year (Morain 1995). A state senator attacked the costs of the "bid and post" system ($36 million a year), physical fitness pay ($4.7 million a year), and bonuses for working in less desirable locations ($3.9 million a year). Indeed, spending for corrections in California has become a major threat to the state budget process (Schiraldi 1994).

The CCPOA recently filed a suit against the State Personnel Board that ultimately could cost the taxpayers of California $81 million (Morain 1994). The suit challenges discipline against 55 members whose cases were supposed to be heard within a six-month period. The California Supreme Court has agreed to hear the case. The California Department of Corrections accounted for 31.5% of the 2,000 discipline cases heard in 1993 by the personnel board. This was up from 24.1% two years earlier. Cases being challenged include a tower guard who left his post to assault an inmate, in his cell, who had refused to follow his command, several other assaults, lying on an employment application about substance abuse, giving drugs to inmates, and having sex with inmates. The head of the union found many of these incidents "sickening" but felt that good officers were often involved because managers did not like them. However, a spokesperson for the state of California said reemployment of some of these individuals could pose significant liability problems for the state.

Correctional officers in California recently were charged with conducting "gladiator days" at one institution in the central part of the state ("Corcoran Guards" 1996). Former officers related their experience with officers arranging fights between rival inmates in the Secure Housing Unit (SHU), betting on the outcome, and shooting those who wouldn't quit fighting. A suit regarding a death of this type has been filed in United States District Court in Fresno (Calkins 1995). Claims are that inmates were being forced to fight and that officers were making "split-second decisions on life or death" ("Corcoran Guards" 1996, p. A6). Mike Wallace (1997) did a CBS *60 Minutes* show on these incidents at the California State Correctional Institution at Corcoran. Eight deaths were said to occur, and one permanently injured inmate told about the incidents (Wallace 1997). Administrators claim the shootings were within departmental policy. If proven, however, these are clear violations of these officer's duty to protect inmates from harm. The fact that at least four former officers came forward and told of the incidents is encouraging.

Conclusions

Unions and other forms of employee organizations have forced greater participation in management and improved working conditions for correctional officers. They are not without problems because correctional institutions are difficult places to work. Union leadership must be concerned about these problems and issues, or it may face the same difficulties that eventually reduced participation in unions in the private sector. The unions must retain the confidence of the public and its representatives.

Associations represent a positive voice for the field and have shown great progress in the past 20 years, both in increasing membership and striving for professionalism. Their work in providing continuing training and certification efforts and their recognition of correctional officers, both locally and nationally, contribute greatly to the future of correctional officer professionalism.

CASE STUDY: PRIVATIZATION

California represents a unique situation in privatization. As a result of the crowding of its facilities, the California Department of Corrections (CDC) saw the creation of facilities operated by local governments (mostly cities) as one solution to the problem. These facilities were administered by the Parole and Community Services Division of the CDC because they were originally intended to manage only returned parolees, a role that later expanded to first commitments. Five small towns in the state received contracts to operate what came to be known as Community Correctional Facilities (CCFs) after an initial period of use just for parole returns.

The CDC's parole division entered into contracts with cities, counties, and private entities to house inmates (first commitments) and parole violators in CCFs, with the goals of relieving crowding at state prisons and reducing the number of new prisons required. Six similar facilities were operated by private organizations (see Sechrest and Shichor 1993, 1996, 1997; Shichor and Sechrest 1995, 1996).

CCF screening criteria contain 18 guidelines for admission. Exclusions include length of sentence; offense history of arson, sex crimes, psychotropic drug use, assault on a peace officer, or assault with a deadly weapon; serious or recent (five years) escapes; protective custody or difficult medical cases; active felony holds; life term; and, media sensitive cases. The facilities offer programs for inmates, such as work, education, drug and alcohol counseling, individual and family counseling, and vocational evaluation and training.

In contacting for the management of state inmates the delegation of state authority over the control and punishment of inmates by publicly operated or private contractors is a concern. For this reason, at each CCF some CDC personnel are assigned as contract monitors, who have responsibility for interpreting CDC policy to the facility director. These include decision making in areas such as major disciplinary actions and payment of additional costs for medical care not included in the facility budget. Minor infractions usually are handled by facility staff. CDC personnel on site for monitoring purposes can be either correctional officers or parole agents, depending on the type of facility.

The number and type of state personnel required is based on the number of inmates in the facility and who operates it. All functions for both types of facilities are monitored by the CDC parole division. The publicly operated (city) facility does not have CDC correctional officers on site, because their administrators are sworn peace officers, but the facility has parole agents assigned who have ultimate responsibility for the inmate classification process. The facility handles both first admissions and parole violators. Inmates stay at this facility an average of 8 to 9 months, although they can stay up to 18 months. It is a high-security facility, with just nine inmates working in the community on a given day, operated by the local police department, using sworn and nonsworn personnel. The sworn personnel are in command positions: a captain, two lieutenants, five sergeants, and four police officers. The police department is responsible to the city council. Forty-seven correctional officers, who are nonsworn personnel, wear police uniforms with patches indicating "corrections." While on duty they have sworn status. The four state parole agents make up the state personnel for the facility, with a part-time supervisor based in another community. The parole agents at the facility may override decisions made by the facility administrator because they represent the state (CDC).

The privately operated CCF has CDC correctional officer coverage and parole agents assigned. The facility houses 400 inmates in 17 dormitories. The average stay is four months, although six months was seen by staff as more desirable. First-termers can do up to 18 months at the facility. Inmate turnover is high, with as many as 165 new inmates arriving each month. Outside crews of 4 to 30 inmates are sent out daily to work on community projects. Four state correctional officers (one lieutenant, three sergeants) and three parole agents, supervised one-third of the time by an area agent, were stationed at the facility.

An exploratory survey was conducted, aimed at finding out staff attitudes and opinions regarding the organizational climate of these institutions and state-operated institutions. The sample was small, altogether 68 persons, and was based on availability rather than a random sample. Therefore, it could not claim, with any degree of confidence, that the attitudes and opinions gathered in the survey were truly representative of all the employees in these facilities. Staff responses to a large degree were concerned with the same issues as the inmates responses to a similar survey.

All staff members in the facilities studied were of the opinion that their facility is completely safe for the inmates. In contrast, only about two-thirds (64–67%) of the staff in the state institutions held the same opinion. In all the facilities, fewer staff members felt that it was safer for them than for the inmates. With regard to crowding, the CCF staff members did not see their facility as "overcrowded," while the large majority of state prison staff members (66–71%) saw their facility as "overcrowded."

Concerning the question of whether the facility is run well, again there was a major difference between the staff members of the CCFs and the state prisons. In the CCFs, 83–90% of the respondents maintained that their facility is well run, whereas in the CRC, 57.2% and, in the CIM, only 44.5% did so. Privately operated facilities were seen as having a better physical plant, and the food was seen as better by a somewhat greater number of staff members.

Another component centered around staff job satisfaction. The majority of respondents never filed a grievance about their job. There again was a difference between the CCFs (94–100% never filed) and the state prison respondents (61–79%). Regarding the authority that the respondents feel that they have, the highest percentage that claimed to have as much authority that needed was CCF staff members (83–88%), with the lowest percent at one state facility (39%). Opinions concerning the fairness of the promotion standards were generally favorable. The highest percent of respondents who agreed that these standards were fair was CCF staff members (100%), and state employees came in a bit lower. Staff respondents were asked whether they plan to look for another job. Results were mixed between the CCFs and state operated facilities, with CCFs personnel slightly less likely to plan to look for another job overall. The job satisfaction indicators show that the respondents from the CCFs seemed to be the most satisfied.

Even though the small sample sizes and use of a method that could not provide random samples of facility employees limited the ability to come to highly reliable conclusions, findings are of interest to correctional officers for at least two reasons. First, conditions may be better in smaller facilities, whether privately operated or not. Second, one day they may be assigned to a privately run facility, like a CCF, in which case they must be trained in overall facility management and the ability to work independently.

REFERENCES

Allen, H.E., and C.E. Simonsen. Corrections in America, an Introduction, 7th ed. New York: Prentice-Hall, 1995.

"Corcoran Guards Arranged Inmate Fights." *Daily Press* [Victorville, CA] (August 22, 1996).

Benton, F.W. , and E.D. Rosen. *Correctional Employment Attrition: Summary of a National Survey*, pp. 5–6. New York: National Center for Public Productivity, John Jay College of Criminal Justice, 1982.

California Correctional Peace Officer's Association. *Member Benefits Handbook.* California Correctional Peace Officer's Association, undated, c. 1996.

California Department of Corrections. Correctional Officer, job description. Sacramento: State of California Department of Corrections, 1996.

Calkins, R. "Prison Staff Violent, Suit Alleges." *San Bernardino Sun* (April 2, 1995): B7.

"First Certification of Academic Program." *Keeper's Voice* (Winter 1996).

Hurst, J. "The House That Don Novey Built." *Los Angeles Times Magazine* (February 6, 1994).

International Association of Correctional Officers. Brochure. International Association of Correctional Officers, c. 1996.

Lane, L.M., and J.F. Wolf. *The Human Resource Crisis in the Public Sector: Building the Capacity to Govern.* New York: Quorum, 1990.

Logan, C.H. "Public vs. Private Prison Management: A Case Comparison." *Criminal Justice Review* 21, no. 1 (1996): 62–85.

Matlock, C. "Prisons Paradox." *Government Executive* (1995): 60–63.

Morain, D. "Suit Challenging Firings, Demotions May Cost Millions." *Los Angeles Times* (October 19, 1994), p. A14.

Morain, D. "Veto Steps up Debate on Prison Spending." *Los Angeles Times* (August 7, 1995), p. A3.

"1996 Annual Correctional Officer/Supervisor of the Year." *Keeper's Voice* (Summer 1996).

Osborne, D., and T. Gaebler. *Reinventing Government.* New York: Penguin, 1992.

Public Employee 51 (May–June 1986): 27.

Sechrest, D.K., and D. Shichor. "Corrections Goes Public (and Private) in California." *Federal Probation* 57, no. 3 (1993): 3–8.

Sechrest, D.K., and D. Shichor. "Private Jails: Locking down the Issues." *American Jails* 11, no. 1 (1997): 21–36.

Sechrest, D.K., and D. Shichor. "Comparing Public and Private Correctional Facilities in California: An Exploratory Study." In G.L. Mays and T. Gray (eds.), *Privatization and the Provision of Correctional Services: Context and Consequences.* Cincinnati, OH: Anderson, 1996.

Shichor, D., and D.K. Sechrest. "Delegating Prison Operations to Public or Private Entities." *Corrections Today* (1996): 56–65.

Shichor, D., and D.K. Sechrest. "Quick Fixes in Corrections: Reconsidering Private and Public For-Profit Facilities." *Prison Journal* (1995): 452–465.

Shiraldi, V. *The Undue Influence of California's Prison Guards' Union: California's Correctional-Industrial Complex.* San Francisco: Center on Juvenile and Criminal Justice, 1994.

Teves, J.C. "Taft Prison Privatization Steals Hopes for Economy." *Bakersfield Californian* (September 16, 1996), p. A1.

Thompson, J. "The Privatization of Prisons Misses the Mark." *Peacekeeper* (1995): 19.

U.S. General Accounting Office. *Private and Public Prisons, Studies Comparing Operational Costs and/or Quality of Service. Report to the Subcommittee on Crime, Committee of the Judiciary, House of Representatives.* Washington, DC: U.S. General Accounting Office, 1996.

Walla, R.K. "Privatization of the Jails—Is it a Good Move?" *American Jails* (1995): 73–74.

Wallace, M. "The Deadliest Prison." *60 Minutes*, Columbia Broadcasting System, 1997.

Weintraub, D.M. "Prison Guards Set Record with Gift to Wilson." *Los Angeles Times* (October 30, 1994).

11

Recommendations and Conclusions

The personnel of a corrections department are its greatest assets. All the way, from the top to the bottom of the agency, the caliber of personnel sets the stage for standards of performance in the delivery of correctional services. The caliber of a correctional agency almost completely is determined by personnel policy and, to a large part, its ability to select, train, and retain high-quality officers.

Although the professional status of correctional officers continues to grow, opportunities for professional advancement within the ranks of corrections have not kept pace. The current state of career development within these agencies raises questions about the future relationship between educational requirements, training, job experience, and the time frames that should be associated with career development and the appropriate career path required for advancement within the organization. It has become evident that a mechanism must be developed to give career correctional officers an opportunity for recognition among their peers and within the organization.

Promotional opportunities within a "paramilitary"-based organizational structure are somewhat limited. The number of supervisory and management positions is relatively small when compared to the total personnel strength of the agency. This circumstance tends to freeze personnel in the lower ranks for extended periods of time. Line and staff officers may wait several years for a promotional opportunity. Few officers are content to remain in positions offering only limited opportunities for advancement. Competent, hardworking officers can become unfulfilled, frustrated individuals who will begin looking elsewhere for career gratification. Career immobility generally is reflected by low morale and poor work performance, thus, an environment is set that breeds mediocrity. A reward structure must exist to recognize the valuable efforts of these officers.

What has previously been written about career development, in terms of opening the channels of successful officer retention, is self-evident. A successful career development program is one of the most important mechanisms in the entire field of personnel management. It gives expression to the opportunity for personal achievement and success, with all this can mean in terms of morale and initiative. Career development, if properly implemented, can breathe life into an organization. Coupled with other aspects of a personnel management system, it can become an effective method for developing an organization's human resources.

A positive career plan can provide for annual salary increments based on an employee's achievement, job performance, educational progress, and greater value to the organization. This contrasts with the normal personnel process, providing annual increments to all individuals in an organization unless they demonstrate extreme negative organizational input that management cannot ignore. The first career development model described here provides for occupational growth based on career and educational incentives. Referred to as the *Correctional Peace Officer Certification Program* (CPOST), this model is a "generic" certification project similar in content to the highly successful law enforcement educational certification program. The second career development model (a tuition reimbursement, educational assistance program) was developed at the request of a number of state correctional department managers in response to an earlier national research survey on correctional officer education.

MODEL PROGRAM 1. CORRECTIONAL PEACE OFFICER CERTIFICATE PROGRAM

Overview and Purpose

A certification program for correctional officers must state minimum eligibility requirements. It should include at least three types of certificates: a basic certificate, an intermediate certificate, and an advanced certificate. The outline for a "generic" correctional officer certification program is presented here.

To establish a certificate program, it would be advisable to create a Commission on Correctional Officer Standards and Training, similar in nature to the Police Officers Standards and Training (POST) model used in law enforcement. The mission of the commission would be to raise the level of competence of all correctional officers designated with "peace officer" status. The commission, through its certificate program, would strive to improve the administration, management, and operation of the correctional agency.

The commission would have four basic purposes:

- To establish minimum selection standards for correctional officer candidates;
- To establish minimum training standards for correctional officer recruits;
- To certify training courses for the improvement of correctional officer performance;
- To provide management assistance and research services to the correctional agency.

Minimum Standards for Employment

Every correctional officer recruit selected by the agency would be required to meet the following minimum criteria:

- No prior felony convictions;

- Clearance by a search of local, state, and national fingerprint files to reveal any criminal record;
- United States citizenship or have applied for citizenship;
- At least 21 years of age;
- Clearance by a thorough background investigation and determined to be of good moral character;
- A high school diploma or successfully passage of the General Education Development Test (GED);
- Clearance by a physical examination to determine the absence of physical, emotional, or mental condition that might adversely affect performance;
- Successfully passage of an oral interview by the agency head or representative(s) prior to employment to determine suitability for correctional service;
- Ability to read and write at the level necessary to perform the job of a correctional officer.

Minimum Standards for Training

Commission regulations would require specific training for every newly appointed correctional officer and every officer promoted to supervisory and management positions. In addition, each officer below the first-level management position would be subject to a *continuing professional training* requirement. This requirement could be satisfied through a series of premanagement advanced officer in-service training every two years after completion of the apprenticeship requirements. In addition to the mandated training, discretionary training shall be provided in management and supervisory development courses.

Eligibility

To be eligible for the award of a professional certificate, an applicant must be a full-time correctional officer with the designated agency. The officer also must have "permanent status" (e.g., successfully completed all mandatory probationary and apprenticeship requirements).

Education, Training, and Experience

To qualify for certificates, applicants shall have completed combinations of education, training, and experience.

1. *Training points*: Twenty classroom hours of corrections training would equal one training point. Such training must be conducted in a classroom or other appropriate site, in increments of two hours or more, taught by a qualified instructor, concluding with appropriate testing, and for which records are kept.
2. *Education points*: One semester unit shall equal one education point and one quarter unit shall equal two-thirds of a point. Such units of credit shall have been awarded by an accredited college or university.

3. *Supporting documentation*: Education and training must be supported by copies of transcripts, diplomas, and other verifying documents attached to the application for certification. Units of credit transferred from one accredited college to another should be documented by transcripts from both colleges. When college credit is awarded, it should be counted for either training or education points, whichever is to the advantage of the applicant officer.
4. *Point accumulation*: Training acquired in completing a certified basic course (academy and probationary program) may be credited toward the number of training points necessary to obtain the intermediate or advanced certificate. When education points as well as training points are acquired in completing the basic course requirements, the officer may select, without apportionment, the use of either the education points or the training points.
5. *Prior experience*: Previous experience with an out-of-state accredited correctional agency may or may not be accepted by the commission as "required experience." In any case, out-of-state experience shall not exceed a maximum of five years accredited experience. Documentation shall include the name of the organization(s) indicated, years of service, duties performed, and types of responsibility.

Professional Certificates

The Basic Certificate

In addition to the previously mentioned requirements, for the award of the basic certificate, the applicant officer

1. Must have satisfactorily completed the period of probation, of no less than one year, and continuous employment with the correctional agency, for a minimum period of 24 months. Officers employed before the agreed-on starting date, must have completed a period of satisfactory service of no less than one year. An advisory committee shall have the authority to determine the manner in which the time periods are calculated, when there is change in employment status, injury, illness, or other such extraordinary circumstances over which the applicant or department may have little or no control.
2. Must have successfully completed the department's required and approved basic (preservice) training academy.
3. If employed before the specified date, the applicant must have completed all required mandates as established by departmental guidelines.

The Intermediate Certificate

In addition to the previously mentioned requirements, for the award of the Intermediate Certificate, the applicant

1. Must possess or be eligible to possess a basic certificate;
2. Must satisfy the prerequisite basic course training requirement;

3. Must have acquired the training and education points or the college degree designated and the prescribed years of correctional officer experience in any *one* of the following combinations:

Minimum Training Points Required	15	30	45		
Minimum Education Points or Degree Required	15	30	45	Associates Degree	Bachelors Degree
Years of Correctional Officer Experience Required	8	6	4	4	2

Using this table, a correctional officer with 30 training points, 30 education points, and six years of experience would be eligible for the intermediate certificate.

The Advanced Certificate

In addition to the previously mentioned requirements, for the award of the Advanced Certificate, the applicant

1. Must possess or be eligible to possess an intermediate certificate;
2. Must satisfy the prerequisite basic course training requirement and have acquired the training and education points or college degree designated and the prescribed years of correctional officer experience in any one of the following combinations:

Minimum Training Points Required	30	45			
Minimum Education Points or Degree Required	30	45	Associates Degree	Bachelors Degree	Masters Degree
Years of Correctional Officer Experience Required	12	9	9	6	4

MODEL PROGRAM 2. EDUCATIONAL ASSISTANCE PROGRAM

Educational Incentives

Professionalism requires a commitment to lifelong learning. The modern correctional agency should have a program of reimbursement for education related expenses for those employees who wish to pursue educational goals concurrent with their career goals. The purpose of a comprehensive training and education policy should be as follows:

- To establish a process for the on-going identification of the necessary knowledge, skills, and abilities needed for today's corrections professional;

- To systematically integrate the department's curriculum development and lesson plans in conjunction with local colleges and universities;
- To develop standards for staff trainers to ensure a consistency in the quality of instruction;
- To enhance career development through increased training and education;
- To ensure compliance with standards that may be developed by the reimbursement program;
- To provide procedural guidelines for a comprehensive tuition reimbursement program;
- To reduce departmental turnover due to motivational stagnation and reduce employee "burnout."

For these reasons, the following "education assistance" concept has been developed as one alternative for correctional officer career development.

Model Policy for Educational Assistance

The following text describes a model policy for establishing a program of educational assistance for correctional officers. It has been derived from similar departmental policies and can be modified to meet the legal and organizational needs of a particular department.

1. *Authority*. This policy and procedure for administration of the Education Assistance Program is established under the authority of (here the department can cite the appropriate statute, regulation, etc.) and has been approved for implementation by the (add the name of the correctional agency).
2. *Purpose*. To establish policy and procedure for the administration of the Education Assistance Program for the agency.
3. *Applicability*. This policy and procedure is applicable to all permanent full-time correctional officers (or others as applicable) of the agency who apply for funding through the Education Assistance Program.
4. *Definitions*. Here, *education assistance* means a program for payment to approved colleges, universities, correspondence schools, and other approved educational sources, for legislatively approved *job-related* training for which individual employees have received prior approval.
5. *Policy*. Officials of the department support continuing education for all employees to increase their job skills and provide for individual career development.

Equal access to educational opportunities shall be provided through education assistance for all permanent, full-time correctional officers (or others as applicable). Any employee who is refused education assistance by his or her supervisor, office, or institutional personnel officer or denied approval by the personnel officer shall have the right to a written explanation for the denial.

Policy Guidelines

Sources of Funds

Funds for payment of education assistance may come from total funds appropriated by the state legislature to each budget unit. To provide equal opportunities for employees of all budget units, a set formula should be developed by the (personnel office or division, etc.) based on an average cost per authorized employee. Each budget unit then would be directed at the start of each fiscal year to set aside a sum certain, based on the formula, to provide educational opportunities to staff members within the limits of their respective budgets. Tuition assistance funds should be approved within each budget unit on a first-come, first-served basis.

Payment of Funds

The Education Assistance Program provides for the payment of funds directly to the educational institution after the employee has received approval for the courses authorized by the (specify the responsible authority).

Educational assistance for courses in pursuit of a second undergraduate degree should not be granted. Requests for specific courses (not associated with pursuit of a degree) may be granted if the courses are related directly to the employee's work with the department. Requests for an employee holding both an undergraduate degree and a master's degree may be granted if the courses are directly related to the employee's work with the department.

Maximum limits on the number of college hours for which tuition assistance shall be granted are as follows:

- Undergraduate degree (B.A. or B.S.): 130 undergraduate hours or its equivalent in quarter hours.
- Graduate degree (M.A., M.S., M.P.A.): 36 graduate hours.

Eligibility to Receive Education Assistance

1. Permanent full-time correctional officers who have satisfactorily completed the initial probationary period would be eligible to receive education assistance (individuals who are separated from the department at the time course work is completed should not receive partial payment of expenses).
2. Officers carrying a grade of *I* (incomplete) from a previous course for which education assistance was received should not be eligible for further education assistance until the course has be satisfactorily completed (unless the individual has reimbursed the agency for the amount expended on the course).
3. Officers who have not complied with the policies and procedures relative to the Education Assistance Program should not be eligible for further education assistance (unless the officer has reimbursed the agency for the amount expended).

Requesting Education Assistance

An officer may initiate the request for education assistance; the officer or institution may suggest to the individual that specific courses might help that officer perform job duties more proficiently, or the officer or institution may direct that the employee undertake specific or related courses.

1. Courses taken should have a clear and direct relationship to the work of the agency and to the improvement of the officer's job effectiveness in his or her present position or a position in the department to which the officer can reasonably aspire.
2. The appropriateness of courses is determined by the course requirements (i.e., established curriculum) for the degree being pursued or the relevance to the officer's present job classification. Officers applying for tuition assistance should attach a copy of the prescribed curriculum for the degree to the appropriate departmental office. Officers requesting tuition assistance for courses not associated with pursuit of a degree should attach a "memorandum of justification" to the appropriate departmental office.
3. Education assistance would be granted for courses offered by public colleges, universities, accredited correspondence schools, vocational and secondary schools, and any approved others. Assistance should not be granted without justification to cover the costs of courses when the same or substantially the same course is available to the individuals at less cost from another educational institution. The dollar amount approved for tuition assistance at private colleges or universities should be limited to the current tuition costs at a four-year state university located nearest to the officer's county of residence. Tuition assistance should not be granted for attendance at "out-of-state" educational institutions unless the specific course work is not available within the state, and the dollar amount approved for tuition assistance should be limited to the current tuition costs at the four-year state university located nearest to the officer's county of residence. The correctional agency, on a case-by-case basis, may approve exceptions to this policy when specific justification exists, if in the best interest of the department and state government.

Approval and Limitations

The personnel office or division should review all applications for tuition assistance prior to approval. A review board, selected by the director or other designated department head, should be the final authority for determining the appropriateness of questionable tuition assistance requests and for ruling on any problems or exceptions to stated policies. The "board" may be composed of representatives from the Department of Community Services, the Department of Corrections, the Office of Administrative Services, or any other appropriate agency member at the discretion of the department(s) director or its designate.

Educational Assistance Limitations

Educational assistance *may be granted* for (1) tuition and routine registration fees, (2) laboratory fees, and (3) basic and normal costs charged by the institution for actual instruction. Educational assistance should *not* be granted for (1) late registration fees, (2) graduation fees, (3) parking or transportation, (4) specific courses taken previously by the employee for which employee received a passing grade without prior approval for tuition reimbursement, and (5) textbooks and other required course supplies.

Maximum Allowable Hours

Agency paid tuition and expenditures for an employee should not exceed the following: (1) graduate or professional studies, six semester hours for each regular semester, and three semester hours for each summer semester; and (2) undergraduate studies, nine semester hours per regular semester, six semester hours per summer semester.

Applying for Assistance

Educational assistance must be authorized in advance. To receive education assistance, including tuition reimbursement, the employee would apply through his or her supervisor and obtain written approval from the central office or institutional department head.

Officer Obligations

An officer who voluntarily requested approval for and received educational assistance should be obligated to complete the courses for which approval was given, provide proof of a satisfactory grade for completion of the courses within 30 working days after completion of courses, and be required to continue working for the department following completion of the course(s) for a specified number of months, as prescribed in a written contract with the agency.

An officer voluntarily applying for educational assistance should be required to sign an individual contract acknowledging his or her obligations and authorizing the department to recover all of the educational assistance moneys expended in its behalf, if

1. The course is dropped, regardless of reason, without the prior approval of the appropriate department;
2. The officer receives duplicate payment for the same course from any other source (for example, scholarship, veteran's benefit, Pell grant, state grant or fellowship);
3. Any courses are substituted for the courses originally approved, regardless of cause, without the prior approval of the appropriate department;
4. The officer is dismissed or voluntarily leaves prior to the time limit as specified in his or her individual contract with the correctional agency;

5. The officer fails to provide the agency, within 30 working days after scheduled completion of the course, evidence of satisfactory course completion; that is, actual grade report for the course in which assistance was authorized (satisfactory grade means a *C* in undergraduate studies or a professional degree program, and a *B* in graduate studies; a grade of *I*, or incomplete, is not satisfactory);

Student Evaluation of Academic Instruction

Student officers should be required to complete a student evaluation of academic instruction for each course taken under the Education Assistance Program and submit the evaluation form, together with official grade report, to the appropriate office.

Equal Opportunity

Offices and institutions of the correctional agency must ensure that race, color, creed, religion, national origin, ancestry, sex, disability, marital status, political affiliation, sexual orientation, or age are not factors in approval of tuition assistance moneys to its student officers.

THE CHALLENGES TO CORRECTIONAL OFFICERS

The role of the correctional officer is changing, ranging from hiring and training to the implementation of new technologies. Unions and privatization represent significant issues for the future of correctional officers. Legal liability is a constant in the lives of all correctional officers and their supervisors. The crowding of correctional institutions simply exacerbates all of these issues. Leadership and sound administration are required to address many of these problems, which include the implementation of policies and procedures, addressing national standards, reducing liability, and the training of staff. Although less active, the courts will continue to hold us accountable for poor performance where we do not follow established minimal procedures, as in the cases cited, such as *Hudson v. McMillian*, which indicates that the field will be accountable where "deliberate indifference" is found in relation to accepted standards of good practice, and certainly where there is a "wanton, deliberate intent to deprive or injure."

Some states are having difficulty in providing correctional services. The largest state correctional system, in California, has experienced many problems in recent years that have "reflected upon the integrity, professionalism, and competence of staff from front-line officers all the way to the Director's office" (Lewis 1996, p. 6). These have included riots, a major lawsuit against their super-maximum facility at Pelican Bay, alleged correctional officer induced violence at one facility where inmates were pitted against one another in "gladiator" contests, a gag on inmate communications with the media, and several problems with employee misbehavior (including sexual harassment of female officers).

Training and education represent some real answers to problems of poor job performance, negligence, and the related lawsuits, as well as public concern. Some of the disturbances at privately operated facilities have been the result of poorly paid, undertrained staff members (Sechrest and Shichor 1997). States cannot hire correctional officers or other staff members at low salaries and expect high performance. On the other hand, the public is foolish to pay high salaries without the requirement for minimal education and training. Professional associations and unions have to be concerned about these issues.

At the bottom line, improved performance will depend on good screening and selection and sound programs of preservice and in-service training that use both internal and external resources. Correctional officers must be prepared to protect society by carrying out the judgments of the courts in confining criminal offenders. At the same time, correctional officers must assist other staff members in correctional facilities by maintaining a secure, safe, and humane environment for those in their custody and care. They must protect the inmates in their care. They must balance the concepts of punishment, deterrence, and incapacitation with the delivery of programs designed to assist inmates who want them.

With these concerns in mind, the correctional officer will be better equipped to carry out the mission of the department and evolve through a process of continuing professionalization. The United States is a world leader in the corrections field, and it will continue in this role only as it upgrades performance at all levels.

REFERENCES

Lewis, R.V. "California Department of Corrections in Serious Trouble." *21st Century Crime and Justice* (December 1996): 6–7.

Sechrest, D.K, and D. Shichor. "Private Jails: Locking down the Issues." *American Jails* 11, no. 1 (1997).

Index